RONAN MCMAHON'S

BIG BOOK OF PROFITABLE REAL ESTATE INVESTING

THE SIMPLE SECRETS OF MAKING A FORTUNE IN REAL ESTATE

D1377367

International Living
www.InternationalLiving.com

Ronan McMahon's Big Book of Profitable Real Estate Investing: The Simple Secrets of Making a Fortune in Real Estate

Author: Ronan McMahon

Editor: Aine Flaherty

Cover photo: © istockphoto.com / Bulgac

ISBN: 978-1-911-260-90-5   120B0044A2

TABLE OF CONTENTS

WHAT PEOPLE SAY ABOUT RONAN MCMAHON

"When I was given a copy of Ronan's new book, I feared the worst. Working as a CFO, with exposure to diverse sectors and geographic markets, I spend my days dealing with numbers. Numbers. Numbers. Numbers. So reading a book about investing, with complicated formulas, charts and more numbers, isn't exactly how I like to unwind. Thankfully, Ronan's book isn't anything like I was expecting...

Instead, it's a simple, in-plain-English book with interesting stories and big picture strategies about how to be a successful real estate investor.

And as someone who regularly evaluates real estate opportunities, I can wholeheartedly endorse what Ronan shares. Use what's in his book and you'll see the only numbers that really matter, those on your bank account statement, steadily rising." — **Bob Compton, CFO, Playa Financial**

"As his publisher of 14 years, I've traveled from the rice paddies of Thailand to the sun-kissed beaches of the Riviera Maya with Ronan. I've seen him in action as a real estate scout, and I've seen the difference his work has brought to thousands of people. I can safely say there is nobody more dedicated to finding and delivering great real estate deals to his readers. If you have an interest in profiting from real estate overseas, then this book is a must read." — **Jackie Flynn, publisher, *International Living***

"What Ronan has built, both for himself and for his community of readers and investors, is a whole new way of looking at the world...and a modern way of living in and around it. I've always said he has the "coolest job in the world." Whenever I call Ronan for one of our podcasts, he's always standing on a pristine coastline somewhere or talking from the back of a golf buggy or just about to board a plane. There's a "man of mystery" element that recalls Graham Greene novels, or perhaps something by John LeCarré. But having known Ronan for nearly two decades, I can see it's actually much more than that… more than simply a jet setting lifestyle, more than airport lounges and the age-old quest of chasing the eternal summer. He's figured out how and where to pursue the greatest opportunities in real estate all over the globe." — **Joel Bowman, host of Fatal Conceits podcast, Bonner Private Research**

"Ronan has really taken the bull by the horns! The unique business model he's developed over years of putting great deals together has proven to create great opportunities for expats and investors alike. If you're looking for a seaside abode to hang your hat affordably, Ronan's your man. He's also your man if you want to invest and make money from a classic alternative asset—international real estate." — **Addison Wiggin, The Wiggin Sessions**

"As CEO of a publishing company for 27 years, I've helped publish hundreds of newsletters, reports and books. And though some of our books have made *The New York Times Best Sellers* list, most of what we publish is simply too unconventional and too controversial to ever be a mainstream success. Unfortunately for Ronan, I believe the latter is going to be the case with his newest book…

You see, in *Ronan McMahon's Big Book of Profitable Real Estate Investing,* he reveals unique ideas I know most people won't take seriously. I know this because that's just the way people act, when confronted with revolutionary thinking. For example, when we published that the Berlin Wall will fall, or Dotcom stocks will crash—long before these events ever happened—people thought we were crazy, stupid, and perhaps both! Time has proven us right. And in time, maybe Ronan's ideas will be proven, too. But by then, the biggest opportunities will have passed most people by.

Oh well! Their loss. I hope you don't make the same mistake. Read Ronan's book carefully and with an open mind, and you'll see Ronan's ideas aren't crazy at all, but a downright genius way to make loads of money from real estate." — **Myles Norin, CEO, The Agora**

"I will never spend a cent on real estate without getting Ronan's sage advice. Ever since my first scouting trip for *International Living*, when Ronan took me under his wing in Colombia, I've been impressed with how he thinks about real estate, travel, and the world. And having met and talked to many of his *Real Estate Trend Alert* members, I know how incredibly unique and valuable his investing service is. There's simply nothing else like it...the best and most exclusive real estate deals in the world delivered to your inbox!" — **Eoin Bassett, Executive Editor, Pangea Research**

"Ronan provides a great service. I like the metrics and parameters he uses." — **Jeff Chambers, business owner and *RETA* member**

"You provide a very robust number of opportunities and do a great job of explaining them. You provide a great deal of background rational for why to invest and the presentations of material is first class." — **Richard Shelton, real estate investor**

"You do the leg work and we profit!" — **Jerry Robbins, retired, *RETA* member**

"Information from people on the ground is priceless." — **Mason Rowe, Los Angeles, luxury real estate appraiser**

FOREWORD

Youghal, Ireland

Can you imagine it?

You earn your living by staying in resorts—usually luxury resorts on the ocean. You visit one, for a few weeks—where you are treated like royalty.

You talk to the owners, developers, chefs. You play golf with your fellow visitors. You dine with investors. And then, you go visit another one.

From the coast of Portugal to the shores of Montenegro...and then down to Mexico...and why not...to Belize, Nicaragua...and even Uruguay.

But wait. You get tired of the seashore? You long for something different? How about a trip to the mountains, or a visit to a medieval town with its stone church spires and quaint corner cafes, before returning to home base?

When I first heard about Ronan McMahon's remarkable career, I could scarcely believe it. He is paid to be on vacation. And paid very well.

Years ago, he figured out that real estate development—and property prices—follow certain patterns. Usually, some technological advance...perhaps combined with a demographic change...or a social trend...sets in motion a bull market in property that can last for decades.

Looking back, it is easy to see why Florida property has done so well. Railroads and highways—along with better automobiles—made it easy for people from the cold northeast states to go to Florida, 'for the season.'

Then, widespread air-conditioning made it agreeable for them to stay there all year round. Since the 1920s, four generations of Americans and Canadians have been moving to Florida.

Nor is it any surprise that the East Coast of Mexico is booming. Or the West Coast of Costa Rica. Or the Adriatic Coast of Croatia. In a nutshell, these places are much cheaper than Florida. They are more beautiful, too…and with convenient, low-cost air travel, they can be as easy to get to as Miami.

And one more thing—in Europe and America there are now more than 150 million 'baby boomers' eager for a better lifestyle. More relaxed. Richer. Healthier.

They have spent much of their lives, walking on city pavements. Now they want to walk on the beach. They've worked for years—9 to 5. Now, they want to relax and enjoy life. They've struggled with tight family budgets for years…now they're able to live better than ever, while spending much less money.

Ronan makes it easy for them. And this book explains how.

Looking around the world, there are remarkable opportunities—for retirement, investing, or simply part-time living. The only trouble is the 'border issue.' When you go to another country, you often don't really know what you're getting into. It's hard to 'size up' foreign real estate salesmen or evaluate their deals.

Ronan figured out—the hard way, after years of trial and error—two things:

First, how do you know which areas are going up…becoming more attractive to buyers…with rising property prices, better facilities and more restaurants, museums, and other entertainments?

Second, how do you reduce the risk and the aggravation of buying and owning international real estate?

This book is an eye-opener on both counts. But it is not the end…it is only the beginning. As Ronan explains, his goal is merely to open the door and show you what is on the other side.

It is left to you, the reader, to take the next step.

Regards,

William Bonner
Founder of the Agora Companies, *www.theagora.com*
September, 2022

AUTHOR'S PREFACE

Don't Skip This Author's Preface

"Land is land, and it's safer than the stocks and bonds of Wall Street swindlers." — Eugene O'Neill, playwright

August 2022. It's early morning in Cork airport, Ireland. I have coffee. Laptop. Boarding pass. All set for another scouting trip.

For over two decades I've been traveling light and fast. I'm an international real estate investor. To do this I put my boots on the ground all over the world…or toes in the sand, depending on where I am. Then there's all the travel of my dedicated team. The annual bill for travel and research is usually close to a million dollars. No wonder my long-suffering accountant reaches for the whisky bottle when he wades through our expense reports. His nights are long.

Go forth. Find opportunity. That's my mission.

Why? Because buying quality real estate in fast-growing locations, for less than what others pay, is the best way to make money. As I'll show you in this book.

When my plane takes off in an hour I'm set to go from Ireland to Panama by way of Croatia, Montenegro, Portugal, Mexico…a half-dozen or more stops over six weeks or so.

Airport lounges are where I catch up on the news of the moment, and today the world is full of raging inflation, war in Ukraine, market jitters, and looming recession. Elon Musk is tweeting, politicians are bickering…

What does it all mean?

That depends on your point of view. On my international real estate beat it means stronger and better opportunities than ever.

Inflation is a special kind of canker, eating away at savings and retirement nest eggs. But real estate is the most effective inflation hedge there is…the surest way to protect and grow your wealth.

As I write this, all across the world soaring prices, raw material shortages, administrative backlogs, and other barriers are making it tough for developers to build.

Yet, demand for quality real estate in desirable locations is greater than ever before. Fed-up with rising living costs and now free to work from anywhere they want, people are trading San Francisco for Los Cabos and London for Portugal's Algarve…

There's a global housing shortage. As growing demand meets limited supply and peak pricing, we're entering what I call "The Era of Scarcity," and for most investors, that means there's a real lack of opportunity.

But you and I are not most investors…

If you're reading this then you've almost certainly joined my *Real Estate Trend Alert*.

Throughout this book you'll see many references to *Real Estate Trend Alert—RETA* for short. *RETA* is my investment research service for people interested in profitable real estate. People like us.

This book began as a promise to *RETA* members. I began writing it with the goal of putting everything I've learned in 25-odd years about buying real estate for profit and pleasure into one resource.

For years I searched for a group like *RETA*. I wanted to join like-minded folks eager to pool our buying power and share in the best real estate deals around the world. I searched in vain. For there was no such group.

So, in 2008 I founded my own and called it, that's right, *Real Estate Trend Alert*.

If you're not a member yet, well, you ought to be. The entire point of *RETA* is to put us on the inside of the world's greatest real estate opportunities. And during the Era of Scarcity, membership of *RETA* has more value than it's ever had before.

Outstanding deals are never easy to find, but most investors will find it even more of a struggle as scarcity bites. Meanwhile, *RETA* members will continue to access our pipeline of incredible off-market deals from the world's most desirable locations.

There is nothing like this book. And its lessons have never been more urgent or useful than in the uncertain world of the 2020s.

There are plenty of other books, blogs, courses, and videos out there about real estate. Many bamboozle us with complicated formulas...some are downright dangerous. Very few deal with overseas real estate, and none to my knowledge show you a clear and simple path to the best real estate opportunities in the most stunning corners of the world.

Prepare yourself for disappointment if you are a spreadsheet whizz. Get set for frustration if you are an animal for algorithms. Because in well over two decades of successful international real estate investing, I've distilled what I do into something deceptively simple—something I believe anyone can do.

I get in on the ground floor. I get my boots on the ground. And I have made a lot of money for myself and my *RETA* members doing it. For example:

- In August 2021, I brought *RETA* members an off-market deal in an upscale neighborhood of Cabo, Mexico, in a community called Cabo Costa. As I write a year later, *RETA* members and I are looking at a collective gain of $13.8 million based on today's retail prices. That's on paper obviously, we haven't all sold! I personally intend to rent long term into the hot Cabo market. I'm expecting these condos could gross 15% a year renting long term. That's give or take depending on the individual condo price. (More on this in chapter 8).

- A look at current retail prices in another Cabo deal called Monte Rocella we had in May 2022, shows *RETA* members who got in are sitting on a collective uplift of $10.2 million as I write in August 2022.

- In Playa del Carmen, on Mexico's Riviera Maya, we had a deal in a community called Siempre Playa in April 2017. The *RETA* price for condos was from $193,800. As of July 2022, those condos listed at $371,676. All told, the retail prices today show *RETA* members are collectively up over $15 million.

- Just 45 minutes or so drive down the coast from Playa del Carmen is the beach paradise of Tulum. I brought *RETA* members a deal in Tulum called Samsara in October 2021. Today's retail pricing shows *RETA* members who got in are collectively up over $22 million!

You get the point…big and rapid gains.

Of course, I have a few established processes, and yes, I crunch numbers. The numbers have to work before I'll even consider a deal. But I'll leave the complex formulas and real estate razzmatazz to the binder boys and flash promoters.

Does this all sound suspicious? You don't trust me yet, that's fine. Makes sense. All I ask is that you keep reading, because if using the ideas I share with you in this book leads to just a single successful real estate investment for you, well then! You are up many 1,000% on your investment in this book, and your time reading it has been extremely well spent.

And I'll have done what I set out to do…

That is, share my passion and open your mind to the opportunities out there in the world.

Spectacular real estate opportunities are always somewhere to be found. This is the God's honest truth. An indisputable fact. And after you read this book you'll be able to easily prove this fact to anyone you like.

The problem is that "somewhere" isn't your hometown, your county, state…it isn't even usually your home country.

You have to look beyond…

Everyone knows that getting ahead of big transformational events can make you a lot of money. But few us believe that ordinary folks can make out. It's always the rich that get richer, right?

Sure, you and I can't build a spaceship like Musk, or buy a penthouse for $50 million. But we can think and act internationally and benefit enormously from big transformational events. We can get ahead of the biggest trends in the world and buy the right real estate to profit from those trends.

And together, in our *RETA* group, we have a collective buying power that opens up much more opportunity for us than if we act alone.

That's what I am sharing with you in this book—I'm sharing with you a clear way to profit from the most spectacular opportunities in real estate today, tomorrow, and for the rest of your life.

What do you need?

Just common sense and some money (not necessarily a whole lot of money) will get you started.

You don't need any foreign languages, you don't need to travel, heck, like I say, you don't even need to leave your living room…

What People Say About *Real Estate Trend Alert*

"If you're serious about making money in real estate, I don't think there is any better group than *RETA*. Ronan's decades of research, networking, and negotiating are what makes the difference. The very high-quality threshold *RETA* deals need to meet reduces the risks of investing off-plan." — **Greg Bush, England, retired**

"The best most complete way to investigate international real estate investment." — **Nicole Garner, Arizona, business owner**

"In the past two years, between myself...friends and family, we have participated in 11 of the *RETA* offerings to date. Looking forward for more to come!" — **Patrick Carr, Denver, chief financial officer**

"If you can find a more honest, knowledgeable, and hard-working group than the staff at *RETA*, you should definitely do business with them and let me know who they are." — **Justin Barnett, Miami, retired**

"If a guy wants offshore real estate, *RETA* is the place to be." — **Russell Simmons, Canada, farmer**

"Fantastic real estate information, starting with Ronan and his great team of real estate scouts who travel the world looking for great *RETA* deals. Their informal communication and in-depth knowledge is off the charts." — **Robin Shortle, North Carolina, property manager**

"Smoking 'inside' deals before becoming public. Keep doing what you're doing!" — **Brad Costanzo, seasoned entrepreneur, growth strategist and investor**

"This group gets you on the inside of the most profitable real estate deals overseas. The group buying power allows us to buy directly from the developer at rock bottom prices before the general public." — **Johnny Corbyn, Virginia, business owner**

"No other way to get the best first-hand information on fabulous properties...most trusted source that you cannot match anywhere else. Actually the best kept secret, that we *RETA* members would like to keep for ourselves!" — **Roger Day, optometrist, California**

"Great way to become aware of international opportunities and there's a constant pipeline of opportunities to choose from when you are ready." — **Tom Walton, software engineer, Washington**

"Topnotch! Very detailed analysis of deals." — **Ray Steele, Lake Geneva, WI, retired**

"It's the #1 community for international real estate opportunities, and I would absolutely recommend it!" — **Jim Ballard, retired, Oregon**

"*RETA* is the only platform where you can get incredible deals at incredible locations. They truly deliver, working with best in class developers. Many offerings financing." — **Vince Santos, retired, Denver**

"I appreciate the *RETA* concept of strength in numbers, group members buying at a discount, and in locales with beauty, amenities, and rental income opportunities. I also appreciate Ronan McMahon's boots on the ground experience in international scouting and investment." — **Opal Daves, Model, Actress, writer, California**

"I think *RETA* has some of the most compelling real estate deals..." — **Laura Madsen, Wisconsin, Biotech management**

"A fantastic way to gain exposure to international real estate." — **Carl Barton, lawyer, Washington**

"Great research and connections in a wide variety of properties and countries. Great job people! Exceptional value to members and lots of great opportunities. Yes. One of a kind research and opportunities to grow a retirement nest-egg." — **David Simons**

"This service provides great pricing without the leg work and you have due diligence time to check the boxes to be as sure as possible that the investment fits you." — **Rita Bourne, Florida, real estate agent**

"This service really offers some incredible opportunities that are at great prices." — **Camelia Wintringham, California, designer**

"I love the research you guys do, and the detailed explanations of places, trends, contact with developers…" — **Joey Kimmons, Boston, retired teacher**

"Join now. When you see the right investment, jump in." — **Sally Barlow, Texas, firefighter**

"It's a wealth of information that you could never get on your own. And it could change your life for the better." — **Maxine Wilcher, Ohio, customer support analyst**

"I have recommended *RETA* to several people… I'm excited to finally be in process for my first *RETA* purchase and look forward to another after I've had my Social Security pension added to my income." — **Vanessa Warner, USA**

"Lots of timely information and specific properties in recommended locations." — **Milo Holland, Forth Worth, copywriter**

"Solid experienced advice with demonstrated track record of success." — **Franklin Naga, Colorado, travel and logistics concierge**

"*RETA* offers great analysis on what's going on in hot markets and creates unique opportunities through its group buying power." — **Archer Ray, Florida, physician**

"Find someone who really knows the markets and what they are doing, and I feel that *RETA* fits that bill extremely well." — **Cheryl Gibbs, Denver, retired finance & contracting officer**

"It is an established and reputable organization that brings members outstanding real estate opportunities around the world. Hop off the fence and join!" — **Warren Snyder, Colorado, training co-ordinator**

"Good education. Will help you get comfortable investing internationally. Good support." — **Chris Quinn, Dallas, financial executive**

"The deals are extraordinary." — **Virginia Hunt, California, banker**

"Just do it. A project will come along eventually that fits what you are looking for." — **Jordan Mitchell, Illinois, software engineer**

"Great on-the-ground intel, path of progress focused, reasonable but in-depth, international coverage." — **Jasmine Pearson, Bogota, senior management consultant**

"Great way to get into a network of foreign real estate ownership." — **Edgar Bell, Arizona, Chief Operating Officer**

"Best way to find a real deal and location outside of the USA." — **Kyla Cummings, Iowa, dermatologist**

"Introduction to best projects in diversity of markets, with best developer financing." — **Fred Todd, Salt Lake City, commercial real estate broker**

"Get into international investments at the right level and feel backed by the professional team at *RETA*." — **Robert Tenny, Sydney Australia, engineering consulting**

"Great way to explore opportunities around the world." — **Marc Howard, Florida, airline pilot**

"*RETA* finds all the best investment opportunities and deals all over the world." — **Jamie Harris, California, finance**

"The research, contacts, and educational information are unparalleled." — **Maurice Keller, Texas, life insurance agent**

"*RETA* does its homework and has only the best deals. I've been a member for a number of years and wish I'd gotten in to the properties from 2016 and prior." — **Bonnie Armstrong, Connecticut, nurse**

"I have told so many friends about *RETA*! My summary is something like this: About 20 years ago this guy from Ireland asked himself why he should spend another winter in Ireland. So, he didn't. He became fascinated by investment opportunities along what he calls The Path of Progress. Over the years he's formed relationships with first class developers in Spain, Portugal, Mexico, Costa Rico, Panama, and so many more. You pay a relatively small fee for access to Ronan's advice, insight, experience, connections, and amazing investment opportunities where he's done most of the heavy lifting. *RETA* tees up a real estate volume discount to some of the most sought-after destinations in the world." — **Eve Powers, Atlanta, real estate investor**

HOW TO USE THIS BOOK

By the time you finish this book you will have an incredible edge as a real estate investor. In fact, even a few short chapters in you'll *already* have a major advantage…

Because just a few chapters from now you're going to be the keeper of a powerful secret—the secret of making a fortune in real estate. It's deceptively simple. It's tried and tested by pretty much all the richest people in history. And I've made it my life's mission to unlock and share the power of this secret…

In addition to this powerful secret, by the end of chapter 5—not even the half-way mark of this book—you'll know exactly where in the world to invest in real estate for spectacular gains.

Stay with me from there and you'll have my D.E.A.L. system— my tried and tested system for deciphering the spin of smiling estate agents and seeing through the flashy brochures to gauge whether an investment is solid.

I also give you my five "R's" of successful real estate investing. A simple and easy-to-apply method for assessing real estate opportunities anywhere in the world.

And that's only the first half of the book…

In chapter 7 I introduce the most powerful driver of rental profits in the world today. Understanding this can set you up to own income-producing property in the world's most beautiful destinations. Income for life and a home in paradise. Appealing huh?

In chapter 8 I drill down on how you can maximize your rental yield like a pro. I also give you my hard-won lessons on how to pick the right rental manager so you can enjoy your income and your property hands-off and hassle-free.

Chapter 9 is all about how to use other people's money to make yours. You can make a lot of money and use none, or almost none, of your own cash to do it.

No book on real estate would be complete without a good crisis. Anyone who's lived knows there's always some crisis coming, it's just a matter of when. It's not something to fear, but to prepare for. Because incredible fortunes can be made when a big crisis occurs. For instance, I'll reveal how *RETA* members made many times their money after 2008. The key to successful crisis investing is knowing when and what to buy. In chapter 10 I give you that key so that when the next crisis comes along, you'll be ready.

Whatever you do in real estate investing, the most important rule of success is expressed in just three simple words. It's the most critical thing you can do to protect and grow your wealth through real estate. In chapter 11 I give you those three words and explain how to apply this rule when you're buying overseas real estate.

From there I reveal in-depth how you can create a life of fun and profit from just a few well-bought properties. Even one property in fact—just one property—bought at the right price and in the right location can generate annual yields of 15% or more.

Of course, there's travel and adventure too if you want those things. But travel is entirely optional. I'll show you ways you can successfully invest in real estate overseas without ever leaving your living room or office, never mind the country.

By the end of this book you'll be well on your path to success-fully investing in real estate overseas. And as a member of my *Real Estate Trend Alert* you'll have plenty of incredible deals to consider in some of the world's most beautiful and internationalized places.

But we're going to start where most investors start. With a mistake…

CHAPTER 1

The Worst Real Estate Play I Ever Made

"There are no mistakes in life, only lessons." — Robin Sharma

My whole life and portfolio is real estate. I own no stocks, no gold, nor crypto. I have no collectible coins, no cellars of fine wines nor classic cars. Instead, I own properties around the world. I travel. I scout for opportunities to invest in real estate globally. And—almost all the time—I make a profit.

It's my "job" and I love it. I'm an international real estate investor and scout. One of the few who do this full-time. Perhaps the only one. And I've now done it for close to two decades. I'll never stop.

When I'm not "boots on the ground" looking at property, land, or scouting a market somewhere, then chances are I'm on a call or messaging with a contact from some corner of the world. Even in my down time my wife sighs when she sees me surfing listings on my phone, buried in research for my next trip.

In recent years I've established a routine.

I have a base in Cabo San Lucas, Mexico, where I like to spend time between scouting trips in the winter. Every March I take a final stroll on the beach in front of my Cabo condo and say *adios* to the Pacific Ocean. Whales are common close to shore and it's usual to see one breaching the blue waters from right there on the sand.

Shortly afterward I'm in Cabo airport, en route to my base on Portugal's breathtaking Silver Coast to enjoy the summer in Europe.

Months later, as winter weather arrives in Europe, I say good-bye to the beaches and forests of Portugal and to my condo in the upscale Praia D'el Rey community…back to Cabo.

Whether going east or west across the ocean my ritual is largely the same when I leave a base. You can boil it down to two things: I take a final farewell walk on the beach. Then I hand my condo keys back to a trusted rental manager, safe in the knowledge that my condo will shortly start making me money.

And while my condos make money I'm elsewhere, doing what I want with whom I want…enjoying the weather I like.

How I Scout for Real Estate Across the Whole World

I'm not entirely alone. Over the years I've recruited and mentored a small and dedicated team. Seasoned travelers and scouts, they are based all over the world and help me to cover more ground and evaluate many more potential opportunities than I could by myself.

I spend a lot of time on the road. My team likewise are regularly traveling. There's always someone…somewhere… reporting back to me on something exciting. There's no substitute for boots on the ground research. And the more of this in-person scouting my team and I do, the more opportunities we uncover.

All this travel and research does of course cost my company a lot of money. It's worth every single cent as you'll see…

Weather is important to me when choosing a property to invest and spend time in. While I'm "at home" in one of my bases, I never want to turn on air-con or heating. I don't like humidity either. I'm like Goldilocks, except instead of porridge, I want my weather "just right" all the time.

I also want the ocean. Any property I own *and* spend time in must also be close to the ocean. And golf. The closer the better.

Another of my criteria is that my property must have rental potential.

Now, and this is important: these are some of the criteria for a property I'm spending time in for part of the year. This is one of the perks unique to being a global real estate investor. But for a pure investment property I have a different set of criteria.

We'll talk about *your* criteria and how to create them in this book as well as a great many other things that I believe can lead you onto a path of riches and freedom through real estate.

You do not need to travel. I know, sounds strange, but it's true. Choose the right deals and you may not even need to leave your house. We'll get into all that in this book.

Personally, I have always loved to travel and my trips to and from Cabo and Portugal are never direct. I travel to many places in between. I visit friends and family back home in Ireland, scout real estate and meet up with contacts in Mexico's Riviera Maya…Costa Rica…Panama…Italy…

Some years I've been in Asia, others I dig deep in Europe or hit the road in South America. As a full-time international real estate investor, putting my boots on the ground to run the rule over opportunities in person has been crucial to my success.

What does that success look like?

Well, for me today it means financial freedom, plus owning real estate in six countries, having passports for two, and residence in another three. It means leading a group for other real estate investors in a unique club I founded in 2008 called *Real Estate Trend Alert*.

(If you're reading this then you're likely a new member. Welcome to the club. In chapter 12 I'll explain how to get the best from your membership.)

But that's not where I started.

My own real estate journey started like that of most greenhorns: I started with luck and mistakes.

It was 2005 and I was on a roll. I was a keen and green real estate investor, hot to do deals and expand.

I had made my first real estate investments in my home country of Ireland. They were working out gangbusters and I'd just made the leap to international real estate with a highly successful play in Panama. (I'll explain how I ended up in Panama later, that's not important now.)

I was on a high and feeling smart. Around me I saw people making even more money. What seemed like easy money.

Through a friend of a friend I heard about a deal…

He told me there was a great opportunity to buy an apartment in the city of Newcastle, in the U.K., and bank serious rental returns. A big part of the appeal was the attractive financing. I listened as he walked me through details of how Newcastle was booming.

It sounded good. Here's how it worked…

For the sake of round numbers, the price was €200,000. But, I'd seen valuations of €230,000. I could get the mortgage based on the valuation of €230,000 which meant I could buy with little money down. Magic. Hardly any of my own money for immediate equity and what appeared to be positive cash flow. We had projections of rental income of €900 per month.

The deal was on pre-construction apartments. I saw that the population of Newcastle was around a million. This was the same as the Irish capital Dublin, where I was living and which was booming. Surely the economic vitality would be the same I reasoned. And in my naivety that was about all the due diligence I did.

The reality of Newcastle's economy vibrancy was very different. Employment levels were limited. Jobs were mostly low-level service. The market for those high-end apartments was limited. And once a bunch of them were delivered, projected rental rates fell from €900 a month to €700 a month.

The number that didn't change was the holding costs. The HOA fees were huge relative to the income, and there was also ground rent...all on top of the usual management charges. And when the extra supply hit the market not only did rents fall, but values did too.

I knew I'd made a mistake when I finally visited. I checked into a hotel near the apartments. It was late when I arrived so I couldn't make out much but the neighborhood seemed pretty quiet.

The next day was a Wednesday. And pretty much as soon as I left the hotel I sensed a problem. I couldn't find anywhere to get coffee. I could see nobody rushing to work. The streets were empty. And when I did find a café it was staffed by locals—not a foreign worker in sight—which is not a good sign of economic vibrancy in a city.

None of this was a scam. It was just a serious schooling that has informed the many real estate investments I have made since.

I had made a classic mistake. I got greedy. I got carried away by the crowd. I didn't even run the numbers properly. Even writing this today I flush with embarrassment. It seems so crazy to say it out loud. I had believed what I wanted to believe. And this is by far the biggest mistake I see investors make. We humans excel at creating stories to suit ourselves.

But, I don't regret this Newcastle investment. Truly. It was an incredibly valuable lesson and one I'm glad I learned early in my investing career. Since Newcastle, I have never lost money on a real estate deal. (I still own the Newcastle apartment and expect to sell it soon for about what I paid all those years ago).

These days I have a process of exhaustive research. And I have a team to help me. In 2021, my team and I spent close to a million dollars on travel and research to pinpoint opportunities for overseas real estate buyers.

I always run the numbers. But those only come 80% through the research process. Remember, the really big thing I'm looking for is unstoppable trends

I keep the emotions of fear and greed where they belong—a million miles away from my investment decisions. I have learned to be emotionally detached in the face of windfalls or setbacks. And I believe it's as important to pay attention to the dumb things you could do as it is to educate yourself about the smart things you should do.

We're only human. By understanding how our brains and emotions work we can hone our instincts for profit opportunities.

Every morning I remind myself to "Be Process Oriented." This is the top of my daily "to do" list.

Because I know if I follow the processes I have learned as a global real estate scout and investor, then the outcome will usually take care of itself.

In this book I'm going to share with you the processes I follow. The lessons I have learned. They have enabled me to create a life of travel, fun, and freedom as an international real estate investor. Whether you're looking to build an empire or just want to find a good deal on your dream home, my hope is that you will find what you need to get you well under way in these pages.

CHAPTER 2

The Simple First Step to Successful Real Estate Investing

"Knowing yourself is the beginning of all wisdom" — Aristotle

The first step to owning spectacular and profitable real estate is simple. It's the same first step to take wherever in the world you are planning to buy…

You can take this step right now. Because step one is to honestly profile yourself.

To do it, I suggest you get your smartphone out, or open up your computer and type out your answers. Or use a pen and paper.

You're going to interview yourself. And be truthful.

Why are you buying? Think about it before you write down your answer.

Are you purchasing as an investment or buying a vacation home? Is this a place you are going to spend a lot of time or will you rarely visit? Is it a mix of these things, are you seeking some income to cover the holding costs of the property? Are you hoping for big increases in capital appreciation or do you just love the view?

You need to be clear from the start what you want to get out of a property—and also how much you are willing to put in.

What is your time worth to you? Your energy. If you're working 60-hour weeks and are well-paid for it, you don't have much time.

So, buying a renovation project in France or Croatia—however profitable it might seem on paper—might not stack up as a good play for you. Buying a turnkey condo in Panama or Mexico with onsite property management might though.

The good news is that whatever your answer, there is almost certainly a good real estate deal out there to suit your circumstances.

If you are buying purely for investment, your real estate choices should depend on your financial objectives, your existing portfolio (real estate, stocks, bonds, etc.), your tolerance for risk, and simply the reasons you're in the game.

In other words, it depends on what kind of investor you are.

At first, determining what type of real estate investor you are might seem like a simple task…one that hardly deserves more than a few moments of your time. This is far from the truth. In the end, the type of investor you are will go a long way toward determining the type of properties you look at, and the type of property you'll eventually buy.

Although there are hundreds of factors that will eventually go into your final decision figuring out the basics below will get you started:

- Your reasons for making the investment
- Your tolerance for risk, and how much you have to invest
- How you intend to finance the property
- The needs of your existing portfolio
- Your level of experience in the market
- The level of involvement you want to have managing the property

Let's look at these one at a time…

Why are you making the investment?

I like to think of an investor's motivation as falling along an investment range.

At one end of the range, there's the buyer who wants to use and enjoy the property, hold it for an indefinite period, and eventually pass it along to his heirs.

Eventual resale of the property is not an issue for this buyer. Arguably, this may not even qualify as an "investment" in the financial sense, but more of a long-term investment for the family.

At the other end of the scale, there's the buyer who only cares about the investment potential of the property. It's not important what type of property it is, where it is, or what it's for, as long as the potential for a good return is high. Some of these investors never even see their properties. I own a car park in Northeast Brazil. I've visited once for four minutes, and I don't plan to ever return there. I didn't invest in it to park my car there. I invested in it purely to make money.

Of course, there's a wide range between the two extremes. Many of you will fall somewhere in the middle: you want to buy a property you like, in a place you enjoy visiting, *and* you want a reasonable potential for capital appreciation or income from rental returns.

And it's possible you'll evolve from one sort of investor to another over time, just as I have. I was initially pursuing profit and now enjoy a lifestyle of travel among my international properties.

Knowing why you're buying and where you sit on this investor's continuum helps you make the right decisions for you.

And you could be at different points for different properties…

You might buy a historic village home in the mountains of Tuscany as a place to spend time and a condo on Portugal's Algarve or Mexico's Riviera Maya to lock in enormous investment potential.

Your tolerance for risk

Ask yourself "How much money do I have to invest, and how much am I willing to put at risk?"

This is a critical question.

I like a restful night's sleep. I don't like stress or worry. And I invest accordingly. You should too. Life's too short to spend it stressing and juggling things.

So how much money can you invest without breaking into a sweat at the thought of it...

To answer the question, you need to consider several factors. Among these are the percentage of your overall assets required for a potential investment, how close you are to needing the money for retirement or another financial commitment (people five years from retirement will generally assume a lower risk than people 20 years away), and perhaps most importantly, your overall comfort level with risk.

Why is comfort level important? Because perhaps more important than your loss of sleep—at least from a financial perspective— is that being uncomfortable with an investment can cause you to make hasty or rash decisions if the market fluctuates in the future. Comfort allows sober thinking, the most important thing for an investor.

How does this relate to buying an investment property?

In the same way that it relates to any investment. You choose an investment that matches your risk profile. For example, buying pre-construction can mean you double, treble, or even 5X your money fast, but it comes with more risk than buying a completed home in an established community.

You are supposed to get higher returns for taking higher risk. The world is upside down right now in this regard. The high-risk, developed world is showing measly returns.

Historically, due to their relative instability and lack of regulation, investing in developing countries is generally perceived riskier than in First-World, developed countries. Yet, I see strong opportunities to get in at the ground floor in developing markets.

Done right, a strong rental yield will pay for your real estate. Renting to pay for your real estate is a proven strategy. I employ this strategy and so do many of the most successful real estate investors I know. Even some highly leveraged deals can be positive cashflow with no money down. (This is the case with my condo on Portugal's Silver Coast as you'll see later in this book.)

You need to be hyper conservative though…thoroughly understand your costs and stress test your income projections. Remember that renting short term can be more exposed to all sorts of shocks… these can range from a pandemic to a war…and costs will be higher…plus it usually takes time to build up your rental business. (I tell you how to do it in chapter 8.)

Another way to mitigate your risk is simply take your time. I'm a big believer in making a manageable step…bagging a win…doing it again…grow fast by making steps that never take you out of your comfort zone.

As I told you in the last chapter, my worst investment happened when I wanted to move too fast and missed steps. You can create a snowball effect with success. If you over stretch and find yourself chasing bills and dealing with setbacks you will get stuck.

Your options for financing

How you categorize yourself as a real estate investor has much to do with how you intend to finance the purchase. If you're a cash buyer with no desire to leverage your position through financing, the process will be simple for you. Otherwise, the options you have for financing depend largely on which country you're buying in.

Cash buyers can find themselves with very big advantages when it comes to income properties overseas. As a general rule, markets where finance isn't available have less liquidity and fewer buyers, thus lower prices...it's a way you can maximise yield. Also, in some markets finance isn't available on older buildings. This deflates their values. But, they still rent really well, meaning yields can be strong.

A big distinction here is the parts of the world—mostly Europe—where mortgages are available to foreigners. You might not need financing, yet you still finance to keep your capital to invest elsewhere. There are places on my beat where North Americans can lock down attractive bank financing. For example, in Portugal, where I've known of foreigners securing 80% mortgages at 1.6%.

Your financing options will, to some extent, influence what kind of properties you will be in the market for. For example, if you have cash to spend, you can really invest in anything. On the other hand, if you need finance and don't own property to use to secure a loan back home, you may want to focus your attention on projects where developer financing is available—as is often the case with the off-market deals I bring *RETA* members—or on teaming up with other investors, or on "off-plan" investments where you don't need all of the money up front.

Don't forget that financing becomes even more attractive when borrowing in currencies which are expected to fall in value against the dollar, since you'll be paying the loan back with the equivalent of fewer dollars.

What fits well in your existing portfolio?

Within real estate holdings, many investors like to create a mix similar to that of their overall portfolio. That is, they mix aggressive, higher-risk investments with longer-term, steady-growth investments. For example, if you're 20 years from retirement—or otherwise needing the capital—then your investment mix would include a higher percentage of aggressive real estate investments focused on growth and capital gain.

On the other hand, if you're close to retirement and need money, your real estate investments should lean closer to more conservative, steady-growth, income-producing properties.

Investment in undeveloped raw beachfront close to Tulum, on Mexico's Riviera Maya 20 years back is a good example of an aggressive investment. Values increased by 20 times or more as infrastructure and development rolled through...but that huge increase was because development was not a "sure" thing.

Crisis investing in Venezuela today is another good example of an aggressive-style investment. There's no clear path to the country's recovery, but you could buy a beach home for $15,000 from someone who just wants out. And it just might work out...or not.

On the other hand, an apartment in an established European second city would be considered a more conservative buy. When I say "second city" I'm talking about places like Montpellier or Bordeaux in France, or Verona in Italy. I think "first cities" like Paris and London have seen prices pushed too high because of their status as safe havens.

Your level of experience in the market

The level of experience of an investor should match the type of investments they are making. New investors will be best-suited to—and more comfortable with—some of the less complex investments.

For example, undertaking a development project on your own in a far-flung corner of the world may be fine if you have some experience in the country, know the language, and have participated in this type of investment before, but may not be right for your first overseas experience. You could stay close to home, the next state over, or in an established place like Mexico's Riviera Maya where you have property managers to hire.

Managed vacation rentals or a long-term rental to some digital nomad newly freed from their office are relatively safe and easy investments, as are investments in businesses in which you have significant experience.

It all depends on your experience.

How hands on?

Before you ever lay down a red cent for a piece of real estate with a view to generating rental income, you need to ask yourself one important question: How hands on do I want to be?

From the beginning, you need to decide how much work you're willing to put in. If you're looking to buy in a place where there's no established rental management companies or tourist market, you need to be a lot more hands on to make a success of it.

You'll need the time, motivation, resources, and skills to draw in vacationers and manage the whole rental process. If you don't want to be hands on, you need to find a place with an established rental market (long or short term) with excellent rental managers so that you can stay hands off.

The level of participation you can apply to the venture tells you a lot about the type of investment you should be making. One thing is for sure…it will flag certain investments as ones you should NOT be doing. There are investments that require minimum personal involvement, and others that require a lot of your attention.

Determining what kind of real estate investor you are takes into account many factors. You should rate and profile yourself. When you have a better idea of what kind of global real estate investor you are, you'll have an easier time narrowing down your many options.

Generally, more effort means more profit. But, if you're inexperienced and your time short, giving a property manager a cut can be very worthwhile.

"Beware Geeks Bearing Formulas"

A few years ago, I traveled to Portugal's Algarve in the company of a friend. He said he was seriously interested in buying. He was especially interested in a bank fire-sale deal I was looking into at the time for members of my *Real Estate Trend Alert*.

Bank seizures and fire sales are different overseas than what you might be used to in the States where the entire process happens in a quick and transparent way. It's an opaque and muddled process in most of the world. This can be played to your advantage when you know how. Often the bankers and bureaucrats left handling the real estate haven't a clue what they are doing and aren't even interested.

I was paying close attention to a 16th-century convent in a historic town in Portugal's eastern Algarve.

The convent was in ruins until an ambitious developer moved in to convert this building into a condominium complex. The developer had a good eye...and brought in a world-renowned architect to make the conversion a reality. The potential was there. The vision was there. But the timing was off. The project was completed in 2012 as recession was ripping through Europe. The developer got into trouble. So, the developer slashed his prices. But not enough. I first visited this project in 2014. I kept going back to check in on how things were playing out...the noose was tightening on the developer. The bank moved in and took possession of the final condos. The bank then slashed the prices 25% below what they were when I first visited—and way below what the developer had been asking for at launch.

Then the bank offered discounted mortgages on these condos of as little as 1% for EU residents. Non-EU residents paying closer to 2%...still an amazing cost saving over the life of your mortgage. The bank just wanted these condos off their books.

So, you could get access to finance for 90% of the condo's cost, through a discounted bank mortgage, and you could qualify up to 75 years of age.

I told my friend the way I saw the deal working out was this: You could have got in for just 10% of the condo cost—as little as €21,000...and immediately start targeting an income. There was already an established rental market. I expected gross $2,700 a month from 50% occupancy in a year—that's $32,400 annually.

So you could be in for a mortgage as small as €534 a month...and make an average of five times that a month from rental income. Done right, it looked as close to getting free money as you'll ever find.

I expected steady (albeit not stellar) capital appreciation... maybe 40% to 50% rise in value over a decade. Figuring that you could be only into this for 10% (mortgage down-payment) and your cash-on-cash capital appreciation becomes more than stellar.

Of course, there were closing costs to consider—about 6% to 8% in Portugal. And the cost of rental management, anywhere from 11% to 20% maximum per year.

All things considered though, this was a great deal and my friend loved the amenities, the salt-water swimming pool... the feeling of being inside an old palace. He liked Portugal, and especially the Algarve, with its 300-plus days of sunshine, beaches, world-class golf...my buddy was a big golfer.

But my friend didn't buy. Instead, he put every number he could find into complicated spreadsheets. He hummed and hawed...he tortured himself with numbers, got into microscopic detail on all the "what if's." In the end he let the deal pass him by...

Buying real estate is a big decision. Buying overseas or out-of-state is an even a bigger one maybe. So, I get it. You want to get it right.

But, just like my friend, some folks want to get things so right that they never make a decision. I've met dozens of folks who paralyse themselves with spreadsheets and drown themselves in numbers and sums. They let their doubts and fear stop them.

If this is you I'm here to tell you that, if you have put your processes in place and you are true to them, you should trust your instincts. Sure, crunch the numbers. That's critical. But don't let formulas rule you. Even mighty Zillow has realized that algorithms alone can't make you a successful real estate investor. In November 2021, the company pulled out of the buying business after paying over the odds for thousands of homes. Using algorithms to buy and flip houses cost Zillow more than $300 million in a few months.

There are countless "experts" out there with "sure-fire" formulas. They lure you with the promise of magic numbers, iron-clad laws of real estate investing. Don't let them waste your time and energy...trust yourself. As Warren Buffet says "beware geeks bearing formulas."

As I've told you, personally I keep it deceptively simple: I follow big unstoppable trends. Then I position myself ahead of these big unstoppable trends. I find the right location... the right real estate...at the right price. And I make a point of doing business with the right people.

I get in on the ground floor. I get my boots on the ground. And I have made a lot of money doing it.

"We've Been in Six *RETA* Deals"

My wife and I joined Ronan McMahon's *Real Estate Trend Alert* in 2011. I was an international business executive, eventually the COO for a $2-billion, U.S.-based chemical company.

This allowed us to travel the world and live abroad. We spent 18 months in Shanghai, China, and travel gave us the desire to own real estate in different countries. Plus, with all of the turmoil in the world we felt like having different options for the future made a lot of sense for us.

I own stocks and bonds, gold and silver, commercial real estate...I landbank some property and even own some cryptocurrency. (Just for fun and to try and understand the technology.)

I consider overseas real estate for both investment and lifestyle. I own properties that I don't rent and I also own properties that I've never stayed in for pure investment.

I have successfully been in five *RETA* deals. The sixth deal lost government funding so the developer had to back out but I got my entire deposit back because of the structure of the *RETA* deal.

Our first *RETA* deal was in 2011 or 2012. We bought a lot in Costa Rica's Southern Zone. We had plans drawn to build on the site but we decided that it was just a little too rural for our lifestyle. We decided to landbank the lot and are currently sitting on 35% paper gains.

Our next adventure was to Spain's Costa del Sol. This was where I got our first international rental property—a two-bed, two-bath apartment in Puerto Banus. It is hard to say about profitability, because of the COVID crisis. Currently this year I have about 4% net profit and am sitting on around €50,000 paper gains.

The next adventure on the Costa del Sol was buying a three-story townhouse with a rooftop terrace, overlooking the town of Sotogrande and the Rock of Gibraltar. This was truly an adventure as I bought the townhouse, sight unseen, out of foreclosure and in need of major renovations. It took us some time to get the extensive renovations completed. Then we furnished the home with high-end furniture. It was at that time, that my wife decided this was our second home and a lifestyle buy and thus we would not be renting this house.

I am currently writing to you from this townhouse. Two or three times a year we travel from our home in the U.S. to spend time here—six or eight weeks at a time. We have made many good friends here in the community. I am probably sitting on paper gains of around 35% but it is our getaway place.

Every time I arrive at my Spain house and I look at the view and meet our friends, I say to myself "this beats the hell out of a condo on the Gulf Shores." I find it quite fun when people ask "where are you going next month?" and I say to my house in Spain. They do not know it cost less than a condo in the U.S.

When a *RETA* deal in Playa del Carmen on Mexico's Riviera Maya came along, I was very interested in the properties for investment. I decided to buy two condos in this pre-construction project called Siempre Playa. That was around 2017.

I bought a one-bedroom on the ground floor, and a two-bedroom on the second floor. I bought premium apartments to get the floor plans and location I wanted. The COVID crisis caused some delays but all in all we were not in bad shape timing wise. I took possession of the properties, furnished them nicely, and put them in the rental program. After a couple of months, I had inquiries about long-term rental opportunities and decided to look at long-term rentals. Although the rental income may be less, the wear and tear on the properties is much less. After the initial start-up costs, the condos have rented long term without a gap. That has allowed for a 9% net profit and about 35% in paper gains on the units.

Down the coast from Playa del Carmen, I am under contract in another *RETA* deal in Tulum for a unit to be delivered in a year or so.

I haven't yet taken the opportunity to use leverage on any of my deals. However, I will probably use developer financing on the Tulum deal.

I could not have sourced these deals without Ronan and *RETA*. It has added stability to my overall portfolio in that it has been very steady with value and rental income.

Things can go wrong and you need to understand the situation you are investing in. That is the reason I prefer pre-construction deals that are with a solid developer.

As part of a balanced portfolio, overseas real estate gets some of your assets out of your home country and thus reduces your investor bias risks. Plus, it is a lot of fun figuring out which deals fit your current situation and how to make it work. I have no regrets about getting involved in international real estate, especially with guidance from *RETA*.

I met Ronan early on and found him to be very genuine. I often question his early evaluations of the deals as being optimistic. I continue to be very conservative when I look at the *RETA* numbers but, I will say, most deals and all of the pre-construction deals have been better than he predicted.

My advice to you if you're new to *RETA* is to be comfortable with your first deal and make sure it makes sense for you and your family. I have made solid gains and made some great friends along the way. Also, go to an event to meet like-minded people. Very few of your current friends will be supportive of international real estate investing...only because they do not understand it or have the tolerance for the risk or the time and interest to understand it.

My wife Pam loves the ride and the fun of seeing different countries. I have to remind her that the properties are for investments and that we need to keep them rented versus using them. She often reminds me that we have not stayed in our Mexico apartments...ever.

I will continue to expand my exposure to international real estate as I think it is a buffer to any one economy. I also think it is a great way to teach my children about different types of investments and ideas for the future. I will continue to look for the right opportunities through *RETA*. There is simply no way I could source these quality deals on my own."
— *Chet Cross, Puerto Banus, Spain, September 2022.*

CHAPTER 3

6 Kick-Ass Reasons to Own Real Estate

"Real estate is an imperishable asset, ever increasing in value. It is the most solid security that human ingenuity has devised. It is the basis of all security and about the only indestructible security."
— Russell Sage, American financier and railroad tycoon

"Buying real estate is not only the best way, the quickest way, the safest way, but the only way to become wealthy."
— Marshall Field, billionaire entrepreneur

So, you know what kind of investor you are…

Armed with these truths you are ready to move forward. But resistance! Your heart is filled with fear. Uncertainty is your bedfellow. Buying real estate in a foreign country. "Are you crazy!?" says your wife, husband, mistress, barber, doctor, co-worker…

Relax. Smile wisely. Hand them a copy of this book. You are sane and sober.

I'm about to give you the seven best reasons why *anyone* with some money to protect and a desire to make more should love international real estate. In this chapter, I lay out six of those seven reasons. I have so much to say about the final (and number one) reason to own overseas real estate that I've devoted the entire next chapter to it.

And let's get one thing straight upfront: You don't have to look very far. A lot of the best deals I've uncovered over the years are just a short flight away in familiar places. I'm talking about places like Cabo, the Caribbean, Mexico's Riviera Maya, Panama, Costa Rica…

It's of massive benefit to you and your family to own the right real estate in places like these.

And here's why:

1. Protect Your Wealth

To make money, first you need to ensure you don't lose any. Let's talk about your retirement portfolio…

Your retirement account is likely to be almost 100% allocated to U.S. and dollar-denominated assets. That's a bet that the U.S. will continue unchallenged for our lifetime and beyond.

As all of us saw after the last financial crisis, that's not a smart bet to make. If there's a big problem at home, your portfolio is going to take a pounding, maybe with no chance of recovery. Knowing this alone makes its prudent to look beyond your home borders.

Having a strong stable of foreign real estate in your portfolio can help insulate you against market changes—and reduce your exposure to your home market.

I'm 100% invested in real estate. No stocks, bonds, nor crypto. Yet I still consider myself diversified across countries, markets, and real estate asset classes. For example, I own property in Mexico (Caribbean and Pacific), the U.K., Brazil, Portugal, and Ireland. This means I am tapping into very different markets. Middle-class renters in Brazil, Spanish and Dutch vacationers in Portugal, Americans in Cabo…and so on.

2. The Best Asset for Building Wealth

Real estate is the most versatile asset you can own. It offers many different ways to maintain and grow wealth. You can rent short term or long term. Use it as leverage to secure a loan or refinance and free up money. Hold and watch it appreciate in value…or buy cheap and flip it for a profit. You might even decide to live in it yourself, or use it as your winter getaway.

This flexibility is one of the reasons real estate has created more millionaires than any other asset class. In fact, over the last two centuries, about 90% of the world's millionaires have been made by investing in real estate.

It's simply the most reliable asset there is for building long-term wealth. Even when the housing market takes a dip, history has shown that it always recovers and continues on its path of appreciation.

In 2017, when a team of expert economists from the Federal Reserve Bank of San Francisco studied the return of four major investments from 1870 to 2015 (that's 150 years of data crunching), they discovered that real estate came out on top. They looked at treasury bills, bonds, equities, and real estate.

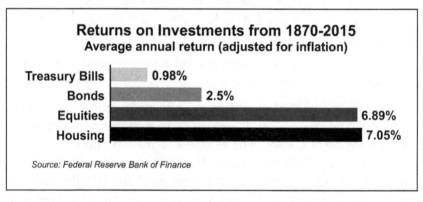

Real estate wins: The average return taken from 16 of the wealthiest economies.

Residential real estate, not equities, has been the best long-run investment over the course of modern history. And although returns on housing and equities over the long term are similar, the volatility of housing returns is substantially lower.

Essentially, this means that with real estate you can have the benefits of stock market appreciation, while protecting yourself from the same levels of volatility. And that's something especially important in any retirement portfolio.

While the stock market generally does recover from crashes, it takes time. Time you might not be able to afford if you're planning to start drawing from your savings soon. For this reason, the rule of thumb is that you should be diversifying away from stocks and other volatile assets as you get closer to retirement.

3. Use Inflation as a Moat

Inflation. According to President Ronald Reagan, "as violent as a mugger, as frightening as an armed robber and as deadly as a hitman."

Most economists will tell you inflation is how governments secretly and unobserved take money from you. Some call it a "stealth tax."

Whatever you call it and whatever causes it, the effect of inflation is the same. Your dollars are worth less as time passes. Prices for goods and services go up. And the more rapid the rate of inflation, the faster your savings are eroded. A $100 sitting in your bank account drops in real worth to $80...then $60...then $20...

Inflation is particularly dangerous if you're close to retirement. Nest eggs get mauled by inflation. Stockpiled cash and savings decline in value.

You'll find people piling into real estate during periods of inflation. It's without doubt the best hedge against it.

Real estate values tend to rise with inflation. According to data from the U.S. Bureau of Labor Statistics, from 1967 to 2021 the price of housing has gone up 4.16% per year, versus an overall inflation rate of 3.93%.

If you bought a $100,000 home in 1967, it would be worth $901,165 today. This doesn't account for any rental income you could have also collected, and over 54 years that would be a significant amount. Just like real estate values, rental income also tends to rise with inflation.

But here I'm talking about if you buy ordinary real estate, in a matured market.

Take a global view, invest in real estate in the right places, and you can hedge against inflation while also benefitting from buying in a market on a major upswing.

I own in multiple markets, across multiple continents. This means I spread my risk and am less exposed than real estate investors who stick exclusively to their home market.

Members of my *Real Estate Trend Alert* and I tend to buy in internationalized places that always have an influx of tourists, expats, or long-term renters. So, even when the world is rocked by war or pandemic or economic catastrophe, I can still do OK from my properties. And when times are good, I can do exceptionally well. In fact, when the dust settles on big crises, the markets in these internationalized places jump to the next level. Fresh waves of people come seeking everything these places offer. Demand explodes. We saw this after the global financial crisis and after the COVID pandemic.

For instance, with my ocean-view condo in Cabo, Mexico, I'm sitting on gains of over six figures. I bought there as part of an exclusive *RETA* deal in 2015. Our get-in price at the time was $336,156. A few weeks ago, as I write this in 2022, a broker wrote to me asking if I would sell for $600,000.

The first summer I rented out my condo it made me $1,800 a month. Not bad, even if renting to a friend of a friend meant that it was below market rate. Then COVID hit, and Cabo's long-term rental market exploded. First, rental prices hit $2,500 a month. That seemed huge...until it went to $2,750 a month. As I write this, in 2022, you'd do well to find a rental like this for $3,200 or even $3,300 a month. This would be a great return for a short-term rental, but for a hands-off long-term rental it's incredible.

When you get in on the right real estate deal, in the right place, positioned ahead of growing demand, then inflation can be a big benefit. It makes future supplies of real estate more expensive to create. The materials for construction go up in price. Labor costs rise. This is a recipe for values to pop.

So, if you've locked in a true deal and a killer low price, your potential gains and yield stand to be even higher than you might first have thought.

You're likely a new member of *Real Estate Trend Alert* if you're reading this book. Which means you may not be crystal clear that you and I have our strong pipeline of desirable deals at exclusive *RETA*-only pricing.

This is thanks to our group buying power and my connections, and later in this book I'll explain exactly how to use your *RETA* membership to make wise and profitable investments in chapter 12.

My point here though is that when we invest right, inflation can be good news for us.

4. Real Estate is...Real!

Real estate is the only asset you can live in. You can't admire the view, make a cup of coffee, or take a dip in the infinity pool of your stock certificate or Bitcoin.

Real estate is a tangible asset and inherently valuable. Folks will always need homes to live in, land to farm, and commercial space to run their business from. And when you own it, you can use it yourself too.

This is one of the things I love most about real estate. Especially real estate in desirable locations…

For instance, my condo in Cabo has not only seen capital appreciation rise to six figures, it also provides me with incalculable value as my winter base. It's an incredible place to spend time. I can watch migrating whales from my terrace. Spend time on the golden-sand beach. And enjoy endless days of sunshine. When I'm not there, aside from renting it out, I can lend it to friends and family. You can't do these things with a stock certificate.

The other advantage to real estate being real is that supply is relatively fixed. Unlike dollars, you can't print 2 trillion homes overnight. Supply is limited by a complex mix of land, permits, capital, machinery, materials, and skilled entrepreneurs.

In some places supply can be relatively easily added—think Vegas rolling out into the desert. In others it's fixed—think a historic apartment in Paris.

I like to buy in places with supply constraints and growing demand. I find the right location, the right deals, the right people, then I negotiate a *RETA*-only deal with a developer.

You don't need a complex equation to figure out what happens when more people want a scarce thing: the price goes up. As the price goes up people start panicking that it will go up more, so they feel they need to act, and someone offers you more money than the property is worth and you sell.

Buy in the right place, and at the right moment, and you can see values double in as little as three years on top of income. Over the course of my investing career, I have found these buying moments in Ireland, Panama, Spain, Brazil, Mexico, and elsewhere.

The other side of having a tangible asset is its "liquidity." By liquidity, I'm referring to the volume of transactions the market can handle and the speed at which it's possible to buy or sell at any given time. I love real estate's lack of liquidity.

When an asset is illiquid and limited it creates the conditions for much greater profits. The crowd surges at the top of the bubble so you have a lot of buyers when it comes time to sell, pushing prices even higher.

Remember at the start of this book when I told you emotion is the investor's number one enemy? For liquidity to be your friend you need to be comfortable and able to ride things out. With time, even bad situations can work themselves out (once you follow the basic rules)…and strong situations can truly snowball.

I guess the point here is that this is a medium-term journey, no rash buying or selling.

5. You Can Buy with Other People's Money

Leverage is so powerful a tool that I've devoted an entire chapter to it later in this book explaining how to exploit and use it.

The essence is simple: When you buy real estate with borrowed money you can increase your returns. And it means you don't need a huge pot of money to get in on deals.

For instance, if you wanted to invest in a condo for $200,000, you could do it with as little as $40,000 down, using a mortgage or financing to cover the remaining 80%. And you'd still get to keep 100% of the profits from capital gains.

Rent out the property and the income can cover the entire mortgage, and make you plenty more besides…essentially giving you free real estate.

This is what I've done with two properties in Portugal. In 2020, a Portugal contact and I snagged a home in Vale do Lobo, a top-tier resort community in the Central Algarve, at bargain basement prices and no money down.

This was a bank firesale property and the bank just wanted to offload the property.

The price was €410,000. And we put €37,000 into furnishing and cleaning it up.

Soon after I saw an identical apartment listing for €830,000. With no money down, that opens us up to incredible returns. Plus, this condo has been renting for €3,500 a week peak season.

Big warning here: You need to be prudent. The right deal is key. I've looked at lots of deals that have 100% finance at less than 2% and never recommended them to *RETA* because the deals didn't stack up. Don't buy a bad deal just because of cheap and easy credit.

But, with the right deal you can 5X…10X…even 20X your money using the miracle of leverage.

I've seen this strategy work time and time again, across my global beat. In fact, I've personally used leverage in almost every real estate investment I've ever made. And it has consistently delivered strong returns.

We've looked at my recent use of leverage in Portugal. Now, let's look at an old *RETA* deal from Spain…

North Americans can get mortgages from Spanish banks. Not a possibility in every country on my beat, but in countries where you are able to, it can be the road to those huge profits I'm talking about.

One Sunday afternoon back in 2019, I was reviewing some old recommendations I had made to *RETA* members to see how they were doing.

I came across a listing for an apartment in La Duquesa on Spain's Costa del Sol. A two-bed unit listing for €245,000.

In 2013, *RETA* members could buy here from €95,000.

It was one of the very first Spanish deals I recommended in the wake of the last big global crisis.

Turning €95,000 into €245,000 in six years (from 2013 to 2019) is quite the gain. More than double your money!

But let's assume the buyer bought with an 80% mortgage from a Spanish bank, which was available then to foreign buyers.

That would have put you into the deal for €19,000 and shows gains of €150,000.

That's nearly eight times your money.

My analysis of course is somewhat simplistic. I have ignored the rental income you could have banked from renting short term to vacationers here. The Costa del Sol greeted more than 13 million tourists in 2019. I also ignored purchase costs and holdings costs. In Spain there are high upfront buying costs. Figure on 10% but it can be a bit more or less. Your ongoing holding costs are tiny—€40 a month should cover your HOA fees and taxes.

But you get the point…you could double your money or using leverage quintuple your money!

Of course, using other people's money to buy an asset isn't unique to real estate, but it's rarely as favorable. That's because when ordinary investors borrow to buy stocks, they have to use margin loans, which usually carry high and variable rates of interest and include terms that allow the lender to force them to repay at a moment's notice. An extremely risky play.

Using leverage to buy real estate changes the playing field. Indeed, it changes the game.

That is to say, in many places you can borrow with low interest rates…which means the cost of borrowing is very cheap. And unlike borrowing on margin, you won't suddenly be asked to pay it back all in one go. In fact, you'll typically have between 20 and 30 years to pay it back, all spread out in small monthly installments.

And when you're doing it ahead of big unstoppable trends set to drive prices up, as you can see, it makes for an amazing investment.

Income of €72,000 a Summer and a Villa in Portugal

My contact on Portugal's Algarve, Chris White, is a 14-year veteran of the real estate industry. Originally from England, Chris has helped hundreds of people buy property there, including many *Real Estate Trend Alert* members.

As a real estate investor, Chris has walked the walk, too. In 2018 Chris snagged a bank foreclosure property that had just come on the market.

It was a villa on a big lot of about 3,000 square meters (32,292 square feet) with over 100 trees and a swimming pool. But, it was a wreck. The pink paint was crumbling, palm trees were growing into the pool, and it had been left empty for over eight years.

Still, he saw the potential. He bought it at asking price for €420,000 with a plan to spend another €80,000 to €100,000 fixing it up, and then flipping it.

He got a fixed rate mortgage of 90%, so he paid just €42,000, borrowing the rest, and has repayments of just €830 a month.

Today, the villa is fully refurbished and now valued at as much as €1.9 million.

However, Chris doesn't plan to sell anymore. It's now his primary residence and a huge income earner when he's not using it. In the summer of 2022 he made a whopping €72,000 renting out his home while he and his family took

---

a seven-week vacation across Europe and Southeast Asia. This covered his entire mortgage for the year and handed him another €62,000 in gross profit, paying for his lengthy and exotic vacation and then some.

By renting his villa for just seven weeks of a year, he generates a gross yield of over 17%. (That's figured on how much he is into it including mortgage. Cash on cash yield is much more.)

Then there are the benefits of using a fixed-term mortgage, which allows you to keep the same rate of interest for years. It means that you can save a truckload of money during times of high inflation.

Say, for example, you borrow $400,000 with a fixed-rate mortgage of 2.5% over 30 years. If inflation is then running at 5% it means that the value of your payments fall, in real terms, by 2.5% a year for 30 years.

So, while you are paying $568,974 in total, adjusted for inflation, you are paying just $293,715 in real terms. A difference of $275,259— just under half the value of the total payment.

I know this is a very simplistic calculation. Inflation will never remain at the same rate for 30 years, and it can go down as well as up. The purpose here is to illustrate just how powerful a fixed-rate mortgage can be during prolonged periods of high inflation.

Of course, a mortgage is not the only option for buying overseas real estate with other people's money. With many of the special off-market deals I bring to members of *Real Estate Trend Alert*, our group gets exclusive developer financing.

Developer finance is, as the name suggests, when a developer finances a piece of the real estate you buy from them—they are the bank. This is a useful way of gaining leverage in places like Latin America, for example, where typical mortgages just aren't possible.

Or, at the very least, come with huge costs and soul crushing bureaucratic requirements.

With developer financing, you can bypass the banks entirely. But getting it is tough. In fact, I've rarely seen it for anyone other than members of my *Real Estate Trend Alert* group because of our contacts and our group buying power. Most ordinary retail buyers will never get this option.

For instance, with a deal I brought to *RETA* in Playa del Carmen on Mexico's Riviera Maya in 2022, members could own in a luxurious, amenities-rich community, including a well-regarded 18-hole Nick Price golf course and access to a secluded secret beach, from $258,600. I expect these condos to be worth $400,000 just three years after delivery—a $141,400 boost. Even at that I'm being conservative (it is very much a $500,000-level community and then some).

But thanks to *RETA*'s group buying power, we got in at an exclusive price…and we didn't have to pay it all up front. In fact, members who got in could lower their risk and increase their upside thanks to the exclusive developer financing.

Members who acted on the deal will pay just 50% of the purchase price of their condo through a payment plan. Then, when the condo is delivered, they can pay the remaining 50% over 10 years with monthly payments from $1,468.

With demand for the right rentals in Playa del Carmen so high, I'm predicting $36,500 in annual rental income once they're established—that's $18,884 more than the cost of their payments.

6. Feared, Overlooked, Yet Easier Than at Any Time in History

"You're crazy." Buying real estate in a foreign country can often be seen as a symptom of madness by loved ones.

Fear is a factor. The rules are different, the language is alien… and can you trust those darned foreigners?

I respect scepticism about investments. Especially when it comes from a lack of knowledge. It's smart to be wary when you don't know much of the detail. Remember, that's the big lesson I learned with my first overseas investment when I bought property in Newcastle in the U.K. I invested without doing my homework. I've never made that mistake again.

There was a time when all I knew about Panama was that it had a big canal. Then I spent time there and did a lot of research. I then bought and sold property there for a profit.

"You're crazy" is pretty much the reaction I got from friends and family when I bought that property in Panama. Now, years later my family and friends have enjoyed staying in a bunch of my overseas properties from Portugal to Mexico and have seen how I've made money from owning them. These days I wonder who's crazy, the guy who sticks to "safe" investments in a stagnant home market chasing very modest yields, or folks like you and I, who know that we don't have to...

Because convenience is a big factor, too. Most folks just don't have time to do their own research or uncover the next hot market. They don't know where to look or how. So, when they invest in real estate, they rarely look far from home. They take the easy and most obvious route.

It might seem crazy not to shop around when you're about to make a big money decision, but it happens all the time. People don't consider the benefits of looking beyond their own backyard.

But buying and holding real estate in most countries on my beat is just as easy as buying the house next door. Some folks will tell you it's even easier.

Here's an example: A member of my *RETA* group bought a condo in Spain's Costa del Sol after I recommended a deal there in June 2015. She bought a penthouse for €129,000.

Then she had it furnished and rented it short term into a hot market. Finally in 2020, she sold the condo for €254,000.

And she did it all by email. All remotely. Through dealing with my contact on the Costa del Sol, she sold for a gross profit of €125,000, not including the rental income, and she never even had to leave her home.

"If They Can Get Passive Income... So Can I"

In April 2017, *RETA* member Dede Fulk bought a condo pre-construction in Playa del Carmen on Mexico's Riviera Maya. The deal was great. I had negotiated an exclusive price with a well-established developer starting at $193,800 depending on the condo. The building was in the heart of Playa's trendiest up-and-coming beach neighborhood.

Dede has taken delivery of her condo and started making income. Dede is also sitting on some nice gains. As I write this, one remaining condo in the building lists for $282,900. Our *RETA*-only price on that condo type was $203,991. A *RETA* uplift of $78,909.

Dede has kindly agreed to share her experience. Take it away Dede...

"The keys jingled in my hand. I couldn't believe I finally owned my own piece of paradise. I kept looking at the key chain I had just been handed. Then looking at the bare, two-bedroom, two-bathroom, double-terrace condo in front of me. I had finally made my dream of owning an overseas property come true.

"For years I had flipped through the pages of *International Living* magazine...mesmerized by the stories of others living the life I wanted. That life involved owning a property in an overseas beach destination. A property that would give me a

---

passive income and the option to stay in it whenever I wanted to get away from the chaos of "normal" life. I thought it was a tall order, but I was convinced if these people I was reading about could do it, then so could I.

"Real estate investing wasn't new to me. I used to own four long-term rental properties in Tucson, Arizona. But investing in real estate overseas was. And I wanted to learn more about short-term and vacation rentals. I started researching and that was how I came across Ronan McMahon's *Real Estate Trend Alert*.

"When I tell my friends and sisters that we purchased an income-producing property in Playa del Carmen, Mexico, I get mixed reviews. Many people automatically think that it is extremely risky to purchase outside of the United States. Personally, I think my tolerance is mid-level since there is a strong rental demand from multiple markets year-round.

"As of May 2022, our condo has been booked consistently, and the money we've made is covering the mortgage and HOA fees.

"I diversify my portfolio and invest in some stocks, although my focus is on investing in global real estate. To my husband, Keith, and I, it's all about buying even in bad times and still making money. I'm in my mid 50s so I don't have time to wait for the stock market to go up if it takes a drastic hit. I don't like the volatility in stocks, and I don't like how the government controls what I do with my 401K. In real estate investing, I look where supply is shrinking and demand is rising, which lowers my risk.

"I hit the jackpot when I found Playa del Carmen on Mexico's Riviera Maya and the builder/developer relationship with my property. Being well established, they could offer financing in instalments. I jumped at that, so I was required to put half down over a three-year period during the pre-construction phase.

"Once it was delivered, they financed the other half at 6% for five years. When I took possession of the property, I had already made a six-figure capital appreciation gain. As I continue to finance at $2,000 a month for another four years, I will be bringing in passive rental income. At the end of the four years, I will have full ownership and a title of a property in a tropical paradise.

"I've learned that global investing offers an abundance of opportunities that we don't often see here in the United States. I wanted it all...capital appreciation, income potential, and a place that I wanted to visit whenever I wanted as well as rent out. I only had to be patient to find that little slice of heaven that I could escape to when I needed some rest and relaxation.

"It has been quite the adventure buying overseas, planning, and furnishing our condo with custom-designed accessories rather than using the pre-packaged options. But we managed to decorate and furnish our new apartment for a little over $10,000.

"Because I've owned long-term rentals in Arizona, I know what's involved with fixing things, taking payments, or evicting renters that don't believe in paying.

"Seeing that my property is out of the country in a top tourist destination, I realized finding a property manager to take care of the short-term rentals would be in my best interest. I couldn't be effective at providing the best service to vacationers unless I was there on site.

"I have a list of criteria that I looked for in a property manager and I found one through referrals. I still know what's happening all the time, but I don't have to worry about calling people to fix anything, paying the utilities, handling any complaints, or cleaning my condo after every vacationer.

"As a past real estate agent and present investor, I know you make your money when you buy low. That isn't happening now in the U.S. Even if people sell their homes for top dollar, they still need a place to live. Rentals and mortgage rates are increasing.

"I believe now is the time to take any extra money you might have in the stock market and invest in property out of the country. Or perhaps, this is a time to look at selling your U.S. property and expanding your lifestyle to include living overseas where you get more for your money...which is what Keith and I are gearing up for.

"It was because I was a *RETA* member that I could get a vacation rental, for way below market value, in an upscale neighborhood of Playa del Carmen. It gives me passive income, and anytime I needed a little Caribbean beach and some rest and relaxation, my condo would be waiting for me."

CHAPTER 4

The No. 1 Reason to Own International Real Estate: You Can Make a Fortune

"Find out where the people are going and buy the land before they get there." — William Penn Adair

"The major fortunes in America have been made in land." — John D. Rockefeller

Diversifying, protecting your wealth, owning incredible properties in beautiful places…as we've seen in the previous chapter, these are great reasons to consider property overseas.

But the number one reason to own international real estate is this: Real estate fortunes, large and small, are made at moments of big transformation. I'm talking about exceptional changes that happen so infrequently in your backyard you might never even see one. Once in a lifetime events, seismic social shifts…

Let me show you exactly what I mean using examples from America's past…

- At the dawn of the 19th century, the newly invented steamboat meant farmland became expensive high-end suburbs at the edges of U.S. cities like New York, Chicago, San Francisco and Cincinnati. Millionaires were made. If you had owned farmland in Brooklyn in 1814, within a decade you would have been very, very rich.

- By the 1870s, the railroads were pushing across the country and making fortunes for savvy real estate investors of the day. The word "boom" has its origins in what happened to real estate in Los Angeles when the trains arrived.

- The Florida real estate boom of the roaring 1920s was brought about largely because of a relatively new invention—the automobile—which brought a surge of vacationers on new roads. Scams were rife but wise investors cleaned up by buying well. This was mirrored across the U.S. as suburbs grew thanks to Henry Ford's affordable cars and better access to finance.

- The GI Bill in the 1940s put money in the pockets of millions of Americans to buy homes... Huge new suburbs were created putting vast sums into the pockets of savvy investors.

- The interstate highway system begun in the 1950s was the largest public works in history and turned thousands of acres of cheap agricultural land into valuable commercial and residential land.

Without a time-machine we can't hope to profit from the booms of the past. But we can learn from them...and then go and find today's big transformations wherever they may be.

Because the stories of those who got rich from America's big transformations are—in short—stories of people in the right place at the right time, doing the right things. By looking overseas you can ensure you are in the right place at the right time *all of the time*. And this book is designed to help you do the right things.

When you take a world view, you see these sorts of major "once in a generation" transformations regularly.

If we only look to our own hometowns, or our own countries, then we may never have the chance to invest ahead of a big trend or development set to drive spectacular profits.

And I'm not saying you need to be total pioneer, learn a foreign language, or do wild land deals in some jungle. There are winners and losers from such major transformations. It's critical to buy at the right time. To lock down the right kind of real estate, at the right price.

I like to wait until the momentum is clearly there, until the road is built, the airport is getting flights. I want to see the demand for myself...get boots on the ground, sometimes for months, even years before I act on, or recommend, any deal.

I like to see the upswing underway. The key then is to find the right real estate and do the right deal.

I've made it my mission to identify big transformations across the world. Billion-dollar investments in airports, highways, and other infrastructure. The massive growth of burgeoning middle classes. Sometimes I travel in air-conditioned comfort, sometimes in off-road vehicles...whatever it takes.

Hacking through jungle or arriving exhausted after an arduous dirt-road adventure on a deserted beach, I've made it my business to be in the right places at the right time, and to get the right real estate deals. I've pounded pavements from Chiang Mai to Cancun, Cabo to the Costa del Sol...

The bigger the transformation, the bigger the opportunities for investors like us. We're talking about sea-changes in the development of some of the world's most beautiful places. Billions of dollars poured into opening up new areas of virgin land. Turning fishing villages into beachfront cities in a matter of a few decades. Or millions of people becoming work-from-anywhere professionals, taking their jobs with them to the world's most desirable destinations and driving demand up just as supply gets thoroughly squeezed.

To profit from a major transformation, first you need to see it. Take the birds-eye macro view. Then get ahead of it.

And I'll repeat, I'm not talking about speculating or buying any old property. You need to do the same smart things you would do with any real estate investment. That is, buy the right real estate.

Location, location—you need to drill down and find real estate that will be in biggest demand and is protected from competition, from oversupply. The absolute best real estate protected by moats (more on moats in chapter 6).

And, finally, to lock in the most spectacular of gains you then need to buy it at a low, low price. This is the key benefit of buying at the right moment in a big transformation, you buy ahead of demand. It's also a key benefit of being a member of *Real Estate Trend Alert*...

Members of my *Real Estate Trend Alert* and I have made spectacular gains by doing this. It's at the core of what we do.

I started my *RETA* group in the teeth of the 2008 crisis. I knew there was huge potential for a group like ours to leverage collective buying power. I hit the road for real, pouring money and time into travel and boots on the ground scouting.

I have long thought about it like this: when you look everywhere there is always big opportunity somewhere. As a boy I was bored in school but for two subjects: geography and economics. I was fascinated by travel, foreign places, and always sat up to hear news of world events. I'm grateful and glad, for this interest in the world meant that even early in my investing career I was comfortable looking beyond my borders for opportunity.

Just a few years before the 2008 crisis, I sold some of my property in Ireland. Values had risen to a level that made no sense to me. In just one decade, between 1997 and 2007, prices for new houses increased by more than 200%. (No, that's not a misplaced zero—that 200% figure is correct.) Already built homes sold for even more. The increase was a whopping 280%.

I made a killing and invested the profits in Panama where there was a major transformation underway. And yes, as I've said, my friends and family thought I was crazy investing overseas. But by doing so, not only did I protect my gains, I increased them. I made a profit of over $72,000 on a property in Panama City. Not so crazy then, and I was off…

Today, and for a long time now, it's been difficult to see much sustainable upside in most real estate markets in North America. Most U.S. and Canadian markets are highly leveraged and expensive relative to incomes, very susceptible to interest rates rising or employment falling.

I've watched over the last few years as "little guy" property investment and speculation has come back in vogue. News articles and hundreds of blogs cover investing in Atlanta or Austin. Television shows feature baristas or graphic designers turned house flippers.

I see real estate investors struggling to make the numbers work in America. Increasingly folks are looking outside of their home states. That's smart, and also a lot easier than it would have been a decade ago. Today with the internet and other technological advances, investing long-distance from the comfort of home is easier than ever. The internet is itself a massive transformational event. And it means you can buy, manage, and market a property in another state or country in a way that was inconceivable before.

But I'd argue that they should look farther than the U.S. Because—like a broken record here—when you make the world your oyster, you can play big transformations for enormous profit far more often.

And playing big transformations—as I say—is where real estate fortunes get made.

When you live in Ohio or California, you can invest in Florida or Mexico's Riviera Maya… It's as easy if not easier to get to the Riviera Maya—a highly internationalized place with hundreds of direct flights from U.S. and Canadian cities and millions of potential renters pouring in through Cancun airport to spend time on the 80-mile stretch of Caribbean coast.

Sure, it's in a different country, but that doesn't mean you can't safely buy a property there and make a lot of money. Plus, it means you own and can enjoy a luxury property in the Caribbean.

And here's a key thing to understand about internationalized destinations like the Riviera Maya. You're now essentially renting or selling to the same market you would be in the U.S. Remote work now means millions of people are free to relocate to desirable international destinations and they are doing so in droves as I'll show you in chapter 7. These are people who will want your real estate and who are willing to pay a lot more for it than you did…assuming you get it at the right price. It's likely your guests will be from Ohio or California…

Brazil 2008: "Always Opportunity Somewhere"

My experience of the Global Financial Crisis highlights what I'm saying about big transformations. My experience is an almost unbelievable story to many I tell it to. It's the perfect example of how—when you look everywhere—you can always find a major transformation somewhere and successfully invest in it for a profit.

Back in 2008, many of my friends and acquaintances around the world were in a state of panic. Their retirement savings were being decimated. In the U.S. and Europe, banks collapsed, pensions disappeared, and real estate markets crashed.

U.S. stocks fell more than 50% wiping out nearly $8 trillion in value. In Europe, several countries were brought to the brink of default, barely saved by emergency bailouts and strict austerity measures. Former British Foreign Secretary

William Hague called the crisis "a burning building with no exits."

I was sitting on a beach in Brazil buying condos with a 1% down-payment at launch—the equivalent of just $736. The weekend I bought my condo, the whole community sold out. I sold, for a gross profit of $43,500.

Northeast Brazil was undergoing a massive transformation. There was no financial crisis there. The area was booming as it emerged as a strategic logistics, tourism, and manufacturing center with a strong agricultural hinterland.

In total, during that time in Brazil I bought six condos pre-construction, two lots, a car park, and a multi-unit residential building. This was a classic explosion of new middle- and upper-class story thanks to a global boom in what this region is rich in...logistics and trade, tourism, and agri and energy commodities.

I looked on while news footage in my hotel showed teary-eyed bank employees carrying their stuff out of abandoned offices in the States. Then in Brazil I went back to making money.

So how was I able to make money on the beach? Because when you take a global view with your investing there are always exits. Always windows of opportunity. (I'd argue this is true of your personal life as well.)

When the U.S. and Europe were crashing and burning, Brazil's real estate market was actually booming. See the chart on the next page.

In fact, my success in Brazil is a big reason I launched *Real Estate Trend Alert*. If you've been a reader for that long, you probably remember me writing almost exclusively about Brazil.

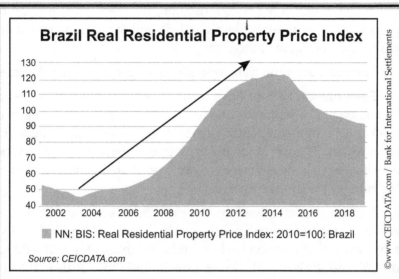

When home prices were falling in the U.S. and Europe, home prices in Brazil were rising. When we buy right using RETA deals in the fastest-growing markets, we consistently and significantly outperform indices like this that capture average returns.

There was so much opportunity there and no one was talking about it. Everyone was talking about the exact opposite: The end of the world.

The lesson? We always have opportunity somewhere. You just need to look everywhere and get ahead of the big transformations.

As I've told you, I own no stocks today. None. I don't own gold, silver, nor any other precious metals or gems. I haven't got a cellar stuffed with rare wines or a garage full of classic cars. I neither own nor do I want a digital wallet packed with Bitcoin or any other cryptocurrency.

I'm all in on international real estate. I devote myself to finding big transformations I can follow, get ahead of, and profit from.

When I've found a big transformation, it's then about finding the right location, real estate, the right deal, and the right people to deal with. And getting in at the right price.

The most common transformational event is a Path of Progress.

Essentially, a Path of Progress is the collision of real estate and technology. The railroads made successes of towns along their tracks. The interstate highway system turned backwaters into boomtowns. The car made the growth of suburbia possible. When a technology changes where we can live or do business, it changes the rules of the property market.

I'm not a speculative guy. I'm more often accused of being too risk averse and conservative in my investments. I only like deals that—even if things don't work out how I think they will—I'll still do OK And the best way I know how to find those deals is ahead of big transformations.

Get the right real estate deal positioned ahead of growing demand and with supply constraints on top of that, it's a formula for values to soar…

In the next chapter I'll introduce you to the greatest Path of Progress transformations I've witnessed around the world. Transformations that in the last few years have thrown up incredible buying opportunities for members of *RETA* and me.

First, let's look to America to see exactly how big transformations make real estate fortunes…

America's Grand Canal

Let me tell you about a felon…a jailbird…and a dreamer. If he had never been put behind bars then America might look different today.

Because his writings from a small-town jail in New York state inspired America's first great infrastructure project, a 400-mile-long canal linking the Great Lakes to the Hudson River.

And that canal turned New York into America's commercial capital and busiest port. It opened the Midwest to settlers who poured inland toward Ohio, Michigan, Illinois, and Indiana. It's even said that the Erie Canal helped launch the consumer economy and led to the birth of the Mormon church. Manufactured goods could be imported into the interior in half the time and a fraction of the cost of before. Ideas traveled along the waterway. Joseph Smith apparently saw the angel of Moroni on his farm close to the canal.

Look at any modern map of New York state today and you'll see that, with a few exceptions, every major city is on the route of the Erie Canal. In fact, close to 80% of the state's population lives within 25 miles of the canal.

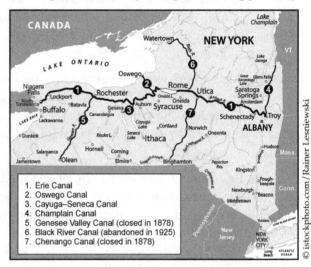

America's first great infrastructural project, the Erie Canal was built from 1817 to 1825. It sparked a canal building boom, opened the Midwest, and turned New York into the economic capital of the country.

So who was the visionary convict who dreamt up the Erie Canal?

It was the early 1800s and struggling businessman Jesse Hawley was a flour seller who bought wheat around Geneva, New York, had it milled in Seneca Falls, and—like other entrepreneurs of the time—ran into trouble with transport.

Getting his flour to the coast on terrible roads was too costly for Hawley. He wound up in debt, and eventually as a result of owing money he was put in debtors' prison.

There, Hawley took up his pen. Writing under the name Hercules he put forth his vision for a canal linking "the trade of almost all the lakes in North America" to "a center at New York for their common mart. This port, already of the first commercial consequence in the United States, would shortly after, be left without a competition in trade...In a century its island would be covered with the buildings and population of its city," he wrote.

Hawley's letters were published in a local paper. Plenty of folks saw them as the ravings of a madman, but Hawley found a few influential readers. He wrote 15 letters in all and by 1810, Hawley's idea had powerful political backers who ran with it and created a Canal Commission.

The Erie Canal opened in 1825, proclaimed by the press of the day as "the greatest engineering feat of the 19th century." Its construction employed tens of thousands of people. Entire cities grew as a result of the canal. Commerce boomed. Vast fortunes were made and in just 30 years, the population of New York quadrupled—from 123,706 in 1820 to 696,115 in 1850.

Small towns like Utica, Syracuse, and Rochester grew into cities. Buffalo went from 200 people in 1820 to more than 18,000 by 1840. The tiny settlement of Lockport was home to just three families before the canal. Thousands suddenly came to live there.

The canal brought tourists too, which no one had imagined, not even the jailbird who came up with the idea of the canal. Thousands of them traveled on steamboats including the writer Charles Dickens.

Across the Great Lakes, the city of Chicago boomed going from a population of 100 people to the fourth largest city in the world in less than 100 years. Chicago became a hub of transport for the entire country thanks to the canal, sucking in money and people at a phenomenal rate, just as the world's internationalized places do today.

By the 1850s, New York City was handling more cargo than the combined ports of Boston, Baltimore, and New Orleans. The fortunes of New Yorkers like Isaac Bronson, Robert Lenox, and John Jacob Astor were made...

Imagine you owned land along the route of the Erie Canal. Imagine too, if you were in the cement business and supplying even a fraction of the material used for the canal!

You would have been ahead of a huge Path of Progress.

The Path of Progress, the most obvious of big transformational events. A new road...a new airport and air routes. It makes the movement of goods and people much easier and can make land and property far more valuable.

America's First Multi-Millionaire

America's first multi-millionaire was John Jacob Astor. He started out as a fur trader, learning about the trade from a fellow immigrant on the boat to America. But in the 1830s, after seeing how vital the port was to trade, he foresaw the rise of New York. He used his fur profits to buy up land for development beyond the city limits. As Manhattan grew and grew, so did Astor's wealth. By the time he died in 1848, he'd acquired the largest real estate fortune in the U.S.

Real estate investing truly created generational wealth for the Astors... John Jacob's great-grandson, John Jacob Astor IV, happened to be on the *Titanic* when it sank in 1912—making his son Vincent the inheritor of the largest personal fortune in the world at the time.

> This is another of the things that makes real estate so appealing. It's a superb way of securing your wealth for your family, kids, grandkids...and on.
>
> I know a lot of *RETA* members who invest with and for their kids precisely because of this.

Steamboat Real Estate Tycoons

Pirates nearly ruined Hezekiah Pierrepont. In 1797, sailing on his ship The *Confederacy from* Canton to Hamburg, he and his crew ran afoul of French privateers. They seized his cargo of tea and sold his ship in France.

But the bankrupt Pierrepont got lucky in love after returning to New York. He married the daughter of a wealthy landowner who gave him a sizeable dowry. Pierrepont then played a savvy hand. He bought 60 acres of farmland atop Brooklyn Heights and invested in a new Steam Ferry Boat company owned by his buddy Robert Fulton.

New York's first commuter suburb was born. Throughout the 1820s, Pierrepont sold

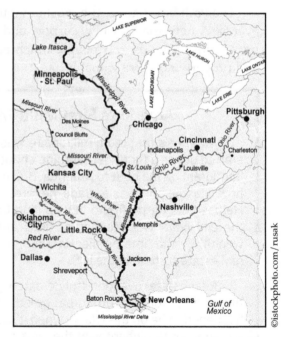

©istockphoto.com/rusak

A great transformation took place on the banks of America's great rivers with the arrival of steamboats in the 19th century.

lots to the rich city merchants who, thanks to Fulton's steam ferries, could easily get to and from their places of business in Manhattan from their leafy new neighborhood.

Pierrpont died in 1838 a rich man and by the middle of the 19th century, 50 million passenger crossings a year were recorded from Manhattan to Brooklyn.

Walt Whitman who had an office overlooking the ferry dock in Brooklyn wrote: "In the morning there is one incessant stream of people—employed in New York on business—tending toward the ferry."

The Brooklyn story was mirrored in cities across the country. Through the early 19th century, steamboats plied the country's great rivers and growing canal systems. Ports were created, towns were born, and in big cities new suburbs thrived.

Urban Americans of the young republic had walked or rode a horse to get where they were going. The wealthy lived as close as they could get to the center of business and political power. But the steamboat gave birth to ferry suburbs. In Cincinnati, wealthy men built homes in Newport...in Philadelphia it was Camden. And across the country those ahead of this transformation—like Pierrpont—made their fortune in real estate.

Surf City and the Railroads

At the turn of the 20th century, Huntington Beach, California, was just a wild, hard-to-reach parcel of stunning beachfront land. Then a visionary pioneer with deep pockets and serious connections arrived.

Born in 1850, Henry E. Huntington moved west with the railroads. He was an executive involved in their construction and his uncle Collis was one of "the Big Four," the tycoons who pushed the first transcontinental railway across the country.

The railroads transformed the United States. In 1862, Congress passed the Pacific Railway Act paving the way for the construction of transcontinental railroads. The first was finished in 1869 and by 1900 there were three more.

The movement of people thanks to the railroads turned once-small settlements like San Francisco into metropolises. San Francisco saw a 3,000% to 4,000% increase in real estate values in a short period of time.

When he got to the West Coast, Henry Huntington stuck around. He sold his interests in the railways and became instrumental in the development of Southern California.

Huntington was a master of anticipating the growth of communities. He was always ahead of demand. And he used his connections and his money to drive a Path of Progress which opened things up…

Huntingdon was behind the Pacific Electric Railway known as the "red cars" which connected L.A. to Orange County. It was in real estate that Huntingdon made his real money, his red car line at one time even operating as a loss leader.

In 1889, Orange County had just three incorporated cities, and a population of about 15,000. Today, there are 34 cities, and more than 3 million residents. Huntington Beach is one of the surf capitals of the world. Vacationers pile into plush resorts and max out the Airbnb rentals. They come for the 10 uninterrupted miles of wide, sandy beach. And for everything else this Southern Californian beach town offers. The swells around Santa Catalina Island, 30 miles off the Californian coast, make for good surfing pretty much year-round at Huntington. Hence its nickname "Surf City USA."

Before the railroads arrived in California, the trickle of migrants to the south of the state was made up mostly of wealthy merchants who came for the climate and a rural retreat. The masses began joining them when railroad competition pushed the fare price down and made the journey affordable to the many.

- Irishman James Irvine was one of those who traveled to California to get rich from gold mining. But Irvine instead became a wholesaler of supplies for the booming population. He used his profits to buy vast tracts of land, including a fifth of Orange County and founded the town of Anaheim.

- William Spurgeon left Missouri for California and bought a 76-acre ranch for $1,000. The story goes, Spurgeon was annoyed by the lack of trees and the high-growing mustard plants on his land so he bought sycamore trees. But to get them onto his property he had to build a road...then he built a store...a bank...and the town of Santa Ana.

- Andrew Glassell was an accidental real estate investor. His law firm was owed money by a large ranching family called Yorba in southern California. Glassell and his partners reluctantly accepted a few thousand acres as payment. In the 1870s, they subdivided a portion of the land in 10-acre lots and founded the town of Orange.

A "Fad Investment" Makes Millions

"The horse is here to stay, but the automobile is only a novelty." In 1903, lawyer Horace Rackham asked his banker for advice. Whether or not he should invest in his client's new venture. The banker scoffed at the idea, like many at the time.

Yet, Racham gave his client, Henry Ford, $5,000 anyway and the rest is history.

The automobile began as an expensive novelty. Dismissed by high-minded experts of the day, few people could afford it. Apparently, J.P Morgan refused to invest in it. Woodrow Wilson predicted the automobile would drown the country in socialism as envy of the rich overcame the masses who couldn't afford a car.

Yet, by 1925, the average American wage earner could afford one of Henry Ford's cars. By the end of the decade most middle-class families had one.

In 1919, there were about 6.7 million cars on the road and by 1929, there were 27 million, or a 300% increase.

But a car alone isn't much good without a road to drive it along.

Before 1920, a traveler in the U.S. would go a very long way before finding a paved road. Travel between cities was best done by rail. American memoirs of the time often talk of being stuck in the mud on dirt tracks. In 1904, only one-sixth of rural public roads had any kind of surfacing. By 1935, more than a third of rural roads were surfaced, and many were paved for motor traffic. New technologies competed for solutions. Asphalt...concrete. Hundreds of millions of dollars were spent through the federal-aid highway program to upgrade the nation's roads.

Cars and the new roads built to accommodate them opened up vast areas for development. You didn't need to be an innovator like Ford or inventor like Edison to profit.

You just needed to own the right real estate.

Tens of thousands of acres around major cities were subdivided into lots and sold. In the countryside, vacation properties were developed. Take Chicago where from 1918 to 1926, the population increased 35% and land values rose 150%, or about 12% a year.

The car and improved road system fuelled a massive tourism and real estate boom in Florida.

Florida towns that had grown with the steamboats, declined with the arrival of rail, and again new towns grew with the arrival of car.

This was a classic transformational event...

Demand soared. Americans now had vacation time and pensions. Banks began lending home mortgages in the 1920s so people could now for the first time use leverage.

Carl G. Fisher was a walking path of progress himself, in many ways. In 1912 he developed the first road for cars across the United States—the Lincoln Highway. And followed it up with the Dixie Highway from Michigan to Miami.

But it's for Miami Beach that he's best known—financing the Collins Bridge across the Biscayne Bay to the resort, the longest wooden bridge in the world at the time. Fisher made millions from Florida real estate. In fact, his Miami Beach was one of the few places in the world that actually experienced a building boom during the Great Depression.

The Birth of Mass-Produced Homes

Before the Great Depression, anyone buying a house faced down-payment requirements averaging 50%, and if you wanted a bank loan you were usually looking at terms under five years with 6% interest rates.

But in 1944, Congress passed the Servicemen's Readjustment Act offering federal aid to help veterans get jobs, an education, and buy homes.

Bill Levitt was one of those returning soldiers. While in the service, he had been producing prefabricated military housing. Upon returning to New York, he bought up some onion fields on Long Island and persuaded his father and brother to switch from building custom homes for well-to-do folks to mass producing affordable housing.

Levitt's innovations in creating mass housing projects coincided with a massive increase in credit availability. By 1955, 4.3 million home loans worth $33 billion had been granted to veterans, who were responsible for buying 20% of all new homes built after the war.

The first community of Levitt and Sons was a wild success and by the late 1960s, Bill Levitt was among the richest men in America with a fortune of over $100 million and a yacht named for his third wife.

The point here is that not all major transformations are infra-structural Paths of Progress. Innovations in construction and easier credit drove a massive building boom in the 1940s and 50s and made fortunes....and it converged with the largest public works and Path of Progress event in American history...

The Nazi-Inspired Highway Boom

Next time you hit the inter-state, think about its origins and how those ahead of that huge transformation made their fortunes.

Phil Patton wrote in *Open Road: A Celebration of the American Highway* that the concrete used to construct the 41,000 miles of interstate highways "would build six sidewalks to the moon."

It also sent property values to the moon... One study in Hartford, Connecticut, found that homes close to the Interstate increased in value by 55% in just a few years. Across the U.S., suburbs in certain areas rose by 3,000% in a decade.

The Interstate Highway Bill of 1956 helped create 47,000 miles of highways. It's considered the largest public works project ever undertaken.

President Eisenhower was a keen supporter. In 1919, he'd taken part in the first trans-continental military convoy in the U.S. and seen the mixed state of the country's roads. Then, as allied commander in the war, he'd seen first-hand the autobahn system in Germany developed by the Nazis. Eisenhower wrote in his memoirs, "During World War II, I had seen the superlative system of German autobahn—[the] national highways crossing that country."

The inter-state highways converged with innovations in construction, with the widescale availability of finance, and created mini real estate booms across the country.

Real Estate Fortunes in Silicon Valley

California's first millionaire, Samuel Brannan, made his money during the gold rush and invested it in vast chunks of real estate in California and Hawaii.

Now, you might think Brannan discovered gold. But Brannan made most of his money selling shovels, picks, and supplies to the mass of prospectors who went West dreaming of riches.

The most famous story of Brannan is of him walking the streets of San Francisco shouting "Gold, Gold in the American River!" He owned the only store between San Francisco and the American River and sold out of supplies at massively inflated prices.

The lesson is simple, during a gold rush, sell shovels.

Among the billionaires in Silicon Valley, there are men who got rich not from owning tech companies, but from owning the land that tech companies like Google coveted as they continued to expand.

The names John Arrillaga and Richard Peery aren't much known outside the Bay Area, but Bloomberg has called them "the Bill Hewlett and Dave Packard of Silicon Valley real estate."

They started buying up cherry and apricot orchards a half-century ago—and today they're worth $6 billion, thanks to development deals. They had the smarts and the luck to be ahead of Silicon Valley's big transformation and they've cashed in, big time.

As of June 2021, Silicon Valley had the highest percentage of homes valued at $1 million or more in the United States.

Mass Air Travel

You could say it began with a Flying Whale. That was the nickname of Boeing's 1946 Stratoliner—the first commercial airplane to have cabin pressurization. Passengers could now breath comfortably at 20,000 feet. A huge innovation followed by others...bigger planes, faster ones...

Travel opened up to the masses through the 1960s and 1970s. And airports were being built to accommodate all these new fliers. Today, across America, easy access to air travel makes cities more attractive to business and contributes to demand for real estate.

And when you look internationally, the construction of airports has been a huge driver of big transformations in some of the world's most beautiful places, putting millions of people just a few hours and a low-cost fare away.

Mexico's Riviera Maya was but a few fishing villages and 80-miles of stunning Caribbean coastline and beaches until Cancun airport was built in 1974. Today it's got four terminals and over 20 million passengers passing through annually. Those fishing villages are small cities, and the entire coast has seen a staggering transformation.

Go back 70 years or so and Spain's Costa del Sol was a hard-to-reach playground for the international jet-set. It could take days to get there. Things really began when a Spanish-born prince of German origins bought land and created the famous Marbella Club in 1954. A guy named Alfonso of Hohenlohe-Langenburg.

European aristocrats were joined by Hollywood royalty...Grace Kelly, Ava Gardner, Marlon Brando, Orson Welles, Brigitte Bardo, Frank Sinatra... Audrey Hepburn lived full time in a private villa in the Marbella Club.

Then, in 1964 the runway at Malaga airport was extended to accommodate wide-bodied jets and there was an explosion of tourism with new hotels and resorts opening. Northern Europeans, mainly British and Scandinavians, poured onto the Costa del Sol.

In 2004, Malaga airport saw over 12 million passengers. In 2018 it was more than 19 million. Post pandemic, in the age of the Zoom Boom, numbers are surging again as millions can now work from anywhere.

Profits in Panama

I mentioned that I got in on Panama's real estate market in 2004. One of my first-ever overseas real estate plays. I invested in a little one-bedroom pre-construction condo in a prime city location. At the time, Panama City was setting off on a wave of transformation.

A change of city zoning had triggered a flurry of construction in prime, central neighborhoods. These were desirable and popular locales. But, until the rezoning happened, the only condos available to buy or rent were very large. They often covered 2,000 to 3,000 square feet. Buildings featured one or two condos per floor. These condos were expensive to buy, run, and maintain.

Thanks to the change of city zoning, a new wave of transformation focused on shiny new condo buildings with smaller units. The condos typically came with high-end finishes like granite counters. They often had amazing views of the city or the ocean. They were in buildings with swimming pools, gyms, steam rooms, and social areas.

They were a huge hit with local professionals and young couples. Once word got out, investors like me jumped in. These condos were priced low (incredibly low for a capital city in an emerging trading hub and world banking center). Potential gains looked strong—the country's economy was booming and the middle-class growing rapidly.

I did very well with my pre-construction condo. I bought for $147,630. I sold shortly after completion for $220,000. My profit: $72,370.

CHAPTER 5

Where to Make Your Fortune

"If opportunity doesn't knock, build a door."
— Milton Berle, Actor

You know my mantra by now…when you look everywhere, there is always opportunity somewhere. But everywhere is a big place. So, in this chapter I narrow it down for you and focus on five huge transformations I have followed overseas.

Each of these transformations has made spectacular returns for real estate investors who have bought ahead. I'm talking six-figure gains in the space of a few short years. That's per deal, and for individual "little guy" investors like us with a modest amount of money in the deal.

I believe you can still make money buying into these transformations—especially as a *RETA* member. The transformations I'm about to tell you about are ongoing, and by applying my five "R's" method of buying right you stand to do very well.

Those five R's are:

- **Right Transformation.** As a risk averse and conservative investor, I purposely seek out opportunities in the world's most desirable and internationalized places. That's because these are destinations where people come from around the world in good times and bad. Places like Mexico's Riviera Maya or Portugal's Algarve. Millions of people driving demand coupled with a major transformation making it easier for those people to get there. A virtuous circle. A crisis like

COVID or the global financial meltdown of 2008/09 are just temporary blips on the growth trajectory of these internationalized places. These places bounce back stronger. All the fundamentals that make these places attractive are even more attractive after a crisis.

- **Right Location.** Then you drill down, where exactly makes the most sense. It might be several or even a dozen different spots. Close to the beach, or golf...airport...in a certain microclimate or sought-after neighborhood.

- **Right Developer.** I'm only interested in doing deals with people with a long track record of delivering. The more storms they have weathered the better. A developer who's been delivering for 30 years has seen a thing or two. I like developer's who are creative, yet conservative. They don't take chances but they do like to innovate. Passion for creating beautiful communities is a must.

- **Right Real Estate.** The longer you are a *Real Estate Trend Alert* and the more familiar you get with our international beat, the more you'll realize how much real estate I don't recommend or talk about. I'm only ever interested in the best in class, that means we retain a competitive edge. So, I seek out the best amenities, the best-designed condos...nothing cookie cutter or pedestrian. By owning the best real estate, your real estate stands the best chance of always being in high demand.

- **Right Price.** All of the above is pointless if you aren't buying at the right price. And that is a lower price than anyone else. The lower your price, the bigger your potential gain and the higher your potential yield. Buying at the right low, low price is the entire point of *Real Estate Trend Alert*. We buy in exclusive off-market deals and use our group buying power to get lower prices than anyone else will pay, and before anyone else has a chance, too. (At the end of this book I'll explain in detail how best to use your *RETA* membership.)

Let's look at five huge transformations I've been following and how my five R's apply…

1. Mexico's Riviera Maya

When I first arrived on Tulum beach in 2004, it was down a dirt road. I found miles of stunning white sand beach, a few rustic palapas, and the warm waters of the Caribbean.

There were no Brazilian models flouncing around, no trendy, adults-only hotels charging a fortune, and Tulum wasn't yet getting regular mentions in *Vogue*.

I could see it all coming though.

Here was a beach paradise at the end of the line of a spectacular Path of Progress hurtling down the Riviera Maya, driving development and profits along the way.

Today, Tulum is among one of the world's most glamorous and chic destinations. It gets millions of visitors each year.

And the Riviera Maya—the name given to an 80-mile stretch of Mexico's Caribbean—draws people from all over the world.

There's a good chance you've been to the Riviera Maya. It's always in the top 10 lists of desired destinations for North American travelers. But it also draws visitors from Europe, Latin America, and other parts of Mexico. According to a travel industry watcher, ForwardKeys, the area was the second-most popular destination in the world, after Dubai, for 2021.

Another reason the Riviera Maya is so in-demand is that it's easy to get to, with direct flights to more than 123 cities in 27 countries, going into Cancun airport, which is the gateway to the region. From New York, for example, it's just a four-hour flight. There are direct flights to dozens of cities across North America, with new flights being added all the time. And tickets are cheap, too.

When you visit the Riviera Maya today it's thoroughly modern, with its bustling towns and cities, a four-lane north-south highway that gets you from Cancun to Tulum in just two hours, big shopping malls, and big-box stores but also gourmet markets, high-speed internet, reliable cell service, and top-notch hospitals. Any comfort or convenience you might need can be found on the Riviera Maya.

It's hard to imagine that until the late 1970s, there wasn't much here except for a few fishing villages along the pristine coast, jungle, and farms, including a vast coconut plantation with a few caretakers on the barrier island where Cancun's resort-packed Hotel Zone is located.

The Riviera Maya's transformation is a classic Path of Progress story. In the 1960s, the Mexican government realized the huge potential of the booming travel market. Cheaper flights had opened up overseas vacations to the masses. They wanted a slice of the action and were very forward thinking in the approach they took.

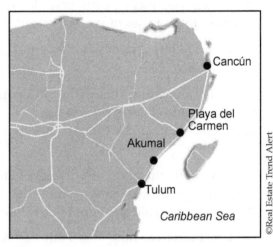

The 80-mile stretch of coast known as the Riviera Maya attracts visitors from around the world.

They didn't just put out an expensive ad campaign in the hopes of drawing investors and encouraging development. They got down to basics, studying what tourists demanded on vacation. Based on those parameters, they selected a handful of possible locations in Mexico that fit the bill.

Cancun was one of them.

The Mexican government, specifically its tourism agency FONATUR, rolled its sleeves up and set to work.

Mexico's Caribbean coast had the basics going for it, including the intrinsic value of being a Caribbean coastline with a huge potential market on its doorstep in the U.S.—only two hours away.

The government's FONATUR tourism authority had the capacity to make good on its promises to deliver infrastructure and accessibility. And it offered effective tax incentives to attract major international hotel groups.

They built an international airport in 1974. They put in roads and water treatment plants and electricity. They lured big hotel chains with promises of tax breaks and finance to help them build.

It took a few decades, but they pulled it off. Cancun became a tourist mecca.

Today, Cancuun is one of the most popular beach destinations in the world, and it's still growing and developing. The international airport has expanded six times. New hotels and resorts are opening all the time.

About 50 minutes south of Cancun, the fishing village of Playa del Carmen was the next spot on the Path of Progress roaring south. And the hippie chic community of Tulum was next after that…

I've been watching this Path of Progress juggernaut on the Riviera Maya closely for nearly 20 years. I've invested in a bunch of properties on the Riviera Maya. That's how hot I am on the market here.

Let's look closer at the two hottest spots for real estate investors on this Riviera….

Booming beach city: Playa del Carmen

About 50 minutes south of Cancun, connected by the well-maintained modern highway, the fishing village of Playa del

Carmen was the next spot on the Path of Progress roaring south after Cancun.

For many years, it was mostly known as the place to catch the ferry to the island of Cozumel about 45 minutes off-shore, which is popular with scuba divers and snorkelers.

Playa was just a few dusty dirt roads. Rustic accommodations by the ferry terminal for the few people who decided to stay the night. Think palapas and even livestock roaming around.

Big change today! Playa has become a sophisticated beachside city with close to 300,000 residents and millions of visitors. It has large malls, an international dining scene, plenty of shops and boutiques, and a very international community, including a vibrant expat scene. In a city so new, everyone is from somewhere else. English is spoken everywhere.

In Playa, back before the road was in, $10,000 bought you a building plot in the unpaved village center. Today, a 1,000-square-foot oceanfront condo in Playa del Carmen can set you back $600,000.

Like Cancun, this sleepy seaside village was transformed into a world-class destination in a matter of decades. But it followed a different path. Instead of most tourists staying in huge resorts on the beach—which they likely never leave—Playa is a real living, breathing city.

It's the type of place where you can grab an espresso and croissant at a French café in the morning on the way to the beach…enjoy a lunch of fresh seafood with toes in the sand…have your choice of any number of gourmet dining options for dinner…with shopping for high-end fashions and artisan creations mixed in—not to mention relaxing spa treatments.

Playa is hip and chic…a vibrant, cosmopolitan city with a bright future that continues to grow and develop. It has an enduring appeal to diverse markets, from those work-from-homers to vacationing families and couples of all ages, groups of friends, snowbirds spending the winter season south of the border, expats…

And it's maturing into a sophisticated, upscale destination increasingly drawing a well-heeled clientele with money to spend and a need for appropriate accommodations. That's why I'm so bullish on my rental income predictions for the opportunities I invest in.

There are so many things to do, see, eat, and drink found nowhere else in the world…with warm weather…sunny skies…and Caribbean vibes. And as a result, it draws visitors year-round.

There's now a lack of developable land in desirable areas. That limits supply, leading to rising land costs. Permitting is getting tighter with each passing year, too. In fact, Playa Del Carmen doesn't allow high-rise construction in the downtown area.

All this means that by doing the right deals, we stand to do extremely well. Apply the five R's here. You can't put your money just anywhere in Playa. You need to buy the right real estate, in the right location, at the right price, and from the right developer…

Take Siempre Playa, a condo community in the Zona Dorada, or "Golden Zone," which is fast-becoming the district known for high-end residential and commercial development. This is like a mini Path of Progress within Playa del Carmen.

Next door to the condos, construction is ongoing for a Chedraui Selecto, which is a high-end supermarket chain in Mexico, as well as an Aloft Hotel, which is a boutique hotel concept from Marriott. And across the road, one of Playa's biggest commercial developers plans to put in a high-end shopping mall.

This is the hottest location in town. The developer is one of the most established in the region, a winner of awards for design and innovation. Their focus is on high-end amenities and they were smart…they bought land way ahead of the big transformation at prices far lower than what other developers pay today.

In April 2017, *RETA* members were able to lock down two-bedroom condos in Siempre Playa from $198,600. As of July 2022, two-bed condos in this community were listing at $371,676 at retail.

That's a $173,076 jump in five years.

RETA members who own in Siempre Playa have been staying in and renting out their condos since taking possession in spring 2021, in this thriving community in a prime location. According to data from the developer, occupancy is between 85% to 90%, with owners setting rates of $95 to $110 per night for the one-bedroom condos and $150 to $200 for the two-beds.

The developer tells me that mid- and long-term rentals have also entered the mix in a serious way. Digital nomads are seeking out three- and six-month contracts, with online entrepreneurs and remote workers looking for year-long arrangements or more. They love the amenities and convenience. Siempre is an ideal place to live and work, with owners charging from $1,500 to $1,900 per month for a one-bedroom, $2,500 for a two-bedroom. That presents an intriguing option for owners, one that I'm seeing elsewhere on my beat...the rise of long-term renting as an attractive option for investors. (More on this in chapter 7.)

In another Playa deal, in June 2021, members of *Real Estate Trend Alert* could buy in a community called Singular Dream from $265,304 for fully furnished two-bedroom lock-off condos (with a furniture pack valued at $23,000), and from $174,600 for the one-beds, also completely turnkey (furnishings valued at $15,000).

Construction of Singular Dream is complete. And condos were being delivered to *RETA* members starting in July 2022. To give you an idea of how well *RETA* members did, the developer's list price for a one-bed condo *RETA* members could buy for $198,600 was $331,073—an uplift of $132,473.

That's just a sampling of *RETA* deals in Playa, but you get the point. Buying ahead of this major transformation has proved incredibly profitable.

The end of the line for the Path of Progress: Tulum

In 2007, Playa del Carmen was reportedly the world's fastest-growing city…today I think that title could easily go to Tulum. You'll see construction everywhere. New hotels, new homes and condos, new commercial development, new roads and other infrastructure.

Tulum is 50 minutes farther down the Riviera Maya. When I first visited Tulum in 2004, at the end of a long journey on bumpy roads, I found just a few rustic palapa bars and restaurants among the coconut trees that fringed a white-sand beach. It was paradise, the quintessential tropical beach and—to this very day—among the most beautiful places I have ever been in all my travels.

Tulum beach is still postcard-perfect. It's said to be one of the most "Instagram-able" places on earth. But much has changed over the years.

On that initial visit, Tulum town, which is inland from the coast, had one ATM—that was often not working—and a supermarket.

In its early days as a destination, most visitors, from resorts to the north, came to Tulum simply to visit the famed Mayan ruins along the coast to the north of town. In fact, they still draw about two million visitors a year. If you're in the area, it's well worth the trip to see the stone temples and other structures right on the cliffs overlooking the water.

But Tulum also was a stop on the backpacker trail, a favorite of hippies and the like. It was a place to "drop out"—a so-called counterculture haven.

By the early 2000s, it had been discovered by hipsters and fashionistas from Manhattan and elsewhere and soon enough it was a must-go for the international jet-set and celebrities who wanted to lounge in a beach bed all day, maybe do a bit of yoga, dine on the chef-created creations at hip eateries, dance the night away at parties in the jungle…and get up and do it again the next day.

Now, Tulum is very much entering the mainstream. Couples young and old, retirees, snowbirds, families, remote workers…they are all coming to Tulum. The population has grown from less than 7,000 when I first visited to over 46,000.

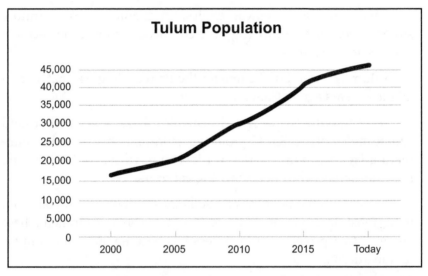

The population of Tulum is growing fast, same as what happened in Playa del Carmen which went from a fishing village to 300,000 people in a few decades.

Like we saw in Playa del Carmen, Tulum is on a trajectory to becoming a city in itself.

As the Path of Progress flowed straight to it, Tulum "grew up" in many ways, although it still has that bohemian feel and vibrant dining and nightlife scenes.

Tulum has several banks and several supermarkets, including one offering all manner of gourmet items like French cheese, Italian wine, Japanese sushi rice, and crusty fresh-baked bread...not to mention a whole section of vegan, gluten-free, and organic items. The choice of places to dine has gotten much bigger.

There are cool cafés where baristas offer up coffee creations... chic Italian and Argentinean places with homemade pasta and thin-crust pizza...sidewalk eateries offering pulled pork tacos and grilled chicken. Every time I visit, there's a new place to try out. There's even a Starbucks.

There are also medical clinics, mechanic shops, furniture stores...everything a thriving little city needs to meet the needs of visitors and residents.

Tulum is the end of the line for the Path of Progress that started all those years ago in Cancun.

To the south is the Sian Ka'an Biosphere—over a thousand square miles of UNESCO-protected wildlife-rich wetlands, shimmering lagoons, and deserted Caribbean beaches. To the north are the stunning beachfront archaeological ruins.

You can't build near the archaeological ruins nor can you build in the biosphere. Because of these limitations on development, these "moats" that protect Tulum, access has become incredibly important in Tulum.

That's why this location is so special...and land prices are increasing steadily.

Tulum is where I've seen some of the most impressive deals in recent years. Tulum is booming, no doubt about it. This has pushed prices up.

But thanks to the group buying power of *Real Estate Trend Alert* and my relationships with some of the top developers in Tulum, we've been in a unique position to pick up best-in-class real estate at a fraction of the cost that others pay.

This means that *RETA* members are able to lock in huge potential upside right from the moment they buy. And thanks to Tulum's booming rental market, they're sitting on income generating machines once they're delivered.

For instance, Tao Tulum is within the master-planned Aldea Zama community, which has its own gourmet market and other little shops, restaurants and cafés, and a weekend organic farmers' market—and a cycle path to Tulum beach and Tulum town. Two-bedroom condos that *RETA* members could buy for $208,440 in October 2017 are, as of June 2022, listed at $311,000. That's an uplift of $102,560. Myself, I bought one of the entry-priced two-bed condos in Tao Tulum (Members-only price was $154,500) and sold it in early 2020 for $225,000.

In the Edena community, *RETA* members could buy two-bedroom homes for $149,000, and the developer threw in a free pool valued at $7,000. I bought one of these homes. As of October 2022 they listed at retail for $249,000, although the developer sold one in May for $252,000.

In October 2021, *RETA* members could buy luxury two-bed condos for $198,600 in Samsara, a stunning community overlooking the archaeological park. In July 2022, the developer opened up the remaining condos in Samsara through a local broker to retail buyers. Condos that had had a *RETA*-only price of $212,300 were retailing at $298,200. An $85,900 boost.

The transformation of the Riviera Maya has been one of the world's most spectacular, and most profitable for savvy real estate investors. I've spent a lot of time there as a result and I've developed an extensive network there that puts you and (in our *RETA* group) on the inside.

But it's not the only place in Mexico I've found a huge transformation for real estate investors to get in on...

2. Los Cabos, Mexico

I spend my winters in one of the most beautiful places on earth. A place that, for nine months every year, has the *perfect* weather. Never too hot, too humid, nor cold...

Just the ideal climate.

I wear short sleeves, I play golf when I want, stroll on the beach, dine outdoors, and when I open my laptop it's usually with an ocean view from my terrace or one of the many beautiful spots around.

No snow, ice, oppressive heat...no air con needed.

And amazing weather is only the beginning of Cabo's appeal...

There are excellent reasons that Hollywood stars and the world's super rich have been hopping in private planes or sailing luxury yachts to visit Cabo since the 1940s.

For one thing, it's uniquely gorgeous. Golden-sand beaches fringe a desert landscape, with the fingers of giant Cardon cacti (some of which are 500 years old) pointing to the bright blue sky overhead.

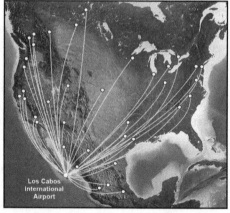

The desert is a place that feels primeval...unspoiled. Where you can get back to nature. At night, the glimmer of millions of stars lights up the dark skies, a magical experience.

Cabo is simply one of the world's most prestigious and beautiful getaways... the scene of a phenomenal transformation...

Once hard to reach and a playground of Hollywood stars and European royalty, Cabo is now well-connected with direct flights to the U.S. and Canada.

You could say it started with a starlet...

Lucille Bremer was a dancer who went from stage to screen and starred in the 1944 smash hit *Meet me in St Louis*. She danced on screen with Fred Astaire, made friends with the likes of Bing Crosby and Lucille Ball...worked with the greats of MGM.

Yet Hollywood wasn't for her...

In 1948 she fell in love with a dashing entrepreneur who had discovered a sleepy oceanfront paradise right at the bottom of the Baja California peninsula.

Abelardo Luis Rodriguez was the son of a Mexican President and he dreamed big...building an airstrip and the first-ever resort, Rancho las Cruces.

His new wife, Bremer, spread the word among her Hollywood friends about a place away from it all where you could snorkel and fish all day and sip cocktails without prying press.

The great and the good of Hollywood came in private planes and by boat. There was no other way to get to Los Cabos, making it the perfect exclusive escape.

With the Pacific Ocean to the west and the Sea of Cortez to the east, Cabo was and still is a fisherman's paradise. Jacques Cousteau labelled it "the world's aquarium."

That's a great description for a place where you can see blue whales, dolphins, giant manta rays, sea lions, and more than 900 species of fish. Whales close to shore are such a common sight in season that I've stopped pointing them out to friends.

Celebrities like John Wayne arrived from California to another world, where 500-pound black sea bass lurked in the harbor and sailfish and striped marlin were close to shore. Today Cabo hosts the world's most prestigious fishing tournaments with pay outs of millions of dollars to the winners.

Although today anyone can catch a flight to Cabo from all over the U.S., the lack of infrastructure kept Cabo super exclusive for a very long time.

And that helped firmly establish Cabo as a favorite destination for Hollywood. Robert DeNiro, Leonardo DiCaprio, Cameron Diaz, Jennifer Lopez, George Clooney...the list of celebrities who visit and invest in Cabo is long.

That's one big reason it's become the epitome of luxury in Mexico. And along with the famous, the plain old super-wealthy hang out here.

As the years rolled on, it became easier to get to Cabo. A new road connected it all the way to Southern California. The Cabo international airport hooked up flights across North America.

Just as we've seen happened in the past in America, a major transformational event occurred.

The real estate market in Cabo followed the jet-set lead. When you attract visitors on the level of George Clooney, you build second homes for that market. In Cabo, you'll find plenty of choice in the market for homes with price tags of $5 million plus.

And the condo market offers a range of options in the $500,000 to $1 million price band.

Multi-million-dollar homes are aimed at those with deep pockets. This kind of buyer doesn't go bargain hunting. They want the most expensive, most decadent, and most enviable real estate they can find—and they'll get it in Cabo. They are often buying a third, fourth, or fifth home to add to their portfolio, and more concerned with adding ridiculously overpriced upgrades than getting any kind of gains.

Then there are the luxury timeshares, which are big business in Cabo. My impression of timeshares was formed by aggressive salesmen in Europe…pitching two weeks a year in a cheap condo for a few thousand euro in popular tourist haunts. But timeshares in Cabo are on a whole different level…aimed at aspirational "ordinary rich" folks who want a slice of the jet-set lifestyle but can't afford a multi-million-dollar home.

To this day, I'm still shocked by the number of people who shell out $100,000 for a timeshare. (A high-end timeshare goes for $100,000 and more, that gets you a week or so.) It seems crazy to me to spend this kind of money and not own anything. All you get is the right to vacation in a swish home for a couple of weeks a year. And you'll pay annual maintenance fees on top, which could be as much as $7,000.

It's even crazier when you think that *Real Estate Trend Alert* have had deals like Copala, where in 2015 they could get a luxury oceanview condo from $336,156 that today could sell for $600,000 and rent for $3,500 a month. (Over 12% gross yield. In chapter 8, I give you my yield calculator so you can properly assess deals based on income after all costs.)

Prices had reached fever pitch in Los Cabos before my first visit in 2014. In the early 2000s, beachfront homes in Los Cabos would have set you back 20 times more than any other comparable Pacific coast lot. Prices had sky-rocketed to incredible levels.

Then in 2007, the global economic crisis hit. In Los Cabos, construction ground to a sudden halt. Buyers and investors were no longer willing to pour millions into vacation homes…or spend hundreds of thousands per year on a timeshare—a place they didn't even own.

And that's where our first *RETA* opportunities came into play…

I knew that Los Cabos would bounce back. But, in the interim, there was opportunity for doing deals…especially using *RETA* group buying power with smart developers who knew how to adapt to the market conditions.

And one of them, the developer at Copala, gave us our first-ever Cabo opportunity. The developer's business until then was primarily timeshares…but they knew that to stay nimble after the crisis, they had to do something different. So, they offered us luxury condos at a deep discount. It was an opportunity so good, I acted myself. That was in 2015 and like I've said, the *RETA* price on a two-bed, two-bath ocean view condo was $336,156. (In September 2022 I got an email from a real estate agent saying they had buyers ready to pull the trigger and asking would I sell for around $600,000.)

The real estate market was at a low point in 2015 when we seized the opportunity. But that low point didn't last. Even as we seized that chance Cabo was gearing up to roar ahead…

When financial crisis hit the U.S. in 2007, the music stopped. Buyers stopped coming to Cabo. Timeshare sales fell off a cliff. And then Hurricane Odile swept through…compounding Cabo's woes.

But as we've seen in other international jet-set locales on our beat, a low point is often just a breather before the music plays louder than ever.

The big groups in Cabo took a deep breath in the wake of the financial crisis and set their sights on a major transformation.

It is the perfect example of what I call "a Path of Progress." Since then more than $4 billion has been substantially ploughed into infrastructure, new golf courses, and some 20 new resorts. Among those are big names: Montage, Ritz-Carlton, Four Seasons, Hard Rock, and Nobu. These resorts aren't all dipping into the same pool of wealthy clients. They all target specific segments.

And these powerful resort operators are highly skilled at pressuring the local government and tourism authorities to support them by adding more flights and funding more infrastructure.

Cabo was on this $4 billion Path of Progress tear when COVID swept the globe and shut down travel. After COVID, it was back to the races big time and the pace of the Path of Progress picked up.

Demand was through the roof and it's easier than ever to get to Cabo.

Before the pandemic, tourism was booming in Cabo. In 2018, passenger numbers at the airport were up nearly 7% on the year before. 2019 saw the same increase again.

In the wake of the pandemic, tourism bounced back bigger and faster than before.

I saw this with my own eyes…

When I arrived in October 2020 to spend my winter in my condo in Cabo, things were quiet. As fall turned to winter, more remote workers arrived. By the time I left for Europe, at the end of April 2021, it felt like Cabo was back in full swing.

It wasn't the government that came up with a plan to handle the pandemic and re-opening. The powerful interest groups behind Cabo's $4 billion Path of Progress worked out a plan for safely re-opening. Companies like Marriott, IHG, and Hilton. The authorities followed their lead.

The opening of new luxury resorts is continuing at the same rapid pace as before.

Cabo is a tourism juggernaut and a destination for the rich and famous. Which means lots of high-paying jobs. Resort managers, executives, 5-star chefs…they all need a place to live.

Since the outset of the $4 billion Path of Progress, I've watched as the number of these professionals increased, increasing demand for condos in that sweet $250,000 to $500,000 range (and creating the critical shortage that is getting worse.)

And now the pandemic's freed millions of people from the office. And this is where it gets *really* interesting…

Before the pandemic I regularly met professionals—especially from the West Coast and Texas—who were spending a few weeks or months running their businesses back home from a terrace in Cabo. The internet and ease of getting to and from Cabo gave them this flexibility.

They were everywhere…my neighbors in Copala…folks down on my favorite beach in Santa Maria…on a Sunday day-trip to trendy Todos Santos…at a gourmet restaurant in San José…

Los Cabos is a short flight from many U.S. cities. The weather is perfect, the lifestyle incredible, and the views—if you have an ocean-view condo—are amazing. It boasts sun and sand, sea and surf, super-luxe hotels and day spas, fine dining, and some of the world's best golf and fishing.

In January 2020, when my wife and I attended a neighbor's cocktail party, we were the youngest by far. Our neighbors were retirees and snow birds. They chose Cabo for weather, its beautiful setting, and ease of visiting family back home.

As the pandemic raged, many older neighbors stayed home, waiting for the vaccine. But the gym was packed through the day with 30 somethings…the party room became a co-working space…

And here's the rub, these younger arrivals have no plans to leave Cabo. Plus, all those I chatted with told me they had friends and family mulling the same move. And of course our older neighbors were itching to get back and they have.

I have bought three properties in *RETA* deals in Cabo. I bought in Copala, in Cabo Costa, and in Monte Rocella.

I've already told you about Copala where *RETA* members could buy in 2015 from $336,156 and I've lately been told my condo could sell for $600,000. In terms of rental income, I figure these condos could rent for $3,500 a month.

Next was Cabo Costa, due to be delivered in 2024. I brought this deal to *RETA* members in August 2021. The starting price for *RETA* members was from $188,200 for two-bed, two-bath ocean-view condos. As I write in September 2022, these mezzanine condos would retail starting from $300,000.

In May 2022, I brought members the chance to buy in another upscale community called Monte Rocella. Our *RETA* start price for a two-bedroom ocean-view condo was from $234,600. Also available were two-bedroom condos with views over the community's cactus garden from $198,400 and two-bedroom penthouses from $318,800 with a spacious rooftop terrace.

As I write just four months later, condos *RETA* members could buy for $234,600 are listed at $269,790. The condos for $198,400 are $228,160. And those penthouses for $318,800 are at $366,620.

It's worth noting *RETA* members had access to exclusive developer financing in all the above deals.

I would love to be able to present more deals to my *Real Estate Trend Alert* group. I believe in this market that strongly.

I keep a very close eye on the real estate scene. I'm often zipping around town to see potential projects with my own eyes.

But the vast majority of opportunities simply aren't up to snuff in terms of location and amenities. And there aren't many of them, in any case.

That's because there are serious barriers to development in Cabo. Permitting for new construction is tight and complex. Appropriate land with views (in Cabo people want ocean views) and in convenient locations is in short supply.

But this isn't a bad thing for real estate investors like me and members of my *RETA* group. It just makes the opportunities I do find all the more valuable.

Cabo has been the site of some of my strongest investments, personally and for members of *Real Estate Trend Alert*. I think we're just at the beginning of its full potential, and I think the transformation taking place here, with Cabo turning into the ultimate high-end destination, will run for the next 30 years...

3. Costa Rica

It was 1948, and a bloody civil war in Costa Rica had just ended. The experience was so traumatic that the government disbanded the army and put the money into education and a national health-care system.

I share this little history lesson because it set the stage for turning what had been a largely rural and sparsely populated country into what it is today and made the transformational events I follow here possible.

Costa Rica is safe, with a stable democratic government (it's longest continuous democracy in Latin America) and a decades-long history of growing economic prosperity. In fact, it has been called the Switzerland of Central America.

That, along with an educated population, has attracted dozens of multinationals (including Hewlett Packard, Microsoft, and Pfizer) operating manufacturing plants, corporate headquarters, and more within its borders.

And, of course, Costa Rica is a destination of choice for millions of tourists seeking to immerse themselves in its natural beauty of stunning beaches, soaring verdant mountains, and wildlife-filled jungles. Costa Rica pioneered the concept of eco-tourism back in the 1980s. And since then, the industry has become a major economic driver. And it's not all trekking in the jungle. There are also top-end resorts from the likes of the Four Seasons, and bustling beach towns offering dining, shopping, nightlife, and other fun.

In 2021, there were only 1.3 million visitors due to pandemic travel restrictions. But before, tourism numbers were on an upward trajectory. In 2019, there were 3.14 million visitors, a jump from 3 million in 2018…and 2.9 million in 2017. According to the Organization for Economic Cooperation and Development (OECD), international tourism has grown, on average, 7.4% annually since 1990. This in a country of just 5 million.

Costa Rica is also a favorite of the tens of thousands of expats, primarily from North America, who call it home. In *International Living*'s Annual Retirement Index, it's a perennial top five finisher. They come to this country the size of West Virginia for the warm weather year-round, natural beauty, lower cost of living, high-quality, low-cost healthcare, modern conveniences, and the welcoming locals.

Costa Ricans are laidback and friendly. You'll hear the unofficial national motto "Pura Vida" (rough translation: life is good) dozens of times if you visit. In fact, it has earned a top spot in the Happy Planet Index, which is based on factors like life expectancy and wellbeing, four times in a row.

Costa Rica, wedged between Nicaragua to the north and Panama to the south, has a Caribbean and Pacific coast.

Eco-Friendly Costa Rica

Nearly 100% of Costa Rica's electricity is generated by renewable resources, including wind, hydroelectric, and geothermal. The country has a tremendous commitment to conservation, with 25% of its territory protected by national park or private reserve.

Remember this, as it, and other building restrictions, plays into how real estate is developed here in a big way. Specifically, it can lead to scarcity, which drives up prices.

In a region known for its difficult history, Costa Rica is a success story. It's trajectory from humble agricultural producer to a center of business and leading tourist destination within a matter of a few decades is impressive...along with the infrastructure improvements that have gone with it.

This has had a huge impact on the country as a whole, of course. But there are some regions that have particularly benefited and been the site of significant—and ongoing—Path of Progress events. There are two main transformations I've tracked in Costa Rica.

The Southern Zone

For decades, the Southern Zone, far south on Costa Rica's Pacific coast near the border with Panama, stayed off the radar of tourists, investors, and second-home buyers. Everyone knew where it was. Some understood how much potential it held. But very few scouted it or spent time there. For one very good reason: it was difficult to get to.

The coast road south of the town of Manuel Antonio, long one of the top tourist spots in the country on the Pacific, was unpaved to the town at the start of the Southern Zone, called Dominical. A section that looked like it should take 20 to 25 minutes to drive based on distance took at least 90 minutes bouncing along the rutted, pot-holed road…and crossing some scary bridges.

In all, the drive from the main international airport in the capital, San José, took most of the day, which discouraged all but the most adventurous visitors.

Tour operators would tell you to give the Southern Zone a miss unless your idea of vacation heaven involved the wilderness, exotic critters, and basic digs. It's a shame as I consider the landscape there as some of the most stunningly beautiful in the world.

Picture jungle-covered mountains looming above a coastline that alternates between wild, sandy beaches fringed by palms and rocky coves. Monkeys, toucans, sloths, macaws, and dozens of other species populate the surrounding rain forest. And you don't have to be in one of the area's nature preserves or national parks to see them. You are surrounded by nature here.

And although there are modern conveniences like high-speed internet, cell phone services, and shops selling any item you might need, you won't find big-box stores, malls, large resorts, or condo towers on the beach. Many people compare this region to Hawaii 30 years ago.

There are three main population centers. The aforementioned Dominical, which is a funky village right on the beach whose surf break is known world-wide. There's a microbrewery, a sushi place, a little organic market, cute cafes, and artisan vendors arrayed under the palms on the beach road. There's a weekly farmers' market too. A place to spend a pleasant afternoon.

Uvita is about a half-hour south on the coastal highway. It has a few larger supermarkets, hardware stores, banks…it's somewhat of a commercial center, a hub for residents of the region.

Then there is my favorite: the little jungle village of Ojochal. There is not a defined town center here, rather roads snake through the jungle, with homes and businesses quite spread out.

This is the "Foodie Capital of Costa Rica." Gourmet dining in the jungle, whether its French cuisine, Asian fusion, or nouveau Costa Rican. A few years back a little plaza opened up that has a gourmet market, restaurant, cute boutique selling home décor and stylish beachwear, and, of all things, a Belgian beer bar. Ojochal is hip and chic. Upscale in flip flops.

I first visited the Southern Zone in 2011. The tricky access and rough-around-the-edges feel put real estate in the Southern Zone into an asset class that many avoid, but one that I target: unloved, overlooked, and undervalued. Then, a transformational event flipped this locale from no-go to a buy-now commodity.

After 30 years of rumors and promises, new roads opened in 2010, making the Southern Zone easily accessible for the first time. It was a game changer. The drive from the international airport is now an easy three hours…with panoramic ocean views along the way.

Since 2010, tourism numbers have increased significantly, expats have moved down in droves, and land values have skyrocketed.

There is huge demand in this region for both finished homes and lots, which many buyers prefer so they can build their dream home. The homes dot the hillsides and can also be found in the jungle. The most desirable homes have views over the treetops to the Pacific, although some people do like those mountain views thanks to the thousand shades of green of the countryside here.

The problem right now in the Southern Zone (and a boon to savvy real estate investors with the right contacts to buy at off-market pricing) is there is limited inventory. The perfect recipe for rapid gains when you buy at the right price.

Sure, there is plenty of land around and much of this region remains undeveloped. But a good portion is protected by national park. The topography of steep ridges, jungle-covered hills, and the soaring Talamanca mountains also makes construction impractical in many areas—and means awe-inspiring vistas when you find a place where you can build.

Finally, the Costa Rican government has tightened its grip on development. Getting the right permits for water access and construction can be difficult and is not guaranteed, which means there are plenty of lots on the market where there could be a lengthy waiting period to start construction—and there might be restrictions on what size home you can put up.

Again, here we see the common thread to the places I invest: barriers to development, "moats," which create a supply crunch and boost prices, meaning supersized gains for those who get in with the right property at the right price.

Word to the wise: in the Southern Zone, anywhere in the world really, don't buy property based on the assurances from the seller or developer that the property will receive the proper permits, get access to electricity and water, or similar, at some point in the future. These types of things are never guaranteed.

I've managed to sidestep those issues by dealing with a developer who is a pioneer in the region.

If the Southern Zone was considered "rough going" before 2010, I can't imagine what it was like when Sylvaine Pilault first visited on a trip from her home country, France, in the late 1980s and decided to make it her home. She bought land from a farmer on that first visit at a serious bargain price.

That was the seed of the real estate development company I and my *Real Estate Trend Alert* group have dealt with many times. In fact, I consider this the finest developer in the whole country. They even have their own home design and construction company.

She bought more property and, over the years, built up an impressive land bank. That's how, even as the Southern Zone grows and attracts more visitors, she has been able to offer lots and homes to my *RETA* group at low, off-market prices—that and our group buying power.

In Costa Rica, which has that commitment to conservation, it's only possible to develop former farmland like this. Plus, it's a master-planned community where all the permits to build, as well as roads and access to water and electricity, are in place.

Being surrounded by primary forest and close to stunning virgin beaches means that development should always be extremely restricted in the Southern Zone. And the strict permitting and tightly enforced building regulations here create a "moat" and mean that the stunning lots like those I've been able to present to *Real Estate Trend Alert* members are extremely rare.

The play here is capital appreciation and rental income.

As far as rental income, gross rental yields of more than 13% are driven by a critical shortage of rentals in the Southern Zone. There are only boutique hotels and eco-lodges. Small establishments. The alternative is a vacation rental, of which there are a limited number due to the restrictions on development here. There are those moats at play again…

At the end of the day, it means the increasing number of visitors are having a tough time finding accommodation. Those who own the right type of property are in prime position.

One of the deals I presented my *Real Estate Trend Alert* group, which was delivered in October 2019, involved two- and three-bedroom homes with pools—called Villas Ojochal. They are close to Ojochal, as you might expect, actually a brisk walk or quick bike ride away. This location is great for vacationers. The two-bedroom villas are going for $180 a night, the three-bedrooms for $250.

These communities are also ideal for those U.S. and Canadian snowbirds and European vacationers who want to rent for a few weeks or months at a time...even local expats who are looking to rent something long term. With one of these villas, owners have options, including renting a two-bedroom for $180 or a three-bedroom for $250.

On the capital appreciation side, you have options. You could buy a lot and hold it. Values are rising.

For example, in one deal I brought to my *RETA* group from the French developer in December 2018, *RETA* members could buy lots close to Ojochal, perched on hillsides with panoramic views of the ocean and surrounded by lush rainforest from $92,000. Retail prices are now 60% higher.

Of course, you can't forget the lifestyle element here. For the right type of person, one who wants to be immersed in a laidback tropical jungle vibe, buying or building a home in the Southern Zone is ideal, whether you live there full-time or part-time (and rent out to cover your costs when you're not there).

The uplift *Real Estate Trend Alert* members have seen and rental income they can enjoy are only possible because of the Path of Progress that has roared down this coast for the last decade or so.

The Southern Zone has come a long way and still has a ways to go. I'm expecting huge gains here on lots and homes for years to come, as well as significant rental income due to the critical shortage of rentals in the area.

But Costa Rica is a dynamic country. The Southern Zone isn't the only place where growth and development is happening at a rapid pace...and tourists flock in numbers.

Northern Pacific Coast

Costa Rica's northern Pacific coast, near the border with Nicaragua, opened up before the Southern Zone. It has what is perhaps the original Path of Progress story in Costa Rica…and it's still going.

This region of Costa Rica is known as the sunniest in the country and is home to some of its most beautiful beaches. It had boomed big time before the housing crash…and, in recent years, has rebounded and then some.

Way back before Costa Rica's tourist boom, this was a sleepy region of cattle farms, empty but expansive beaches, and good surf breaks. It fit the bill if you were looking for a little fun in the sun…a lazy vacation where you could kick back and unwind.

Getting to this idyllic spot took some doing. The road from the capital city was potholed and in bad shape. It was a bumpy ride that took four or five hours. Or you could take a prop plane. It set you up for the lack of frills when you arrived. Sound familiar?

Your lodgings were small mom'n'pop hotels and B&Bs. Your dining choices were limited. You could forget fancy linen, fine silverware, and white-glove service. You provided your own entertainment. Adventurous types were happy to get off the beaten track. Surfers, sport-fishermen, backpackers flocked here. Mainstream tourists stayed away.

But a savvy group of hotel and real estate developers could see the appeal of this endless-summer location.

The Four Seasons pumped more than $200 million into carving out a top-quality golf course, rooms and suites, and hillside villas with private plunge pools. They needed tourists to fill their luxury rooms and pay their premium rates. A bumpy dirt track or a prop plane simply wouldn't cut it.

The road from the capital San José was paved. The airport at Liberia, the provincial capital just 30 minutes from the coast, was expanded and upgraded. (It was also expanded in 2006, 2012, and 2017.)

In 2002, regular direct flights to the U.S. started on Delta.

Funny story about that... Investors involved in the Four Seasons, as well as Hacienda Pinilla and Reserva Conchal resorts, were instrumental in persuading Delta to fly to Liberia. They put up a $3 million guarantee to offset Delta's losses if there weren't enough passengers.

But Delta never had to tap into the fund. And Continental and American Airlines soon followed with their own flights. Tourists could now get to this location quickly and easily for the first time.

In 2003, Liberia airport saw 50,000 passenger arrivals. In 2008, that number hit 420,000, more than an eight-fold increase. By 2019, 1.2 million passengers passed through Liberia airport. In 2021, visitors dropped down to 388,000 due to the pandemic. At that time, Costa Rica still had serious travel rules and restrictions in place. Since the start of 2022, numbers have surged again.

Starting in 2002, investment in residential development outstripped investment in tourist development. Developers poured into the market, snapping up the best pieces of land. In the three years after those regular direct flights, prime beachfront land tripled in price.

Visiting this part of Costa Rica today, you can stay in fancy hotels with 5-star service and 5-star amenities. The Four Seasons was joined by JW Marriott, Andaz, Planet Hollywood, and the Westin. An investment group from Dubai is planning a super-luxury project. They claim it will be a 7-star resort.

In any number of towns across the region, like Playas del Coco, Tamarindo, or Playa Flamingo, you can play golf, relax in a spa, and dine in chic restaurants. These days, it's highly developed. And home to not just high-rise condos but also fancy gated communities.

Along the way, this region earned the nickname, the Gold Coast.

In short, this is no longer a low-cost destination, whether you're heading out to dinner or buying a home.

My scout, who was in the region recently, reports new construction in popular towns like Playas del Coco and Tamarindo—high-end condos going for $500,000 or more—penthouses for over a million…ocean-view homes for $2 million and more…ocean-view lots for $200,000 and much, much more.

And the long-planned marina in Playa Flamingo, with an upscale commercial and residential zone, is nearing completion. A charter fishing boat captain my scout met said his slip will cost $1,000 a month—those are California or Florida prices.

What's happening in the rental market is also telling. Long-term rental prices were already among the highest in Costa Rica. My scout, who used to live in Tamarindo, a funky surfing town, tells me he visited the condo he used to rent, a mid-range three-bedroom condo about 15-minutes' walk from the beach. He paid $1,200 a month five years ago. It's now going for $3,000 a month.

And people are happy to pay it. It's always been a popular destination, especially for West Coasters looking for good waves and a laid-back life. Then remote working during the pandemic brought even more folks, pushing prices up. And some of these newcomers are buying too, seeking a refuge in safe and stable Costa Rica.

But there are still bargains to be had…if you have the right contacts. It's taken years for me to track down the right potential deal here. It seemed as if this ship had sailed.

But in November 2021, I met with the developer of a vast master-planned community in the far northern corner of Costa Rica.

It's a place I've flown over a bunch of times on my way to Nicaragua. Lush, mountainous jungle spills down to a coastline of quiet bays and pristine Pacific beaches.

But I had never put boots on the ground in this part of north-western Costa Rica until my trip last November. And boy had I underestimated just how stunning it is. A complex network of bays and points are fringed by beautiful sandy beaches, with lush, tropical vegetation spilling right up to the sand. I saw baby foxes, howler monkeys, colorful birds, and giant butterflies, all protected by a nature preserve.

As of writing, it's still very early days. But I can share some details here, and I do so because it will help you understand how the Path of Progress in this region is playing out today and the big money going into its continuing transformation.

The group behind it is a consortium of Central America's biggest families—big names associated with household brands airlines, drinks, hotel groups, etc. have come together to assemble maybe the most impressive land bank I have ever seen—approximately 7,000 acres. They've already put $200 million into electric lines, roads, and other infrastructure for what will be a high-end community with resort and residential sides, as well as a golf course, marina...

I'm intrigued. I'm digging deep on my research. We'll see if a deal comes together.

4. Portugal's Algarve

What's better than a Path of Progress? Two of them! That's the transformation I tracked along Portugal's Algarve.

For those who don't know Portugal, the Algarve is in the south of the country facing the Atlantic, yet it boasts a perfect Mediterranean climate.

More than any country in Western Europe, I've been drilling down into Portugal over the last few years.

Portugal is getting its act together and doing smart things...the kinds of things that drive growth and create buying moments.

There's a sense of optimism, a confidence that has helped the country go from a global backwater to a trendy tourism destination.

It's foreigner friendly and internationalized. It's a place that has learned how to attract capital investment, expats, and tourists…

Pre-COVID, tourism was on a tear in Portugal. In 2019, the tourism sector grew by one of the highest rates in Europe and contributed one in five of all jobs in the country.

And tourism is bouncing back fast post-pandemic, as Portugal continues to grow up as a country and sell itself around the world.

I continually scout all over the country—I have a base on the Silver Coast north of the capital Lisbon—but it's the far south where I see the greatest opportunity and have found the most profitable potential deals.

The sunny Algarve draws millions of visitors each year.

The Algarve is a place of rich culture, great food…soaring cliffs, white-washed villages, stunning beaches, world-class golf (remember, I'm an avid golfer, so I always make note) and 300 days of sunshine a year.

This has made it one of the most popular seaside destinations in Europe, attracting millions of tourists each year from the U.K., France, the Netherlands, Germany, and beyond. They're even coming from the U.S.

Among the growing North American expat crowd are retirees, remote workers, families, and others who come for the great food, the lower cost of living, pleasant weather, rich culture, and ease of getting around Europe.

I've been visiting the Algarve since 2002. It's where I've found some of the most profitable opportunities on my beat. It has delivered for members of my *Real Estate Trend Alert* group since the first bank fire sales came along in the wake of the 2008/09 crisis.

I own a condo there myself and I'm always keeping an eye out for the right deals.

Key to my recommendations in Portugal, including the Algarve, is that it has a fast-growing tourism market.

Already a mainstay of European tourism since the 1990s, the past decade has seen the country's tourism growth start to accelerate year on year, helped by low costs for tourists and unrest in other European tourism favorites, such as Tunisia, Morocco, and Turkey.

In 2019, Portugal attracted a record 24 million tourists, with accumulated tourist revenue over the past three years growing by 45%. There were 5.9 million in 2021, a year after plunging to 3.9 million during the height of the pandemic.

Millions of those who come to Portugal head to the Algarve.

The Algarve has benefited significantly from twin Paths of Progress that has been driving development here for decades... and if you know where to look, there are still corners of this region benefiting from it. Places where you can buy great value real estate that's undergoing rapid appreciation, with the potential to capture high rental yields too.

When development first came to the Algarve, it rolled out west of Faro, where the international airport is, toward Vilamoura. That's where the major resorts, golf courses, hotels, and condo communities first developed, before moving farther west towards Lagos.

Meanwhile, east of Faro and the international airport was overlooked, despite the fact that you have some of Europe's finest beaches here…and a more traditional Portuguese feel.

In recent years, people have been starting to discover the eastern Algarve around Tavira and Cabanas—particularly well-heeled vacationers. Besides a lot of history and culture there are some incredible beaches close by. To get to them, you have to take a water taxi. (Watch out for flamingos en route.)

The opportunity on the central Algarve is to lock down a villa, something undervalued, old or unloved, and do so with a mortgage at low fixed rates. Done right, it's a way to double your money.

I've already told you the stories of both my contact, Chris White, and my own purchase in earlier chapters, but they are worth repeating here…

My contact on Portugal's Algarve, Chris White, snagged a bank foreclosure property that had just come on the market in 2018. It was a villa on a big lot of about 3,000 square meters (32,292 square feet) with over 100 trees and a swimming pool. But, it was a wreck. However, Chris saw the potential. He bought it at asking price for €420,000 with a plan to spend another €80,000 to €100,000 fixing it up, and then flipping it.

He got a fixed rate mortgage of 90%, so he paid just €42,000, borrowing the rest, and has repayments of just €830 a month. Today, the villa is fully refurbished and now valued at as much as €1.9 million. However, Chris doesn't plan to sell anymore. It's now his primary residence and a huge income earner when he's not using it. In the summer of 2022, he made a whopping €72,000 renting out his home while he and his family took a seven-week vacation across

Europe and Southeast Asia. By renting his villa for just seven weeks of a year, he generates a gross yield of over 17%.

I own a condo with Chris in the beach golf resort community of Vale do Lobo near Vilamoura that we bought for €410,000 in October 2020. (I've since seen the same unit type listed for €830,000.) And we bought with 100% financing at extremely low rates.

The central region around the marina of Vilamoura is the Algarve's "Golden Triangle." It was the first part of the Algarve to develop, starting in the 1960s. Today, you'll find 5-star hotels, multi-million-dollar yachts, and luxury resorts.

Because it's the most established part of the Algarve, opportunities here are thinner on the ground, but with a little digging there's still a chance to find something truly special in this region.

In the eastern Algarve, traveling toward Spain, the region is less developed, more local and traditional, and hasn't been "resortified." And that's part of its appeal.

Founded by Phoenician traders, the town of Tavira once had mighty walls. The Moors ruled from the 8th to 13th centuries leaving their mark in art, architecture, and the town's name.

Orange trees stretch their branches in shady plazas. Whitewashed buildings with wrought-iron balconies fill narrow cobbled streets. Every lane invites you to meander, every café says sit and stay a while.

You stick your head into doorways and wander into cool courtyards to find echoes of North Africa and classical Rome…

Tavira was on its way to becoming a firm tourist favorite, with a Path of Progress rolling toward it. Then the Great Recession hit.

In 2007/2008, just as the real estate market peaked, developers were homing in on the underdeveloped beach towns east of Faro, particularly around Tavira, including Cabanas, just a 10-minute drive from Tavira. Then, crisis hit, and the area managed to stay under the radar and relatively undiscovered.

But still, on the eastern Algarve it's in Cabanas and Tavira where I see the prospect for biggest tourism growth and appreciation.

In the rest of the Algarve, they're used to packing families in for the summer season. Then, in the off season, they almost give the place away to break even. But this area appeals to a broad cross section of tourists (including families), with tourism coming from across Europe, with Scandinavians, French, Swiss, German, and others, along with the British and Irish.

Cabanas will get the shoulder season traffic…golfers, retirees, and other renters throughout the year. That means exceptional potential for rental income.

At the other end of the Algarve, the Path of Progress runs to the western Algarve where Lagos was really starting to tick when the global financial crisis hit in 2008/09.

Luckily, most of the land here is owned by just a handful of families, and they weren't highly leveraged when things took a turn. The crisis dampened development but left much fewer half built condos scarring the landscape than you find elsewhere.

Lagos is the most historic town on the Algarve. I love Lagos. It's my favorite beach town on the entire coast.

There are semi-secret sandy coves, long stretches of golden sand, cliffs, sea stacks and bluffs.

Stand in the shade of a flowering tree beside the 15th-century church of Santa Maria and you can see the entire sweep of the bay. You'll find buildings clad in magnificent azulejos—painted ceramic tiles. You can dine on grilled sardines, eat clams in garlic or try piri chicken, and wash it all down with a delicious local wine.

Because most of the early tourism growth hit towns closer to Faro, where the major resorts, hotels, and condo communities first developed, Lagos has grown differently. It has avoided the same unrestrained development. And instead remains low-rise and protected.

As such, it has a chronic shortage of hotel rooms and demand for best-in-class property is incredibly hot. Supply remains scarce, and there are constraints that put serious limitations on availability.

Lagos is a place where the historic old town spills down cobbled lanes, into shady plazas toward a state-of-the-art marina.

And it's eminently walkable.

You can walk to the beaches. Walk to the restaurants, bars, stores...walk to the train station and hop a train to Faro where the international airport is...

You can walk to the marina and jump on a boat to go sailing, fishing, or cruising around the cliffs, sea stacks, and bluffs of the Western Algarve's awesome coastline. The weather is perfect, with temperatures hovering around 80 F. Mornings and evenings are a little fresher, ideal for getting around.

Lagos has amazing restaurants, artsy boutiques, imposing old fortifications, and a Southern Californian vibe. In fact, I know of at least two Californians who say it's a better place to live than California...more affordable, certainly safer...with weather just as good.

Few cities in this part of Portugal can compare to Lagos for sheer variety of historical buildings and monuments, stretching back through more than 2,000 years of Carthaginian, Roman, and Moorish influence.

The old town's narrow, wave-patterned streets are partially enclosed by 16th century stone walls and easy to navigate on your own, though you never know what you'll find around the next corner. It could be a charming café, a quaint market, or a *pastelaria* selling mouth-watering cakes and pastries.

Lagos attracts tourists from all over the world. Lagos has exceptional access. It's just an hour from Faro airport with good road connections—there's that Path of Progress in action—where you can catch a two- to three-hour flight to almost anywhere in Europe. Faro has direct flights scheduled to 75 destinations in 16 countries.

It's one of the reasons I like this town so much. And not just to visit, but as a place to invest in real estate.

Despite its popularity with tourists, Lagos has a chronic shortage of hotel rooms, and unbending regulations mean development is restricted. This puts powerful demand on short-term rentals. And like Tulum, it's a place that's set to benefit enormously from the next wave of travelers emerging from the work-from-home trend. Owning the right kind of property here puts you in prime position for handsome rental income as Lagos gets even more popular.

I do predict that it will indeed get more popular.

The increasing number of longer-stay folks and vacationers alike have every amenity they need. Lagos isn't like the resorts in the central Algarve. It doesn't slow to a crawl when the tourists leave. It's a lively town with a thriving cultural scene...with schools, supermarkets, café, bars.

Lagos is the only place on the Algarve I recommended pre-construction.

For instance, in 2020 I recommended condos in a community called Adega. One *RETA* member bought a condo there for €480,000. Thanks to rapid appreciation she has since sold it for around €700,000. That's an incredible profit of approximately €220,000.

In 2019, I recommended condos in Santa Maria, another Lagos community where *RETA* members could get in with discount pricing. Thanks to a 10% discount, the *RETA* price started from just €310,500. Since then, two-beds that were selling there for €630,000 have been listing for as much as €850,000. Again, phenomenal uplift.

In December 2021, I brought *RETA* members a deal in Dona Ana, within a stroll of the stunning beaches and clifftops of Ponta da Piedade. Members could own luxury condos at a big discount of €53,000 and more.

The get-in price was €477,000…and I expect buyers could see up to €40,000 in annual income. That's a gross yield of over 8%. On top of that, members who got in are looking at potential gains of €133,000 just one year after delivery.

5. Panama

Panama was one of the first places I invested in overseas real estate. It's gratifying that all these years later it remains one of the spots on my beat where I continue to uncover opportunity.

Finding deals on luxury beachfront property is rare. But finding them close to a global city is next to unheard of. That was until a Path of Progress sweeping along the Pacific coast of Panama from its capital presented an opportunity.

First, a bit of background.

Over the past two decades, Panama has transformed from a sleepy regional outpost to a regional powerhouse.

It's earned the nickname "Baby Singapore," as both benefit significantly from their strategic location for shipping and trade. Singapore sits between China and India, while Panama lies between North and South America. Panama also has an extra bonus: its Canal connects the Pacific and Atlantic oceans.

Panama's strategic location for shipping and trade drives its growth. It lies between North and South America with the Panama Canal connecting the Pacific and Atlantic oceans. Ever since the Canal was handed back to Panama in 1999, the country has boomed.

The Panama Canal is one of the pillars of that growth. It's incredible to think that 5% of all global trade passes through the Canal in this tiny country. Other big revenue generators are tourism, free trade zones and banking, finance, insurance, and gold and copper mining. Big multinational companies such as Nestle, Dell, and Proctor & Gamble have come to set up regional bases. That in turn brings in high-level executives on fat salaries relocating for work.

Panama City has seen a surge of demand in recent years from a growing, upwardly mobile, population. Yet, the city has a shortage of developable land. On one side, it is hemmed in by the Pacific Ocean, and on the other it is constrained by large parcels of protected land and watershed for the Panama Canal.

There's very little room for urban sprawl. And this will put huge upward pressure on existing real estate prices.

A "Big Squeeze" is coming and that means there is a window to lock down the kind of real estate that the well-heeled Panamanians and the foreigners coming want.

The kind of place you could rent long term to young entrepreneurs, older retirees, and executives working for a big multinational in the business districts close by. And where you could see rapid appreciation as demand continues to rise against supply in Panama City.

Like Singapore, Panama has created a robust wealth fund and poured money into infrastructure. It evolved a foreigner- and business-friendly law and tax system. And has cemented itself as a key player in global trade, banking, shipping, and big business.

Today, Panama has the world's second-largest free trade zone. It's the biggest recipient of foreign direct investment in Central America. And, it's attracting more and more multinationals looking for a friendly regional base. It's also home to one of the largest copper mines in the world.

As a result, Panama is set to become the richest country in Latin America.

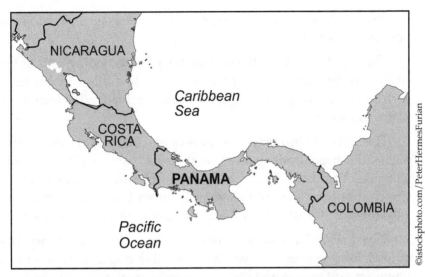

Panama is a crossroads of Latin America and a hub for international trade.

Each time I visit, the transformation becomes more and more visible. You'll see BMWs, Lexus, Porsches, Ferraris, and Lamborghinis on the streets of downtown Panama City. Luxury wings in air-conditioned malls feature Chanel, Louis Vuitton, and Hermes stores. Private planes and helicopters…upscale restaurants…

According to a 2017 Harvard study, over the span of five years the middle class went from 22% to 37% of the population and it's been growing ever since.

The World Bank says that over the past decade, Panama has been one of the fastest growing economies in the world.

On top of this domestic surge in wealth you have wealthy folks from all over the world who come to Panama because it's a safe and stable haven. It's got a fantastic location, smack in the middle between North and South America and close to the Caribbean. The economy's booming. And the country boasts a long history of welcoming foreign investors, real estate buyers, and entrepreneurs.

121

Panama has been displaying one of the fastest growth accelerations in the world.

The rapid growth of the middle class, the economy, and of the city is driving demand for real estate, yet like other global hubs such as Hong Kong and Singapore, developable land is incredibly scarce in Panama City.

This not only increases the value of real estate in the city, it also makes the beachfront real estate close to Panama City far more valuable. The most developed section of coast in Panama is the stretch that runs west of Panama City from Chame to Farallon. It was dubbed the "Riviera Pacifica" by Panama's tourism authority.

This Pacific Riviera is 50 miles or so. The smart money has poured in here over the last 15 years. New hotels, new resorts, a premium golf course and swish new residential communities have popped up. A slew of upper-middle-class housing back from the beach has brought schools, supermarkets, and services in its wake.

The high level of amenities and the proximity to Panama City (a metropolis with a population north of a million) attracts vacationers, snowbirds, and weekenders to this coast. It's long been popular as a beach escape for well-heeled city dwellers.

And it's now a place where folks want to live full time. The Path of Progress that's barreling through is making that easier to do than ever before.

A couple of years ago, I flew over this area in a helicopter to see this Path of Progress in action. From the air, a long orange-brown scar wound its way across the landscape. This is a work in progress, a $370 million project to widen the main highway from the city out to the Pacific coast. Parts of the highway will have eight lanes when it is done.

This road widening is dwarfed by the scale of other planned projects. A fourth bridge will be built across the Panama Canal, improving access from the city to the coast. And plans call for the city's metro system to run out to the western suburbs, close to this area. This will all be a game-changer for the Pacific Riviera.

But there is an anomaly in this Path of Progress. And investors can profit from it by buying the right type of real estate in the right location at the right price.

Playa Caracol is the nicest beach on this whole stretch of coast, but for years it was leapfrogged by the Path of Progress because it lacked road access...much of the land was zoned for agricultural use and owned by just a few families not interested in selling...and it was hard for developers to find a large parcel of land suitable for development.

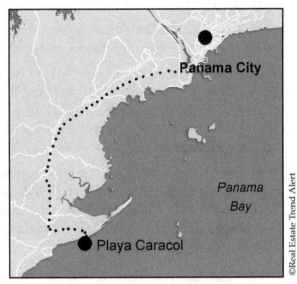

Head west of Panama City and you have some of the most beautiful beaches in the country... that well-heeled city dwellers flock to.

In fact, when I first visited, it was quite a journey to get there. From the turn off of the main highway, we bounced along the rough road and saw just a few discreet beach homes, bars, and eateries, and a handful of people.

We kept driving until the road ran out. The rough ride was well worth it. As we crested the dunes, we were greeted at the end by a pristine white-sand beach.

While beaches and communities farther from Panama City, like Coronado, boomed, Playa Caracol was a sleeping giant. As all-inclusive hotels and expensive high-rise blocks changed the face of beaches west of here, it remained under the radar.

That is, until an established real estate developer with a reputation for getting things done stepped in…a visionary developer I know well. This guy has built man-made islands just off the coast of Panama City…

His plan for the Pacific Riviera was simple: create a best-in-class beach community fronting Playa Caracol's white-sand beach.

When I revisited the region in 2015 on a scouting trip, I was blown away. The developer had got a paved road put in, all the way to the project, and was spending serious money on infrastructure. This was in addition to millions of dollars of government spending on those roads and bridges I mentioned.

I knew then that Playa Caracol was going to become the premier beach destination on this coast. High-amenity beach living on the doorstep of Panama City hits many markets: well-heeled and middle-class Panamanians, foreign executives, vacationers from abroad, expats, snowbirds.

Members of my *RETA* group are already sitting on gains of $100,000 or more in Playa Caracol. In January 2017, I brought members a *RETA*-only opportunity to buy two-bed, ocean-view condos at The Palms from $199,000. In August 2019, a similar-sized condo in Caracol farther back from the beach with only a sideview of the ocean listed for $299,000.

All this was a textbook application of the five R's…a huge transformation, the right location, the right developer and real estate… and the right price.

Now, in the next chapter I want to show you the most powerful thing to look for in real estate anywhere today…something to add to the five "R's"…

An unbreachable and impregnable moat!

CHAPTER 6

Seek Unbreachable Moats!

*"I look for economic castles surrounded by
unbreachable moats."* — Warren Buffett, investor

*"Housing supply is inelastic where location
matters."* — Thomas Davidoff, associate professor

The Croatian city of Dubrovnik has one of the great fortification systems of the Middle Ages.

It's protected by 17 towers, five bastions, three fortresses, walls that are 20 feet thick, and a moat that was once armed with more than 120 cannons.

It's one of the only fortified medieval cities in Europe that was never penetrated by a hostile army (though many have tried).

Even as recently as 1992, during the Croatian War of Independence, the city proved unbreachable...

It's perhaps the most successfully defended city in all of history. It exemplifies why the business analogy of the "moat" is such a potent one.

Made famous by investor Warren Buffett, a "moat" in the business sense is anything that can give you a sustained advantage over your competition.

This competitive advantage can take many forms. It can be a cost advantage, whereby you can undercut the prices of any competitor. It can be a size advantage, which gives you economies of scale. It can be a unique technology or a patent. Or your moat can be high switching costs within your industry (we all know the pain of switching between insurers and cell phone carriers).

Whatever it is, a moat is essential to a great long-term investment.

As Buffett said to shareholders at Berkshire Hathaway's annual meeting in 2000: "The moat and the ability to keep its width and its impossibility of being crossed is the primary criterion of a great business."

Coca Cola has a moat, its iconic brand that's recognized the world over, which has helped it dominate the soft drinks market.

Ikea has a moat in its economy of scale, its network effect, and because its DIY business model keeps prices lower than readymade furniture sellers.

When it comes to real estate, the more moats you have, the stronger your competitive edge and your ability to create profit.

Of course, your moats need to be protecting something desirable, useful, and valuable. Buy best in class real estate in inherently desirable places, with strong demand, in communities delivered by the best developers. And with our moats, we can turn it into stellar gains.

Let's have a look at some of the key competitive advantages a real estate investor can have:

Competitive Advantage #1: Geographical Moat

If you look at the most expensive real estate in the world, it all has two things in common. It's in short supply and it's in high demand.

Take the New York real estate market. In June 2022, the median listing home price in Manhattan, was $1.4 million. The reason it's so high is not because the quality of homes are better there than anywhere else, it's because there is such huge demand to own in one of the world's biggest economic hubs.

Crucially, because Manhattan has limited space (it's on an island, so it literally has a moat around it), building here has become extremely expensive and prohibitive, sending prices of existing real estate skyrocketing.

Another example is the Old Town of Dubrovnik. Like I say, the compact city is hemmed in by old medieval walls. There is no space to build and even if there was it would be impossible thanks to the city's UNESCO World Heritage site status. At the same time, tourism to the city has been booming for two decades, hitting almost 1.5 million visitors in 2019. That's a lot for a city of just 42,000 people. Limited supply collided with high demand and real estate prices exploded.

Limited supply and high demand are crucial. And if you own real estate in a location with these two things you can make a killing—especially if demand is still growing.

Ideally, you want to find an opportunity where the supply is naturally restricted by lack of space to build. This is what I call a "geographical moat." It's an essential element in many of the *RETA* deals I bring to the table.

For instance, a major geographical moat underlies many of our deals in Tulum on the Riviera Maya. Take one *RETA* deal in a community called Samsara. In October 2021, I brought *RETA* members the chance to own luxury two-bedroom condos with an unbeatable *RETA*-only price starting from $198,600.

The land where Samsara will be is set apart, unique…special. A quiet and exclusive enclave off the main drag, yet close enough to get to the white-sand beach and town with all its cool little shops and restaurants in about 10 minutes.

The famed Mayan ruins that put Tulum on the map and that host two million visitors each year are just to the north along the coast. And in front of Samsara, just across the road, is the national park that acts as a buffer zone around them and as a nature preserve…all the way to the beach.

Nobody can build in this protected zone. It is a geographic moat around our opportunity that should keep this enclave, which will be down an essentially private road hemmed in by jungle, high-end and desirable, as Tulum develops further.

There is another moat working in our favor as well…

To the south of town is the Sian Ka'an Biosphere—over a thousand square miles of UNESCO-protected wetlands, jungle, and wild coast. To the north are those stunning beachfront archaeological ruins.

Given all those barriers, finding something as secluded and private as Samsara is very rare. You'll find plenty of projects in bad or average locations in Tulum, but there is a very limited supply of the right type of developable land in Tulum for top-notch communities like Samsara.

In July 2022, condos in Samsara went retail. A mezzanine unit that *RETA* members could buy for $212,300 was listed at $298,200—that's an $85,900 uplift in less than a year.

Like I say, limited supply in itself is not enough to drive values up. There needs to be high demand too…and in Tulum demand is booming.

In fact, there are numerous big trends swirling around right now that are making it the fastest-growing town in this region and one of the most desirable destinations in Mexico.

Once a favored haven of the jet-set and bohemian backpackers, Tulum has "grown up."

It now attracts increasing numbers of so-called mainstream vacationers from around the world. They've seen the trendy influencers frolicking on the white-sand beaches and at the hip restaurants… and they want to do the same.

On top of that is another growing market: the work-from-home set that are part of what my team and I have taken to calling the "Zoom Boom." The pandemic forced them into remote working, they took a liking, and now don't want to go back to the office. So why not make "home" a tropical paradise? I will talk more about this in the next chapter.

Tulum is hot right now, simply put. I'd say hotter than ever. A recent survey from travel booking site Expedia named Tulum—and the wider Riviera Maya—one of the most searched destinations by travelers for 2022.

Trouble is, all these new tourists coming for a week vacation, not to mention those Zoom Boomers looking for places to stay for months at a time…even a year, struggle to find accommodations.

That's what makes our Samsara opportunity so appealing. There are no other condos like ours available. It has incredible amenities and even beach club access with a private shuttle bus. With that moat around it too, I expect a community like this to be a rare commodity for years to come.

In fact, it is already helping to drive prices up. I've recently seen an advert for a two-bed condo in Samsara listed at $298,200. We could own similar condos at our exclusive off-market price of just $212,300. That's a boost of $85,900 in just nine months.

Another recent *RETA* deal in the Village at Corasol in Playa del Carmen, just 50 minutes' drive from Tulum, is another great example of a geographical moat.

RETA members locked down two-bed luxury condos starting from $258,600 that I'm confident could be worth $141,400 more just three years after delivery, and bring in $36,500 in annual rental income once the community is established.

Simply put, there's only one Corasol. It is unique in the Riviera Maya. In fact, it's unique in the Caribbean in terms of location, convenience, amenities, and service.

Corasol is the essence of a "moat" in action. This near 500-acre master-planned community can never have true competition. I can give you a bunch of reasons, but the main one is that there simply isn't any land to create anything like Corasol ever again…

In the case of Corasol, this moat limits supply. So as demand increases, the market can't react to create new supply. It's not possible…the market can only react with higher prices.

And demand is driven by unstoppable trends—we're talking millions of vacationers and a huge surge of work-anywhere folks all coming to Playa del Carmen and the Riviera Maya.

Corasol will remain a desirable oasis within Playa del Carmen even as the city grows. And this is a city that's grown from a tiny fishing village in just a few decades with no slow-down of development in sight.

When you own a condo in the Village at Corasol, you're in the heart of a lush, 5-star master-planned community right next to a vibrant world-class beach city. You wake up to tranquillity, an 18-hole golf course, and awesome amenities. You have easy access to a "secret beach."

There's simply nowhere else to build something as special as our opportunity on the beach and this close to the heart of Playa del Carmen's main tourist district, called 5th Avenue.

Playa will continue to grow and boom but Corasol will remain a best-in-class haven. All the green areas around the condos in the Village will still be protected, the views will be uninterrupted, the beach access the same.

In a master-planned community like this, no one can build a low-standard project next door. High standards are maintained. All of which helps enhance real estate values. In this case, the developer plans to build new communities in Corasol themselves, so that they fit their overall vision.

As you can see from this satellite image, there's simply nowhere else to build something as special as our opportunity this close to the heart of Playa del Carmen's main tourist district, called 5th Avenue. It's the kind of geographical moat that I love...

That vision, from the landscaping to the architecture and amenities, is thoroughly thought out. Right down to the material used in the pool chairs. It's all part of a concerted effort to create a pampered, luxury resort experience, the moment you pass through the gates.

As Playa grows, our condos in the Village at Corasol will get even closer to downtown Playa del Carmen. The city gets bigger, the hotels, resorts and residential areas built farther out, but Corasol isn't moving. It will always be close to the artery of the action, 5th Avenue. Forever close to the beach, which will make it one of the most desirable places to live in the city.

Competitive Advantage #2:
Insider Knowledge and Industry Contacts

Moats don't always need to be physical attributes...

To go back to the example of Dubrovnik. What's often overlooked is how well the city-state—known at the time as the Republic of Ragusa—used diplomacy to defend itself. In fact, it was so good at placating its enemies that most of the time its great walls were not necessary. They negotiated treaties, paid tributes, and expanded their influence beyond the Adriatic.

Indeed, its diplomats were so well renowned throughout Europe that even Machiavelli himself applied to work there!

My point is, the connections you make and the influence you can wield is just as important as knowing where to buy. It gives you the inside track on what's really going on and opens up opportunities that aren't available to most real estate buyers.

That's why I spend six months of the year on the road scouting and creating contacts. Along with my team, we spend close to a million dollars on travel and research each year.

And it's worth it. Each new industry contact we make has the potential to deliver incredible profits to *RETA* members through the deals they can bring. This dedication to building a network of insiders is something few other real estate investors do—and none that I know of can compete with the scale we have at *RETA*.

This gives us a remarkable competitive advantage when it comes to finding the best deals and working with the best people.

For instance, in Costa Rica's Southern Zone, we get access to members-only deals because we deal with Sylvaine Pilault, the pre-eminent developer in the region. She arrived in the Southern Zone in the 1980s and has since created the best-in-class community in the Southern Zone.

Her long track record in the Southern Zone is a moat that keeps her competitors at bay. She bought land at agricultural prices, before the new roads and highways opened the area up. And, she's made the connections, accrued decades of experience, and figured out the best way to get the permits and approvals needed to develop.

A newbie developer trying to break into the market today simply can't beat Sylvaine. On pricing alone, they're paying current land prices which are multiple times what Sylvaine paid.

On permitting and paperwork she's way ahead of her competition, too. She's established a top-notch residential community in the region, setting a very high bar for anyone else trying to do the same thing.

And that's what we plug into by dealing with her. It gives us an edge. She's given us first shot at deals and pricing that no one else saw. Most importantly, we know what we're getting is best-in-class, and by dealing with Sylvaine, we've been handed another moat.

With our deal at the Village in Corasol in Playa del Carmen, we applied the same advantage…

We're working with the best in the business. We are plugged in with the insiders, the big landowners, the savvy developers who had the land in the family for generations or got land at low prices.

Land is key to *RETA* opportunities on the Riviera Maya. The price of land has been pushed way up by the juggernaut Path of Progress that has rolled down the coast from Cancun straight into Playa, turning it from a simple seaside hamlet to a bustling resort city in a matter of a few decades.

And Corasol is a special piece of land, in that it is nearly 500 acres right on the Caribbean coast, and close to the heart of a bustling city.

The Spanish group behind the original project at Corasol got into financial trouble. A Spanish bank stepped in and took possession. As bureaucracy and disinterest took over, the community was left to languish. Nothing happened for a long time.

In truth, the crisis preserved this land…prevented it from becoming a standard, run-of-the-mill community, like the way the eruption of the volcano that coated Pompeii in ash preserved the city's ancient structures and artifacts…

Then the bank sold to a powerful Mexican group. They're the ones who have gotten things back on track.

The developer and his group got a great deal on the land by buying at a time when, due to a legacy of the financial crisis, the Spanish bank were obliged to sell.

That's why the developer can afford to pass on such a low price to us in the kind of premium and special community that will be in high demand.

The developer is a heavy hitter in the business world in Mexico… one of the wealthiest families in the country. They even own the bank offering the financing for our Village opportunity.

In Corasol, they brought in the best architects and designers, with experience in crafting both residential and hospitality projects, to create their communities.

The developer of The Village, who is also the master-developer of Corasol, is not going to let just anyone build within the gates. They're committed to low-density development with a cohesive look that maintains as much green space as possible. And no one is going to be building on the immaculate fairways of the 18-hole Nick Price course that surrounds our opportunity.

All this makes Corasol special, a place destined to be a high-end sanctuary for many years to come. The developer knows this.

They have no interest in creating some run-of-the-mill community. Their plans call for positioning Corasol as a $500,000+ community. Already, they are building condos at that level, with many hitting $1 million and beyond. Luxury villas are double that and more. But the *RETA* get-in price for a two-bedroom, two-bathroom luxury condo with expansive terrace of 163 square feet was from just $258,600.

Which brings me to one of our most important moats…

Competitive Advantage #3:
Group Buying Power

This particular moat is particularly for you if you're a *RETA* member, which I assume you are if you are reading this.

If you've ever shopped at Sam's Club, you know that buying in bulk means big savings. In much the same way, *RETA* members can save big on real estate.

This is possible because the combined power of *RETA* members has the ability to buy real estate in bulk.

It's a win-win for us and the developer we work with. The developer sells a large chunk of their inventory right off the back and in return they hand us big juicy discounts...ensuring we pay way less than anyone else. I call this the "*RETA* edge."

This is an incredibly rare moat to have. It's the kind of competitive advantage that's usually reserved for billion-dollar investment firms. But at *RETA*, we use it just as effectively.

I'll go into detail as to why developers are willing to do these deals with us in chapter 12. For now, there's no shortage of examples:

- Our Cabo deal from August 2021, Cabo Costa, is the perfect example. In August 2021, *RETA* members could buy two-bed, two-bath condos with members-only prices starting from $188,200. Nine months later, the developer sold a condo for $130,000 more than *RETA* members paid. And in April 2022, another of these condos was re-listed at $330,000.

- In Playa del Carmen, we had the opportunity to get in on a limited number of handpicked condos in Singular Dream in June 2021 at incredible off-market pricing: from $265,304 for fully furnished two-bedroom lock-off condos (with a furniture pack valued at $23,000), and from $174,600 for the one-beds, also completely turnkey (furnishings valued at $15,000).

In July 2022, the developer list price for a one-bed condo was $331,073, and that was with a developer discount…without that discount, the price was $348,498. Based on the discounted price, that's an uplift of $132,473.

- In another Playa del Carmen deal, in Siempre Playa, two-bed condos we could get at off-market *RETA* pricing of $198,600 were listing at $371,676 retail in July 2022. That's a $143,342 jump in five years.

And that's just a small selection of recent deals…

In each case, we got in way below what anyone else is paying. And by doing so, it sets us up for exceptional gains down the line.

A Four-Step Approach to Finding Profitable Real Estate Overseas: The D.E.A.L. System

I've been learning about real estate investing as far back as I can remember. My parents owned a couple of investment properties, and my dad would sit me on his lap and explain the business to me. It's all I've ever wanted to do (along with playing golf).

Now I do it on an almost instinctual level. The same way a boxer throws a combination. Unthinking. I've rarely sat and broke down the exact steps I take. But I've sometimes sat down and thought hard about the patterns, breaking it down into the fundamentals I repeatedly look for.

Let's call it the D.E.A.L. System.

D.E.A.L. is a handy acronym for the four major steps of analysis that go into each opportunity I recommend in *RETA*. They are:

- **D**iscount
- **E**arning Potential

- Appreciation
- Leverage

Discount: Pay less, profit more...

Poor ol' Ebenezer Scrooge. His last name has become a synonym of miser. But ask any successful investor, and they'll tell you there's nothing wrong with being tight-fisted. In fact, it's the secret to success of legendary investor Warren Buffett.

Buffett is a proponent of something called "value investing." In short, that means buying companies that sell for less than what they are worth. "Whether we're talking about socks or stocks, I like buying quality merchandise when it's marked down," says Buffett.

Imagine, a man worth $87 billion buying marked down socks! Yet, this Scrooge-mindset is why Buffett is so rich. He holds onto his money tightly, waiting patiently for massive discounts in the market. Then he strikes...

I apply the exact same value investing philosophy to real estate.

Take one recommendation I made in 2014: As the European debt crisis slashed prices throughout the continent of Europe in the wake of the financial crisis, I recommended buying heavily discounted real estate in Spain and Portugal. That crisis created phenomenal real estate bargains. One *RETA* member, for example, paid €99,000 in mid-2014 for a condo I wrote about on Spain's Costa del Sol. When I spoke to him only four years later, his condo was worth €210,000.

And there are many reasons other than a financial crisis why real estate might be selling at a discount. Maybe the seller is just desperate to make a quick sale, or an inexperienced developer has mispriced his condos. When I'm on scouting trips, I'm looking for anomalies like these and others, which can cause real estate to be undervalued.

And sometimes, you can buy at a big discount simply because you're a *RETA* member. Let me explain…

The *RETA* Edge

If you've ever shopped at Sam's Club, you know that buying in bulk means big savings. In much the same way, *RETA* members can save big on real estate.

This is possible because the combined power of *RETA* members has the ability to buy real estate in bulk.

It's by acting in unison with like-minded investors that we get the incredible deals that we do.

Alone, I can't bring much to the table when I negotiate with developers besides my charm. With *RETA* members at my back though, I can bow developers to our will, craft insanely good terms and prices, and leave everyone a winner. And after 14 years in existence our *RETA* group now has a heavy-hitting reputation in the right circles.

Our group buying power is highly respected and sought after. It's how we get deals no one else gets, deals that even the most informed local real estate insiders can't believe. I'll explain why exactly developers give us the deals we get in chapter 12.

Earning potential: Get paid to own real estate…

When I was young, my parents owned a modest real estate portfolio in my hometown of Cork, Ireland. One of my clearest memories from then, is my father explaining rental income to me for the first time: "Essentially son, our tenants' rent pays the mortgage. So when all is said and done, it's like we're getting a free house!"

The idea blew my young mind and set me on course to become the real estate investor I am today. After earning my BSc in Finance, I almost immediately began building my own real estate mini-empire.

By buying discounted real estate in prime locations, and targeting wealthy young professionals, I was able to supersize my rental yields. So not only was I making enough to cover my mortgage and other costs (i.e. getting a free house), I was pocketing extra cash, too.

But it wasn't until I started investing overseas, I realized how much more income I could be making...

While you can do well in some places in the U.S., as a *RETA* member, you're no longer a prisoner to paltry returns in your domestic market. By investing in real estate overseas, you have the chance to make double, even triple what you might make at home.

If you've bought real estate in the U.S. or own dividend-paying stocks, you know how rare it is to find a double-digit yield. But when you're open to following the big transformations wherever they might be, you increase your chances of finding fat yields, because the world is literally your oyster.

Appreciation: The big payday

The other way to make money from real estate is to simply wait for the value of your holdings to appreciate. Sometimes, this might mean waiting decades. I've met plenty of real estate investors with a 30-year time horizon.

Other times, this might mean waiting months. Typically, like in the run-up to the 2008 financial crisis, if you're able to resell for a nice profit within months, you can bet there's something terribly wrong with the market.

I usually target a happy medium holding period of five years. By real estate standards, that's still short—unbelievable to some people—yet it's realistic when you buy real estate overseas.

Leverage: Get rich with other people's money

I've said it before, and I will say it again and again...one of the biggest benefits of investing in real estate is the opportunity to do so using other people's money through financing. This lets you keep your powder dry for other opportunities, and it also lets you harness the wealth-multiplying power of leverage.

Let me show you what I mean...

Imagine a pre-construction condo priced at $200,000.

You buy the condo with $40,000 down. So, you are into the condo for $40,000. If that condo rises in value by $40,000 in the first six months, as is often the case with our best *RETA* deals, you have doubled your money. On paper at least...

This is where the terms you buy at matter.

Or, think of this another way. You buy a home in Portugal for $250,000. You put up $50,000 of your own money and borrow the rest from a local bank at 2%. Then you rent your home. For simplicity, let's assume your rent only covers the interest. In five years' time, if you sell for $400,000, your gain is $150,000, or 300% of what you invested.

As you know, I've personally used this leveraging strategy in Portugal, and I know other *RETA* members who have, too.

But you can't always find bank financing as a foreigner, so finding real estate where developer financing is an option is another top priority for me...

In other words, I'm looking for opportunities that let *RETA* members put a little money down, for the huge potential upside.

While many developers don't want the risk of financing foreign buyers, after over 12 years at the helm of *RETA* I've also connected with enterprising developers willing to offer financing exclusively for *RETA* members...

What you've just seen is just a quick overview of The D.E.A.L. System that's hopefully given you some insight into how we find opportunities to recommend in *Real Estate Trend Alert*. While I always look for a Discount, Earning Potential, Appreciation and Leverage, getting all four is the Holy Grail of real estate investing and not always realistic. Sometimes, appreciation might seem weak, but potential rental income is huge...

The D.E.A.L. System is just the start of my filtering process. As you know, I have a team of nine researchers and analysts, including two chartered accountants, dedicated to bringing you everything you'll see over the course of your *RETA* membership.

CHAPTER 7

The Most Powerful Trend is Demand

*"There are decades when nothing happens, and there are
weeks when decades happen." —* Vladimir Ilyich Lenin

"One day offices will be a thing of the past."
— Sir Richard Branson

Spring 2022 and I'm standing on a dusty hill in southern Spain.
In front of me, the land rolls toward the glittering Mediterranean.
Beside me, a slick-suited developer is eagerly explaining his group's
vision for their new high-end community…

"The villas will all include an office—one with a view. People
don't want to come somewhere beautiful like this and work in their
basement," he says. "They want to see the ocean. Then, in our condo
phase, we will have a co-working space. It's simple, after COVID,
people realize that their second home can be their first home," he
tells me.

Whether or not he realized it, that developer was repeating what
others just like him were saying in many of the world's most desirable destinations. He was pivoting his business to tap into one of
the most powerful trends in real estate globally—a transformation
in how and where millions of people live and work—the biggest
societal shift since World War II.

In the 18th century, wealthy city dwellers lived right in the centers. They needed to be a walk or a horse-ride from their place of

work. In the 19th and 20th centuries, millions of people moved to new suburbs because trains, trams, cars, and new roads meant they could live farther away, own bigger houses with yards or gardens, and commute to the office or factory.

Now, thanks to the internet, millions of people can live wherever they want. This was happening before COVID. For a long time, digital software and online communications have made it possible to work without an office. I should know. My team and I have always worked remotely. Our "office" is entirely virtual. Most of our business is conducted on platforms like Slack, Zoom, and WhatsApp, and my team are based all over the world.

But the pandemic was the great accelerator of all this. Even as the lockdowns began in April 2020, I knew the most powerful impact for real estate investors was going to be acceleration of the work-anywhere trend. Overnight, millions of people stopped going to work.

I predicted that remote viewings of properties would go mainstream…city center office space would become less vital, and—as soon as lockdowns ended—remote workers would pour into desirable overseas destinations in even greater numbers than before, creating huge opportunities for real estate investors like us.

It's a trend that's been called by different names. During the pandemic it was "the Zoom Boom" as millions of people downloaded Zoom to stay in touch and work remotely. Plastic surgeons coined that term when they saw a boom in business as people not only spent more time on Zoom looking at themselves during the pandemic, but had the time and privacy to recover from procedures.

People have different priorities post-COVID too. A lifestyle upgrade is now not just some far-off retirement dream. It's doable now. Just by moving to a tropical beach or a historic southern European town. The rise of remote working means the glue that held workers in close proximity to their work has come unstuck.

The significance of this shift can't be understated. Historic social changes can sometimes be hard to step back from and understand when you're living through them, but make no mistake, this is a transformation akin to the great urban migration during the industrial age.

Why pay $3,000 or even more for a cramped studio apartment in San Francisco or New York, when you can live in a spacious condo and spend your evenings sipping on piña coladas next to a stunning white-sand beach…

Why suffer through a mid-western winter when you can be in short sleeves poolside in Cabo?

Why deal with congestion and high costs in California when the oranges are just as a sweet in Lagos, Portugal?

People are waking up to the possibilities. They can improve their lives, have amazing experiences, lower their costs, improve their weather…

And as I write, this is impacting destinations right across my global beat. I'm seeing it in the *Los Angeles Times* headline announcing that Americans are flooding Mexico City…in a *Lonely Planet* article about remote workers converging on Tulum…even in news reports of thousands of foreigners flocking from all corners of the world to live and work in Georgia—not the state but the small country on the far side of Turkey.

More than anywhere else, the towns these remote workers flock to are what I call "internationalized" places. They have an established tourism infrastructure and familiarity for overseas visitors. They're cosmopolitan. They're easy to navigate…with good access to international airports and a community of expats to plug in to.

In other words, these are inherently desirable places. And also places where large-scale Paths of Progress have made access easy… and access is a key ingredient of an internationalized place.

Remember for example, Mexico's Riviera Maya is a few hours flight time from the U.S. and Canada with hundreds of direct flights. The four-lane highway down its 80-mile length makes it easy to get around. And the weather, beaches, natural beauty, and variety of dining, nightlife and conveniences, are big draws.

So, we have these places where big transformations are underway in terms of connectivity and infrastructure and now you have this incredible increase in the number of people free to go to those places and stay months or years.

For us, this is huge.

The pandemic was just a pause in the growth of these internationalized places. Right after lockdowns were lifted and travel came back, passenger numbers were breaking records. Revenge travel was part of this, and speaks to the huge potential for short-term rental profits.

Now though, this global transformation of work is generating phenomenal gross rental yields on long-term rentals, too. I'm talking as much as 8%, 12%…even 16%…

For instance, shortly after travel returned, my real estate contacts on the ground in the Riviera Maya were reporting such soaring demand for long-term rentals that they couldn't even secure rentals for their friends. One of my scouts, who used to live in the funky surfing town of Tamarindo, Costa Rica, tells me a condo he used to rent near the beach five years ago has gone from $1,200 a month to $3,000 a month.

One of my team interested in a move to Portugal's Algarve told me he simply couldn't find a long-term rental. "I'll try again in the winter. There's just nothing available. I think I'm going to have to network with boots on the ground," he told me.

I had real trouble myself finding a rental ahead of a 2022 trip to the Algarve. In Lagos, in the western Algarve, I found nothing that met my search criteria, even for the last week in October. This is a place that used to have a red-hot, summer season and a more modest shoulder season. Today, demand is almost as high in the shoulder months, which are getting longer and longer. My contact on the Algarve has received offers of €8,000 a month for a villa. When I finally landed a booking for the last week in October, it cost me over €1,600 and it's not even in the neighbourhood I was looking for.

I see similar demand in Cabo, where I spend a lot of time in my condo. The first summer I rented out my place there it made me $1,800 a month. Not bad, even if renting to a friend of a friend meant that it was below market rate. But since the pandemic, things have gone crazy. First, rental prices hit $2,500 a month. That seemed huge...until it went to $2,750 a month. Now, you'd do well to find a rental like this for $3,200 or even $3,500 a month.

When I bought my Cabo condo alongside members of my *Real Estate Trend Alert* group in 2015, our *RETA*-only get-in price was $336,156. That puts our potential long-term rental gross yield at a remarkable 12%.

This is more than pent-up demand from vacationers. Though there is that, too. For instance, the Riviera Maya had a record-breaking July 2022, recording 400,000 visitors a day—the highest the region has ever seen. Cabo is also bracing itself for a record-breaking year, now welcoming 520 flights per week.

High short-term rental demand from vacationers is indeed squeezing supply and driving up prices in these hugely popular towns. But the kind of long-term demand I'm seeing is unprecedented. These remote working folks come for weeks or months on end. They bring their jobs. They bring their family and their pets...

Crucially, they bring their price expectations. They aren't looking for cheap, they're looking for more. More amenities...more space...more sunshine... And they're willing to pay for it.

They don't expect to find a standout rental for $800 a month. But they will pay $2,500 or more to get one with a sea view and a large terrace that's close to a beach. In comparison to what they'll find at home, they're still getting incredible value.

From a real estate investor's perspective, the rise of long-term renting is huge…especially in destinations that are traditionally seasonal, where short-term rentals dominate.

In a hot long-term rental market, you can dictate the term of lease and keep vacant periods between tenancies down to a few days—assuming you have the type of property in the type of location that attracts good tenants.

And then there are the low holding costs you'll find overseas. For instance, for my beachfront condo on Portugal's Silver Coast, my total monthly payments (including mortgage, taxes, HOA fees, and golf club dues on two great courses) comes in at just under €1,110.

That's less that what property tax alone could come to in California.

My HOAs are exceptionally high by the standards of Portugal's Silver Coast. It reflects expenses like one elevator per seven units.

In Portugal, your property tax ranges from 0.3% to 0.5% (or 0.8% in rural areas). Figure on about €900 a year for a €300,000 property.

Then you have a mix of other costs, like maintenance and insurance.

The point is, to really capture the long-term renting opportunity, you need to be buying at the right price and in the right place. Buy well and your rental can capture stellar gross yields of 8%, 12%… even 16%…

Those are phenomenal returns for long-term rentals. Heck, in most places those would be impressive figures for short-term rentals. But in the internationalized places where I've been following big transformations, these numbers are now commonplace…especially when you can apply the edge that we have at *Real Estate Trend Alert*—which is my network of real estate contacts and our immense group buying power.

Call it real estate 2.0… Call it what you like. We're at the early stages of a trend that's set to take global real estate in key destinations to a new level.

Big Yields From Long-Term Renting

At *RETA* we extend our yields by using our group buying power to get in well below retail pricing.

- In 2015, I bought alongside *RETA* members in Copala, which is within the 5-star Quivira resort in Cabo. The *RETA*-only get-in price was $336,156. Today, these condos rent for as much as $3,500 per month. That's a gross yield of 12%.

Plus, we've seen prices rise. As I write there is very little on the market in Quivira. The last property I saw listed in Copala had a price tag of $579,000. And I recently got emailed by an agent saying they could get me $600,000.

Also in Copala, *RETA* members paid from $374,786 for luxury homes back in 2015. Homes that now rent for around $5,000 per month. That's a gross yield of 16%.

And the same home type now lists for $810,000 plus. That's incredible capital appreciation on top.

- In August 2020, *RETA* members had the chance to get in on condos from €164,000 in one of the most sought-after locations on Spain's Costa del Sol. My contact, Geoffrey Donoghue, runs a rental management business and he tells me that these condos would now

---

rent for €1,700 ($1,730 per month). That's a gross yield of over 12%.

Plus, we've seen capital appreciation. A condo similar to what we could get here for €184,000 is now listed for sale at €325,000—€156,000 more than we paid.

- In October 2017 on Mexico's Riviera Maya, *RETA* members got in on two-bedroom condos in Tao Tulum, within Tulum's trendy Aldea Zama master-planned community. Our exclusive pricing was from just $154,500. Recently, I've seen a two-bedroom condo in Tao Tulum listing for $2,500 a month. At our *RETA*-only pricing, that's a whopping gross yield of over 19%. I'd consider this an outlier, as such a yield is incredibly rare for a long-term rental...but still possible.

And then there is the capital appreciation... *RETA* members have seen uplifts of as much as $102,560 in Tao Tulum, with condos that *RETA* members secured for $208,440 now listed at $311,000.

Condos RETA members could own from just $154,500 in Tao Tulum are now listed for rent at $2,500 a month.

- In May 2017, I brought *RETA* members the chance to lock down two-bed condos in a community called Siempre Playa, in Playa del Carmen, for $193,800. The first owners moved into their condos in Siempre in 2021 and many have started renting them out, too. I know of a number of two-bed condos offered at $2,600 per month. With a *RETA* get in price, that can generate a gross yield of 16%.

On top of that, capital appreciation has been phenomenal. The condos *RETA* members were able to lock down for $193,800 were listing in mid-2022 at retail for $371,676. That's a boost of $173,076.

- In December 2019, we had the opportunity to buy in a community called Santa Maria in Lagos, on Portugal's Algarve from €310,500, thanks to a 10% discount. My contact, who runs a rental business in Lagos tells me a stylish property, like the kind that have been delivered at Santa Maria, can generate €2,500 a month or more. That's a 10% gross yield.

Again, we've also seen strong uplift in Santa Maria, too. Two-beds that were selling there for €630,000 are now going for as much as €850,000.

This is just a small selection of the *RETA* deals set to benefit from the surging demand for long-term rentals.

The remote working trend is more than just a trend. There are powerful historical factors at play…

Some 50 million Americans left their offices when COVID became a national emergency. It would have looked like a national walkout if it hadn't been mandated by their companies. And it didn't take long for progressive businesses to recognise the benefits.

Twitter, was one of the first to proclaim employees could work from home indefinitely. Google, Microsoft, and Facebook followed with work-from-home policies of their own. And it wasn't just tech companies. Even Ford Motors, the icon of American's great industrial age, introduced permanent work-from-home for employees who weren't needed on the factory floor.

The result is that two years later, as social distancing restrictions are removed and the world dusts itself off and goes back to normal, huge swathes of society have quietly transformed their lives.

The paradigm change began in the early 1980s with the invention of the internet. Existing computer networks were linked, opening up a whole new world of connectivity, and with it, alternative ways of working. Since then, technology and software has been improving rapidly, making offices all but obsolete.

It's a massive transformation in line with that of the canals, steamboats, and railroads in the history of the U.S. In the same vein as the automobile and the roads that were built to drive on…

It was the pandemic lockdowns in 2020 that sparked the moment of combustion…when the full degree of how far the tech has come got brought into light. For the first time ever, we discovered that entire industries and large swaths of the economy could be operated remotely, from anywhere…and that those giant office buildings that dominate city skylines all over the world might have outlived their purpose.

Indeed, since their inception, offices have always been profoundly flawed spaces. Created to ensure efficiency, they've institutionalised bureaucracy and idleness. They were a clumsy way to adapt the factory model to non-mechanical work. And as paper has disappeared from operations over the last few decades, the office has struggled to remain relevant.

Well before the pandemic, the reign of the office was looking shaky. The digital revolution combined with rising rents and the increased demands for flexible working often made the physical office more of a liability to a business than an asset.

Manhattan, for example, has the most expensive office space in the country at $91 per square foot per year. Yet, today in New York City, office occupancy is as low as 36%, according to data from security firm Kastle Systems. That's a lot of overhead costs for something that no longer serves an essential purpose—at least not to the capacity we've seen in the past.

And businesses are already cutting back. Salesforce recently cut its San Francisco office space for the third time, listing 40% of its 43-story tower for lease. It followed a slew of major tech firms that have downsized or shuttered San Francisco offices, including Coinbase, Pinterest, Block, Taskrabbit, and PayPal.

The reality is, companies now need to offer remote work to attract talent. LinkedIn said in February that remote jobs received 50% of all applications during the month, despite representing less than 20% of all jobs posted.

The office, as we know it, is in its death throes. There will still be pushback of course. There is a big incentive for politicians, landlords, corporate executives, and business owners to get workers to return to downtown offices. To boost footfall, tenancy, tax revenue, etc. However, the winds of change have already blown through... impossible to reverse.

What this means is far bigger than empty buildings. The death of the office has broken the millennia-old relationship between employment and home. Since humans began cultivating farmland, where you live has been intrinsically tied to your employment. Towns and cities have risen and fallen based on the employment opportunities they have brought.

The Californian gold rush transformed San Francisco from a sleepy village called Yerba Buena into the State's major seaport. During American's great industrial age, companies built entire towns to house their employees, creating mining communities in Colorado and lumber towns in California. Even the success of the medieval Venetian city-state rested, quite literally, on the salt they could extract from the lagoon that surrounded the city.

"Work from home" means the glue that held workers in close proximity to their work has now come undone. And it will change how we work and how we live forever.

The last great transformation of this scale in U.S. history followed World War II.

In the years following the war, America's great industrial machine turned its effort to home building, using techniques of mass production that made it possible to build homes faster and cheaper than ever before. Combined with the rapid adoption of the mass-produced automobile and a huge extension of intercity expressway networks, explosive suburbanization followed.

Cheap agricultural land surrounding cities became valuable development ground for suburban growth. For developers who saw the potential of this new way of living, the growth was practically endless.

And with the signing of the G.I. Bill of Rights by President Franklin Roosevelt just two weeks after D-Day—which provided veterans help buying a home, setting up their own business, going to college, or getting a government job—for the first time in history, home ownership become something that was within reach for everyone.

It was the birth of the American dream...the promise that every man could have his castle...

The rise of remote working takes this one step further. It's a global phenomenon. It offers everyone the opportunity to have their castle wherever they want. And many will take it to paradise…and to the places where our *RETA* buying power has the most leverage.

This is why I see our long-term rental opportunity delivering for years to come.

CHAPTER 8

Income While You Sleep

"If you don't find a way to make money while you sleep, you will work until you die." — Warren Buffett, investor

"Landlords grow rich in their sleep."
— John Stuart Mill, philosopher

Money seeping into your bank account. Regularly. Like clockwork. You hop from your comfortable bed after a restful night to find thousands of dollars have magically appeared.

Rental income! It's among the most wonderful things in the world.

I still get a rush every time I see rental income hit my bank account. It's as if by some miracle. Take my Silver Coast condo in Portugal. Thanks to the income I make from summer rentals, I literally own a beachfront condo in Portugal for nothing! I got bank financing to buy the condo. The rental income covers my mortgage, all my costs, and then some. I get to spend lots of time there and then hand the keys to a property manager for the busy summer season when I don't want to be there anyway. Just like that.

It's incredible, hassle-free, and I love it.

Everyone loves this…it's the most thrilling thing about successfully investing in real estate.

And it's why this chapter is the most important.

Because almost every real estate opportunity should be thoroughly viewed through the prism of yield. (I say "almost" because buying land to hold for the long term with a view to capital appreciation is different.)

And in this chapter, I'm going to give you my "yield prism" so you can do just that.

My yield prism comes in the form of a tried-and-tested spreadsheet. You'll be able to download it and apply it straightaway. I know, I said I wouldn't burden you with complicated formulas, but this is simple and incredibly powerful. It's a tool I urge you to use.

That's not the only reason this chapter is vital. I reveal everything that I know about squeezing the most income out of your real estate. You'll get my tips for dressing a rental, marketing it, hiring a property manager...everything I've learned down to the little touches that make a big difference for those all-important reviews if you're renting short term.

And I'm going to show you how, with just a few well-bought properties, you could travel the world enjoying perfect-weather year-round.

Let's drive on...

The Prism of Yield

"Ah, Ronan, you're a two-bed guy, aren't you."

I hear this frequently. From a *RETA* member in an airport lounge...or an email to our *RETA* concierge...

This is not some reference to my wife and I's sleeping arrangements. It's because I so often recommend two-bed, two-bath condos to *RETA* members in our off-market deals.

No, I am not a "two-bed guy."

I am a yield guy. More accurately I am a big yield guy. A huge, unbelievable, blow-your-mind yield guy. (I'm going to assume you know how to work out a yield. If you don't, then google that right now.) I'm also a capital appreciation guy but this chapter is all about income...

I do not have some irrational passion for two-bedroom properties over studios or one-beds or large villas.

I am simply always searching for the best yield. And that is why I most often recommend two-bed, two-bath condos. Because when I look at things through the prism of yield, the two-bed units usually stack up as the best yield-generating real estate.

And two-beds give you some versatility, you can rent to a single person, a couple, a family...a group of friends.

But this is not universal. In some places when you run the numbers, a studio or one-bed offers the strongest potential yield. In Playa del Carmen on Mexico's Riviera Maya, I've recommended one-bed condos.

In 2016, I brought *RETA* members a deal in Singular Joy with an off-market price of just $143,800 for a one-bedroom condo. These condos are just a block off the beach and a block to 5th Avenue, where all the action is found in Playa. That makes them ideal rentals.

Massi is a real estate guy I know who is banking huge rental income from his two suites in Singular Joy. Massi rents his condo out through Airbnb. He has a two-bedroom lock-off but exclusively rents each suite separately. He found that to be the best way to maximize rental income. And boy has he...

He made $55,513 in 2021 with the two suites he owns, which comes out to $27,756 each. Granted he lives in Playa full-time and is able to be very hands-on with his rental, so his results are not what every owner might experience. Massi tells me he had 85% occupancy for 2021.

I have heard of another owner in Singular Joy with a one-bedroom condo. According to data from the developer, they made $27,074 over the last year.

By the way, the last condo that I saw listed in Singular Joy was at $209,500. That's an uplift of $65,700 for *RETA* members who bought. But you get the point...

I don't always recommend two-beds.

I've also recommended large homes over the years. A few years back, from the streets of Porto in the north of Portugal, it became clear to me that the best yield there was likely from buying a grand old historic home, renovating, and renting to larger groups. There was a niche to be filled, albeit you needed to really get the right location and of course, the right price. The price of two-bed apartments had risen to make no sense and everyone and their mother was getting in on the Airbnb act. Tourism was on a tear, but for any large family or a big group of friends, there was almost nothing for rent. (More on what I call the "big home play" toward the end of this chapter.)

When you employ my yield prism—which I'll give you in a second—there is still an important management and lifestyle consideration you have to mix up with your numbers.

You might be happy to spend $1 million for a beloved beach home in Akumal close to Tulum. You're going to spend lots of time there with your family and you're OK with committing time and energy to the management and maintenance. You make say $90,000 a year which is a nice gross yield of 9%.

Let's say your friend might not have any free time to travel. But they have money and love real estate and are primarily focused on squeezing the biggest yield they can from a property. Maybe in 10 years when they semi-retire they'll spend more time in it.

Their best play is likely a two-bed condo in a best-in-class community like say Samsara in Tulum, about 20 minutes down the coast from Akumal. Samsara is where in October 2021, I brought *RETA* members the chance to own two-bed condos from $198,600.

It's set to be a premium community, rich in amenities, and ideally located close to town and the beach. In fact, VIP access to a beach club is something you get as an owner. And can pass to your renters. A major selling point. Once Samsara is delivered and the community established, I figure these condos—because they were bought at *RETA*-only pricing—can command an annual gross yield of over 14%. (In July 2022, the developer opened up the remaining condos in Samsara through a local broker to retail buyers. Condos that earlier had a *RETA*-only price of $212,300 were retailing at $298,200. An $85,900 boost.)

As an owner in Samsara in Tulum, your friend can choose a property manager to handle everything. They don't need to be any more involved than they want to be.

The point here is that what you want from your property and how involved you want to be in managing it, plays an important part in your decision.

But the most important thing to take away is that things can be different from market to market. Using the prism of yield helps us focus in on the best plays. And remember, your yield is always a function of the price you pay. You can never change that. So, buy low…really low.

And here's my new mantra in the wake of the Zoom Boom and the explosion of long-term renting across my beat: We want to buy properties that we can rent short or long term, or a mix of both. The ideal property gives us the option of renting it any way we like. The condo I bought in Vale do Lobo on Portugal's Algarve was rented all August 2022 at $3,000 a week. Heading into the fall, the plan is to rent it for $2,500 a month throughout the winter.

The condos *RETA* members bought in Cabo Costa I figure could rent long term for $3,000 to $3,500 a month…or short term for $250 a night. And you could find a middle path too, experimenting with minimum stays of 20 days or a month to catch the slow-traveling "free rich" who pack their laptop and work from where they like.

As we saw in chapter 7, we now increasingly have the option of renting longer-term to the people who can work from anywhere and want to upgrade their lifestyles, or just change their scene.

And there's something really important to know about these people…

They are the same people you would rent to in the U.S. Possibly even better-quality tenants. It's just that you're buying your real estate at a fraction of the cost and thus increasing your yield!

OK, let's hold up the yield prism to some examples in Playa del Carmen.

As you know, Playa attracts a broad market of millions of vacationers and increasing numbers of folks looking to stay for longer periods. It's been at the center of the Riviera Maya's massive transformation. It is a massively internationalized place meaning it draws visitors in good times and in bad.

We know we need the right type of unit for the type of renters we want to attract. We want the location to be perfect for them, think easy access to the beach for beach-lovers or the local entertainment district…or golf for golfers. And the community has to have the right amenities, like a rooftop pool, beach club…whatever it might be. You always want to have the edge and stand out in whatever market you're in.

Plus, we want our real estate at the right price. (Which is why it's smart to buy ahead of a big transformational event and do so as a *RETA* member.)

So far, we have just spoken about the price we buy at and the income earned...but there are also the costs that we need to pay. This is where my very simple spreadsheet comes into play. (You can download and use it yourself at *RealEstateTrendAlert.com/yieldprism*.)

You input your costs and your income. Costs are everything from purchase price, closing cost to furniture, utilities, taxes, HOA fees, cleaning fees...and property management fees if you get a property manager.

Carefully looking at all the costs is very important both to your buying decision and also when deciding what type of way to rent, short term or long term.

For example, today I could rent my Copala condo in Cabo long term, without the assistance of a rental manager. This really helps. Likewise with a home I own near Akumal on the Riviera Maya. I couldn't manage short-term rentals myself, I'd need a property manager.

Let's look at my yield prism for a two-bed, lock-off condo in Singular Joy in the heart of Playa del Carmen's Zona Dorada. Let's use the numbers from a guy I know called Massi. I mentioned him previously. Massi works for the developer SIMCA and put his money where his mouth is. He now rents his condo as two separate one-beds using the lock-off.

First, we pop in the inputs to calculate Massi's net-yield on short-term rental. All his costs and income. (He says his annual gross income fluctuates between $50,000 and $55,000.

Furniture was included in the *RETA* deal so I have no cost attached to that. Massi's price was $290,000 and Massi manages the rental himself. If he were using a rental manager, figure on paying 20% of the gross income for that.

	Average Rate	Number of Nights	Total Amount
Capital Items			
Purchase Price			290,000
Closing Cost			20,300
Furniture Pack			-
Total			**310,300**
High Season	165	114	18,810.00
Medium	165	102	16,830.00
Low	165	93.75	15,468.75
Total Income		310	**51,108.75**
Gross Yield			**16.47%**
Expenses			
Property Management			-
Booking Fees			1,533
Utilities			1,800
Tax Property			300
HOA			5,520
Other Expenses			800
Total			**9,953**
Net Income			**41,155**
Net Yield			**13.26%**

When all our costs come out, the net yield is 13.26%. Like I say, Massi is managing the rental himself, the cost of a property manager would eat into that yield—I reckon 20% of gross income. That would leave Massi with a net yield of just under 10%.

Now, let's apply the yield prism to my Copala condo in Cabo, which I bought in 2015 when the *RETA* price was $336,156. But, let's look at the yield if I were to rent long term at $3,250 a month. Very realistic.

Note, I have no property management fees in this Copala calculation as this is something I can easily handle myself because I have spent time there and I know who to call when I need help with something.

At today's value for my condo of $600,000, this yield looks a lot less rosy, yet still not terrible—5.24% net annual yield. In theory I should

	Total Amount
Capital Items	
Purchase Price	336,000
Closing Cost	20,160
Furniture Pack	15,000
Total	**371,160**
Rental Income	39,000.00
Total Income	**39,000.00**
Gross Yield	**10.51%**
Cost	
Property Management	
Tax Property	1,680
HOA	3,300
Other Expenses	750
Total Costs	**5,730**
Net Income	**33,270**
Net Yield	**8.96%**

sell this and deploy this capital to other *RETA* deals where I get fast appreciation during construction and then high gross and net yields. I'm not going to though because I enjoy returns in lifestyle from owning and spending time here.

You can download and use my yield prism at *RealEstateTrend Alert.com/YieldPrism*.

Now you're armed with an effective tool for accurately measuring the potential yield of a property, let's move on to how you're going to manage your property for the most income after you buy.

It takes time to build up occupancy, word of mouth referrals, and loyal repeat business if you're renting short term. You need strategies in place to set up and decorate, market, and manage the property to keep a steady stream of renters coming in and putting dollars in your pocket consistently.

Much of the same applies if you're renting long term too.

Whichever way you go, you need to decide how hands on you want to be...

It's All About Reviews

There is no training as effective as experience.

Boots on the ground in the real world, I have spent more nights in Airbnbs and other rentals than I could ever count.

And in more destinations.

I've become an expert on what makes good short-term rentals as a user. It kills me for instance, to arrive in an otherwise excellent, clean, and secure condo or villa, with a stunning view and crisp clean sheets, to find that the owner hasn't left me or my traveling companions a drop of water.

Why not spend a few bucks on water at a minimum? Maybe coffee and a fruit bowl?

What would you leave out for a friend arriving after a long journey? Your guests arrive at night, or in the heat, after long journeys, delayed flights...whatever, they are likely weary. Thirsty.

Don't force them out into the streets to look for the basic necessities. Treat them like your friends and then ask them for a review. And they will be very happy to help you out.

It's not because this is just basic human decency, it's because reviews are the proxy for everything else I am about to tell you. It's why you furnish your property how you do, clean it the way you do. Everything is ultimately about getting that five-star review. Bring the personal touches, text on arrival, show consideration...

There is a psychological principle used in sales and marketing called social proof. Essentially, it means that when somebody says something positive about a product or service, a potential customer reading or hearing that statement is more likely to buy that product or service themselves. They think, 'This person had a positive experience, I will too.'

You are essentially selling your property to potential renters. So, make sure to solicit reviews from your renters with a well-timed WhatsApp or email after their stay. Ask them to post their comments on the booking site. You could also leave a note in your rental asking them to do so.

Good reviews can bump your listing up in online rankings and can encourage more people to book your place. One survey by an online marketing company found that 88% of consumers trust an online recommendation as much as they would a personal recommendation.

Dressing your rental

After its introduction in 2008, Airbnb revolutionized the vacation rental industry. It made it possible for everyday people to rent out their homes in just a few clicks.

In the early years, many homeowners simply listed their home, or sometimes just a room, for some extra cash here and there. They didn't really proactively seek out renters. When they got a reservation, they simply did a quick cleaning, maybe cleared some space in the fridge and closet, and washed the sheets.

The renter would show up, get a key…done. Very casual. It kind of felt like watching a friend's house while they were away for the weekend.

However, as the site exploded in popularity with travelers, savvy rental property owners soon realized this platform, along with other booking sites, could help them create a significant income stream.

But to do so required a whole different approach to setting up the property. No longer would renters be satisfied with a so-so property, especially on vacation.

When furnishing and decorating your rental property, I recommend that you look to model homes or hotel rooms as your initial inspiration. No clutter. No family photos on the wall. Spotlessly clean and well-maintained. Every guest should feel like they are the first one staying there.

And I know that adding something as simple as a hammock or an egg chair can boost occupancy. Own a condo with a large terrace? Ask yourself does it make sense to add a hot tub there? Then make sure that hot tub features in your photos online.

When we took possession of our condo on Portugal's Silver coast, it had already been a rental and the reviews were good because the condo has an amazing view and it had the basics. But then my wife gave it a facelift, removing the dated, generic furniture pack, and the reviews went from good to superlative.

Pro tip: For properties that we rent out and use ourselves, one thing we do is have photos and mementoes from our favorite places dotted throughout the property. It feels homely to us but for the visitor it's not intrusive and weird like family photos.

Beat the competition

If you're asking renters to part with their hard-earned cash, you need to be sure that what you're offering beats the competition. Your rental property is a product. And you need to treat it like one.

Let's take short-term rentals as an example. Say, you're renting at $150 a night, and so is your neighbor, but their identical home is kitted out with A/C, king size beds, and a washer/dryer and yours isn't. In that case, you'll either have to match those amenities or cut your rate.

The idea is to stand out to potential renters who are browsing through booking sites, comparing the look and features of similarly sized and priced rentals in the area they want to be. You want to be the clear choice.

Finding out what your competitors have is as easy as browsing those booking sites yourself.

Comfort

In a short-term rental, you need to look at how comfortable a stay you're giving to your renters.

It's incredible the standard of home that people think they can charge top dollar for. Scratchy comforters… cheap sheets…chipped plates in the kitchen…non-functioning appliances—I've experienced all of those and worse on the road.

It seems like it should be common sense to make the house or condo you're renting as comfortable as possible. But as the saying goes, common sense isn't very common. That's to your benefit: Get the basics right and you'll be head and shoulders above the competition.

Your unit should be well-decorated and comfortably furnished in a contemporary style. Furniture should be clean, plush, and match. The beds should be large (king-sized) and with comfortable sheets, pillows, and blankets. Plentiful lamps to provide light.

The kitchen should be equipped with microwave, coffee machine, blender, good knives, complete sets of dishes and cutlery, plenty of pots and pans, matching wine glasses…you get the idea. You don't want your guest to feel like they needed something you didn't provide or that you went to the thrift store to furnish the place.

Pro Tip: When you're planning to rent a home short term, stay there yourself, as if you were a guest. Sleeping in the home, taking a shower, and using the appliances lets you see first-hand the plus points of your home and any shortcomings (that you can then rectify).

Thinking of your guests' comfort and making their stay as pleasant as possible will set you apart—and earn you good reviews and repeat business. People who plan to return to the area (say they take a beach vacation to Portugal's Algarve every year) would much rather go back to a rental they know rather than have to search for a new place.

Something else to consider is kitting out your rental at least somewhat in the "local" style. In a condo on the beach in Mexico, for example, it would be a nice touch to include a set of margarita glasses. Your décor could incorporate some indigenous handicrafts. You probably wouldn't want to have imposing, heavy dark wood furniture—it just doesn't fit the airy, bright, and colorful coastal setting.

That's for short term.

For long term, folks are typically looking for the same location and amenities as vacationers but they're staying longer. So, you need to really make sure your home or condo is in good repair— properly insulated, comfortable, and any issues sorted quickly and without any quibbles. No one wants to deal with that landlord who'll nickel and dime them when an essential repair needs to be covered… or who doesn't want to help when something goes wrong.

A little goes a long way in forming good relationships with your renters. And, in long-term rentals, that's especially to your benefit. A happy tenant is one who'll take extra special care of your home. Which means you don't have to.

When I rent in Cabo, I've been happy to take a little less than I could ask on the open market to get a tenant I know won't cause me any trouble. I use my friend network to find wannabe renters and there are plenty of them I assure you.

Buying a furnished place

In some cases, when you buy your home or condo, it will come completely furnished. If you check out real estate sites in various vacation destinations around the world, this will be highlighted in the listing. These resales are from folks who've been offering the property as a rental but are ready to get out. Buying a turnkey, ready to rent property can save you time and money.

But not so fast. You'll have to do a thorough review of the contents to make sure everything is up to standard. Are the mattresses old and uncomfortable? Are the plates mismatched? Is the furniture in the living room dated and worn out?

If so, you'll have to start fresh.

In other cases, you can buy directly from a developer, who might throw in a free furniture pack worth thousands of dollars—that's right down to the plush towels in the bathroom and the cutlery in the kitchen.

This can be a huge benefit as you get high-quality furnishings put together by a professional interior decorator—and you don't have to pay for it, which is a huge saving. It'll look great from day one, with no effort (or stress) on your part needed. And, of course, you can always add some of your personal touches later.

In one *RETA* deal in Playa del Carmen, Singular Dream, members of our group secured furniture packs for one-bedroom condos valued at $15,000 and those with the two bedrooms got a pack valued at $23,000.

Little extras that go a long way

Renters usually travel with just their suitcases. They'll appreciate anything you provide that will help them enjoy their stay—or save a few bucks.

I told you my pet peeve is arriving into an Airbnb and the host hasn't even left me a bottle of water. My ideal rental starts with finding water, coffee, and a few bananas.

Providing the personal touches and treating renters as you would a friend rewards you with repeat business and good reviews on booking sites. Here are some items you could throw in (and be sure to highlight them in your listing):

- Bicycles
- If you're by the beach: beach towels, chairs, umbrellas, and boogie boards
- Sun hats
- Maps of the area
- Guidebooks
- Flyers and coupons for local shops and restaurants, including food delivery
- Toiletries (in case they forget something at home)
- Coffee and coffee filters (if they get in on a late flight, having coffee in the morning will definitely be welcome)
- Laundry soap

Consider putting out a little welcome gift basket for each guest with a bottle of wine, chocolates, tropical fruit, fresh-baked muffins…it won't cost you much and delight your guests. You can even bake the treats into your pricing.

The opposite is also true...arriving into a rental with a kitchen full of half-used sauces and random aged condiments is a big turn off.

I also recommend putting together a binder or folder with information on local attractions, gate codes for your development, WiFi password, the cleaning service schedule, instructions on how to use the kitchen appliances and washer/dryer, what to do if the hot water or internet goes out, emergency numbers, pharmacies and hospitals, taxi numbers, and any travel tips for that area, such as how much to expect to pay for things.

All these extras will help your guests relax, settle in, and start relaxing that much sooner if you've taken care of this "admin" for them.

Pro Tip: Travelers these days, especially digital nomads and remote workers, expect reliable fast internet. And even vacationers want to be able to watch Netflix in the evening and post photos on social media.

Marketing Your Property

So, you've given the people what they want as far as amenities and furnishings. Now, you need to get the word out that you're better than the competition.

This is not the time to hide your light under a bushel. If you want to keep your rental filled and keep those income checks coming in, you need to get to grips with advertising and marketing.

It will help to think like a potential rental client...and understand what they're looking for. A little tactical thinking will go a long way.

A contact who has properties in Medellín, Colombia, told me he fitted all his rental properties with air-conditioning—even though the climate is so temperate air-conditioning is rarely needed. His reasoning? Most North American renters will automatically tick "air-conditioning" when searching for a place, even when it's not needed. By including that one amenity, he ensures he's visible to a bigger pool of renters than his competitors who don't offer air-conditioning. Then, make sure your advertisements reflect what they're seeking.

Properly listing your property

I can't begin to tell you how many good rental properties go overlooked because the owner hasn't advertized it properly.

Say you've got a luxury condo that's a few steps from a beautiful beach and a stroll to a gourmet restaurant. It's in a community with top-notch amenities and amazing views. How well do you think it would rent if you're using just a few photos of the interior and simply mention a few features of the condo—but not the community or surrounding area?

That's not a hypothetical question. Believe it or not, this is what I found when I booked a rental condo online. I was scouting and needed a place at short notice. I fully expected to pay a high price for my stay. I knew the community I wanted to stay in. It was high season, and I didn't think I'd find anything available to rent. But one condo had slipped through the net—because its owner is doing such a terrible job promoting it.

Because I knew the area well, I was happy to take a chance on renting her property. I know the community and even the condo block her property is located in, so I knew for a fact that I'd have a comfortable stay in a good location. Other prospective renters likely would not. Based on the photos she had chosen to promote her luxury condo, I guessed most renters would be unwilling to take a chance on renting her condo. Long or short term.

On arrival, I met the owner. My assessment was right. She couldn't understand why her condo wasn't renting as well as others in the community. I could.

Here's what you should do to avoid making the same mistakes.

Highlight the location

Make sure renters know what's close by to your place. Ask yourself, who would find your place a good base? If there's a conference center nearby, for example, mention it in your listing. If it's a foodie destination, describe that and where to go to sample the best food. Near some historic ruins or an expensive ski resort? Tell people.

Come up with a catchy one-line title that makes your home stand out ("Luxury Condo by the Beach and Close to 5-Star Restaurants," for example). It should sound compelling enough to make people want to click on it and find out more.

Additionally, make sure your address and location are as clear as they can be, and if you have the option, add a map or geotag your home on an online map.

Give a lot of detail

Whether advertising for a long- or short-term rental, you'll need to give a good description of your home. Bigger vacation rental by owner sites will give tips on what's expected as standard in a property, down to the number and type of towels in each bathroom.

List what rooms you have and what furniture and appliances you've got, down to the type of bed and how many place settings you're offering. Describe the area around your home—the amenities and attractions nearby. State how close they are to your home. Mention a few good places to eat and shop; give the names of the eateries and the type of food they serve. Most importantly, paint a picture of the dreamy vacation your guests can enjoy.

A word of caution, though. Deliver what you promise. If you describe your home as "luxury", renters will expect fine linens, top-notch furniture, and quality finishes. Don't tick to say you've got a beach view if you haven't...or that your home is a "few steps" to town when it's a half-hour hike. You'll just get unhappy renters and bad reviews.

And, add some information about you. People still trust a face over an anonymous listing. So, if you have the option to add a picture of you and a short, friendly blurb, do so. If you're using a rental manager, make sure he/she does it instead.

Choose the right "keywords" and descriptions in your listing

If you're advertising online, you don't need to be super tech savvy, but you do need to keep in mind how the internet works. That means that you need to add keywords into your listing.

Keywords are the words search engines like Google and websites use to categorize information. They're the words people will use to find you. So, when you are writing up a description of your place, make sure to include the keywords that people might be searching for.

For a home in Playa, for example, you might say you have a "central Playa del Carmen condo," "close to the beach," and "close to Fifth Avenue," that is "comfortable and furnished" and comes with "pool access." (You don't need to add the quotation marks and you should certainly add more detail than those examples.) Thinking about what people will search for to find a place like yours, and using those phrases and words in your description, will help you rank higher in search engine results.

How to take attractive photos for your listing

Airbnb allows up to 100 photos for your listing, but the sweet spot is around 20. Most people won't bother to browse through more than that. But more important than quantity is quality.

Your home is only as good as the photos you show of it. Choosing the wrong photos can put off prospective renters, so you need to make sure yours are top-quality. Get some help with taking the photos if you need it...and use your best photo as your "profile" photo. It's the first thing folks will see when they search.

There are a whole host of studies out there that show that people pay far more attention to adverts with clear, helpful images than ones without. That's because as much as 90% of the information we absorb at any time is visual. So, if you're skimping on photography, you're losing renters.

Make sure you have photos that flatter your rental without being misleading: That means taking pictures of the interiors (including clean and tidy bedrooms, sitting areas, etc.), any outside space, such as terraces, pools, or gardens (also clean and tidy), and any nearby beauty spots. It is incredible to me how many renters with a beach on their doorstep neglect to put a single snapshot of the sand or sea up.

Bad lighting, weird camera angles, and photos of dark corners won't help. Make sure your home looks its best. Stage it as if you're selling it to a prospective buyer. Declutter it and remove any personal items you've scattered around. Take pictures with all the lights on, even in daytime. Photos should be clear. Make it look warm and inviting. If you've got outside entertaining space, show it off. If you're close to a beach, post some nice beach shots.

If you try it yourself and you're not achieving the results you want, consider hiring a professional photographer. It could be a smart investment. Airbnb found that listings with professional photographs performed TWICE as well as listings that didn't use professional quality shots. (For a time, they even offered free photography services to hosts in certain locations—that's how much value the company saw in good photos.)

Pro Tip: Think about what currency you advertise in. One contact rents out his Spanish home on a lot of short-term rental sites. By switching to advertising in sterling when the exchange rate is favorable, he makes more than if he advertised in euro. This, along with other strategies, means he's grossing €30,000 a year on a home that would rent long term for just €14,400 a year.

Where to list your rental

If you're planning on renting short term, I recommend you use an established vacation rental by owner website that's high profile, an established brand. There are several of these: VRBO, FlipKey, and Airbnb are among the most established. You can list your rental on several of these.

If you plan to rent your property longer term, you should check out the most established websites for long-term rentals in your particular destination. You can work with local real estate agents and property management companies also. And, for lots of internationalized places you'll find Facebook groups specifically for long-term rentals.

If you use an agent or management company to find a tenant for a long-term residential rental or a commercial unit, they will usually take a one-off advertising fee equivalent to one month's rent on a twelve-month contract.

Generally, short-term rental sites take a percentage of what you charge your renters as payment for using their service. That's a fee you wouldn't pay if you were to advertise on your own personal website. But there are advantages to using these services that make it worthwhile for a lot of vacation rental owners.

The biggest advantage to sites like these is visibility for your rental property. The big names in the business spend a lot of time and money making sure they come out on top when someone searches online for rental property. That means more traffic on their site—and more potential renters for your property. In turn, it means you won't have to fight to have your property seen by online searchers.

The well-known brands are trusted by renters, too. That's another advantage to using them. Some of them operate a full-refund policy to renters if things go wrong. That helps potential renters feel more secure. It also pushes them from simply browsing to making a booking—these sites handle payment processing too.

If you're going it alone to advertise your short-term rental, get a professional in to help with your website. It should look appealing, be easy to navigate, and laid out properly.

Whether you're using a brand-name site like this or managing your own website, renters should get an easy one-step booking and payment process. Most folks are time pressured these days. The quicker and easier the booking process, the better. Bigger sites allow renters to book and pay on the spot using a credit card.

As an owner, you should explain your cancellation policy clearly, and make it available to renters before they book or pay. You should also give renters a copy of your rental rules.

Even if you still use booking platforms, it can be a good idea to have a website for your rental as it's just one more way to get the word out.

It's Not All About Airbnb

Rental sites like Airbnb and VRBO dominate the online vacation rental book industry. You should definitely be on sites like this—they are established, well-known worldwide, and popular.

But keep in mind that there are other vacation rental sites out there. Know your renter and use different websites to attract them.

Some are favored by travelers of other nationalities. If your renters are Scandinavian, Mexican, American, British,

Irish, etc., seek out the websites they'll use and post your rental there. And you should also translate the listing in the appropriate language. It's easy to hire translators for short jobs like this on Fiverr.com.

There are also "niche" vacation rental sites that are frequented by specific groups. Here are just a few:

- Niche Escapes allows travelers to search for rentals based on their interests or needs, including categories like surfing, nightlife, disability friendly, eco-tourism, and more.

- Pink Vacation Rentals is for the LGBTQ community.

Taking Your Rental to the Next Level by Focusing on Your Niche

If you search for vacation rentals in Central Florida, you'll find lots of available homes set up to attract a very specific audience: families visiting Disney World and other area attractions.

In the homes in the developments surrounding the theme park area, you'll find four/five/six-bedroom homes to accommodate extended families with swimming pools, playrooms stocked with toys, big screen TVs for movie nights, video game systems, and, of course, Disney-themed décor.

It's a great illustration of how establishing a niche can super-charge your rental.

For many families, these ideally located "Disney-fied" properties become their go-to every year—this special home becomes just as much part of the vacation as meeting Mickey Mouse. They recommend the home to friends and family…and the Disney fans they know from fan Facebook groups and message boards.

This is key because when you have repeat customers and referral business, you become less reliant on platforms like Airbnb and VRBO. When you deal directly with these renters, you don't have to give those platforms a cut. You make more money and don't have to do as much marketing.

You want to get to a point that this is where the majority of your business is coming from.

Some potential niches overseas include:

- Surf vacations in Nicaragua in homes or condos along the beach in the area around San Juan del Sur, as well as the Emerald Coast to the north.

- Yoga and wellness retreats in the jungles of Costa Rica.

- Destination weddings in Puerto Vallarta, Los Cabos, or the Riviera Maya.

- Golf vacations in places with many well-regarded championship courses like the Costa del Sol, the Algarve, Los Cabos, and the Riviera Maya.

Profile Yourself

I'm regularly contacted by folks who bought the right real estate in the right area at the right price...and are falling flat on the rental income front while their neighbors are raking in the cash. To see if you should hire a rental manager or no, ask yourself these three questions:

1. Do You Live Close to Your Rental Property?

It's a slam-dunk to manage a property that's almost on your doorstep. But if you live in Texas and the rental property is in Costa Rica, it's much trickier. You can't jump in your car to deal with hassle with tenants, emergencies, or urgent repairs. A rental manager can save you time

---

179

and money when your rental property is far from where you live.

2. How Much Time Do You Have to Spare?

If you're already running a business, working full-time, juggling an investment portfolio, or in a profession that's time-hungry, you should consider a rental manager. Especially if you make more per hour from your job or investments than you'll pay that manager.

3. Are You Experienced?

It takes a while to learn the ropes of managing a rental property. Rookies make mistakes...that can become expensive mistakes. Getting an experienced, established rental manager on board is worthwhile if you don't know what you're doing.

A good rental manager can mean the difference between mediocre occupancy rates with measly rental income and a killer rental that's a little cash machine.

The Big Home Play

Have you ever tried to book a big home for a group to visit and hang out together? I'm talking about a place for everyone...

A pool for kids and adults. Plenty of private space for each person, yet big communal areas where everyone can get together...lots of bedrooms...in the perfect location...

I have booked and stayed in many such properties...for family get togethers, for retreats with my team, and golf trips.

As a renter, finding big homes that tick all the boxes is often difficult, and that's just the first hurdle. The bigger hurdle is the typical price tag. Big homes tend to be priced in the thousands per night.

Any real estate investor might observe this apparent lack of supply and think, there's a gap...a niche we can fill. After all, these luxurious mansions can throw off huge income.

But our yield is based on the price we pay to own a property and typically such a property comes at a huge price. I know of homes in Cabo that rent for more than $10,000 per night but would cost north of $10 million to buy.

The *RETA* idea—the way to fat yields—is to seek out and buy the right real estate really cheap. I'm not talking about owning a place for Kim Kardashian and entourage. I mean just a place where a regular affluent family or group would get together.

Of course, it isn't enough to find a big luxurious home going cheap...

You need a razor-sharp understanding of who makes up your market...you need the right real estate in the right location. This is critical.

This play works best in a high traffic destination. Think Rome or the Riviera Maya, the Algarve or Los Cabos.

With this big-home play you're targeting large, mixed groups. There will be several generations with different considerations. Some will have high-powered work commitments, there'll be kids, and some retirees.

Flight access will be key as some will be more time constrained than others. And, they will come from multiple locations.

You also want to buy in a place that has a broad appeal. A place that has something for everyone in the group...and a place that has the infrastructure to support that...think spa treatments, dive instructors, kids' activities, grocery stores...

Buy in a blue-chip locale and the market comes to you. And, they come with the expectation of high price and a budget to match.

If you go off the beaten track, it's easier to buy cheap, but renting becomes more difficult unless you have a particular niche or can offer a special experience.

In 2018 in Rome, I found a large six-bed apartment operating as a guest house in a historic building for sale for only €275,000.

I was staying right below it in an Airbnb when I visited Rome with family. We were paying $400 a night for our big, comfortable three-bed apartments. The guesthouse at twice the size was renting rooms individually at $60 a night.

The play: Shut down the guesthouse business, save the operating costs and just rent it to groups for $500 to $600 per night.

Italy's the fifth most-visited country on earth and Rome is packed with family groups from North America and Asia who are looking for something other than a hotel experience. Your rental would save them money and offer them the conveniences of being able to have food and their own areas to relax and hangout.

In destinations all across the *RETA* beat, you'll find old and unloved properties that are similarly ripe for fresh ideas. Bring some enthusiasm and perspective to the game and you could be on to a winner.

In some places a whole other approach makes sense. In Tulum in 2019, my team and I rented an 11-bedroom building. A few blocks back from the main drag where land could be bought for a song until a couple of years previously. Six rooms along the ground floor in a line with a garden. Above that was five rooms, and above that, an open area with a big table and kitchen facilities.

I'd say the whole place could have been built for $250,000. And, the land bought for as little as $50,000 five years beforehand. The plot was narrow, the location not prime but accessible to town, so it wouldn't have had many competing uses.

Our group paid $1,100 per night. It was off season. A hotel would have been cheaper but a hotel wasn't what we wanted. We wanted our own space to plan, brainstorm, work on ideas and deals. It was absolutely perfect for us. Everything was tastefully done. Breakfast laid out for us in the mornings. A supply of bread and cold meats. There was a massage area on the first floor and a hot tub on the top floor.

In 2019, I spent four days with three generations of family on Los Cabos East Cape. We rented a waterfront villa. We paid $600 per night and that was a last-minute deal. Everything else in the East Cape that would serve our needs was full, and most over $1,000 per night anyhow.

I was apprehensive as we drove there.

From the photos, the home looked dated at best. I was worried the beds would be uncomfortable, or worse...too gross to sleep on. On arrival I was pleasantly surprised. The house was fine. The setting out of this world. It was a perfect rental.

The house was for sale and I remember noting that many prospective buyers would walk through the door and find things not to their taste. The house was built by the owner...a bit of a hodgepodge...now life had moved on and they could no longer spend much time there. The terrace was this huge cavernous space, the kitchen tiny and unsuitable for cooking for a group...

Who with $1.4 million to spend would buy this home?

But it was heavenly for a few days' rental...right on the water and with our own waterfront pool.

I recently saw the asking price for this house come down to $900,000. If the owner is truly motivated, you could be buying for as little as $600,000. Then, make some minor cosmetic and marketing improvements and you are renting for $800 plus a night.

The location is blue-chip and accessible. There is a private airstrip right behind the house and Los Cabos international airport is an hour away. Much of the drive is on a dirt road, an SUV advisable, but renting an SUV from Los Cabos airport is easy. There's also a little hotel that's part of the complex. Like the house, it too is dated and a bit quirky. But the setting is stunning...you can wander up for a poolside cocktail or a portion of fries.

Close by in the new Four Seasons, the basic room rate is $1,000 per night. A super luxury villa around here would likely cost between $2.5 to $25 million.

You would not be buying that villa to play the big home niche...

We're not looking for that in any blue-chip destination. We want the rough diamond. These rough diamonds can be illiquid at the best of times. As I say...if you are flying in from L.A. to Los Cabos with a seven-figure budget, you are very unlikely to be willing to inherit someone else's quirks or bad taste. You don't have the time, but you do have the money to shop for the turnkey luxury villa you want.

But find a motivated seller and we can be on to a truly special deal.

You never know how low a seller will go unless you ask. And by ask, I mean make a cash offer for a quick clean sale. Many of these rough diamonds were languishing on the market in the good times...there's a smaller market for such properties. Come a crisis—and find the right seller—and you could cut the deal of a lifetime.

Tracking—and Maximizing—Your Rental Income

A key part of managing your rental is keeping track of your expenses…and how much money is coming in. This gauges the success of your "business."

The first part of this is how much you charge.

Setting pricing

A big part of successful short-term rental is repeat guests and guest referrals. This will often be a significant chunk of your overall business. It takes time to build this up, however. Even big-name hotel brands with tens of thousands of existing guests will figure on three years or so to build to maximum occupancy in a new hotel.

Initially, when you start, you won't have any guests…or any reviews. It pays to look at your competition and undercut them for a while, at least until you get some good reviews.

As you set your prices, you must also keep abreast of the price your competition is currently charging and what owners of similar homes to yours are offering. If they've got air conditioning, blackout blinds, and bike rentals, you'll need to match those to charge the same rate per night. Many owners do this initially and then forget about it. That's a mistake.

Keep in mind that you can also adjust your rate seasonally—or to reflect local events such as film or jazz festivals, when demand is higher. You may want to set a minimum stay period in peak season. For example, in destinations that are warm in winter, like Costa Rica, Mexico, or Panama, you'll find many renters from the U.S. and Canada coming down that time of year. You can charge a premium.

And know the holidays—they're when you can raise your nightly rate as demand increases. This is key for getting your pricing right. And, I don't just mean the U.S. or Canadian ones. Familiarize yourself with both local holidays and the holidays of your potential guests from different countries. For example, in Latin America, Semana Santa (Holy Week), the week before Easter, is huge and people head in droves to the beach.

It also pays to price in the currency that your potential guests use. It makes things easier for them. If you add your home to a listings site in Europe and one in North America, show pricing in euros for the Europeans and dollars for Americans. Watch out for currency fluctuations, too. I've seen bargain vacation rentals aimed at Americans and priced in pounds sterling…where the price per night cost those Americans significantly less.

One last thing…don't forget to charge for extra guests. You may want to set pricing based on a "standard" number of guests and then charge an additional fee (per night or per stay) for any over that number.

How much will you take home?

Your gross rental yield is easy to calculate. Just take your gross rental income for the year, divide it by the purchase price you paid for the property, and multiply the answer by 100, and that's your yield.

Generate $20,000 a year in income on a condo that cost you $200,000, and you've got a 10% yield. Kick the income up a notch to $25,000 and your yield goes up to 12.5%.

To determine your potential income, you need to factor in more than the purchase price to determine your net income and assess if a particular market and real estate type are right for you. You might find, for example, that the headline gross rates on short-term rental look very attractive. But once you factor in overhead costs and occupancy rates, they might not look so hot.

Compare short-term and long-term rentals, for example. Short-term rentals have traditionally generated more rental income, but they also carry higher running costs. You need to furnish the unit, kit it out, add little finishing touches. You're not done there. You'll need to keep overhauling, remodeling, and upgrading it to keep up with your competition, as well as replacing expensive items like appliances, sofas, beds, and electronics. You'll also pay the utility bills, cleaning, cable TV and internet, and rental management fees.

In some markets, you won't need to furnish long-term rentals and the renter covers the cost of utilities. Plus, you'll pay a lower management fee for a long-term rental.

Here are some other costs to consider when calculating how much you might take home from your rental:

- Overseas, verify who is responsible for paying things like condo or association fees. In some markets, the landlord pays this fee, even with a long-term rental. In other markets, it's paid by the tenant. The same applies with other costs. In Panama, for example, the landlord usually pays the monthly water and trash fee as well as the condo fee.

- Whether you rent long or short term, you (as the landlord) will pay things like property tax, corporation taxes and fees (if you own the home via a local corporation), rental income tax, and for repairs and maintenance. Plus, with a furnished rental, you'll need to factor in replacing furniture and equipment periodically.

- Investigate your tax liabilities. Property tax overseas is generally much lower than in North America. Tax on rental income varies widely. You'll pay 0% in some Caribbean tax havens, up to 30% in Costa Rica. Find out if you can offset expenses against that tax. Also, look up local property tax rates, and ask if there are any other taxes (wealth tax, luxury tax, school tax) that apply to your property.

- If you plan on sending the rental income back to your home country, ask if you'll have to pay any extra taxes for wiring money outside the country. And remember, you may still have tax obligations in your home country.

All of these things determine your net profit (i.e. the profit you are left with after you pay taxes and other costs).

Buying the right property is the biggest factor in your ROI

ROI stands for return on investment. You can put in time, work, and effort to increase the amount of rent you make. But one thing you can't change is how much you paid for the property in the first place. Yet that determines your yield.

If you pay too much for the home to begin with, you'll always struggle to get a good yield.

You need to do your homework on comps to decide how much the property you want to buy is really worth. If you're buying a home for personal use and any rental income you make is icing on the cake, then you'll probably want nicer finishes, more expensive furniture, bigger living space.

But, if you're buying purely for investment, you can't let your heart rule your head.

Before splashing out on a home with nice views or a gourmet kitchen, investigate to see if it will generate more rental income…or not. Over-ride your personal taste and wants and go with what will make the most money.

Always negotiate when you're buying to get the best possible deal. If the seller won't come down on price, maybe they'll throw in furniture and appliances, for example. That cuts your costs and bumps up your yield.

This is where *Real Estate Trend Alert* membership pays off.

Members get exclusive discounted pricing and finance terms that buyers on the street can only dream of. They cherry-pick premium homes in prime locations…and buy at prices significantly lower than anyone else pays. That means that all other things being equal, members are ahead from the outset—and on track to make the strongest rental yields.

I Like Lock-off Condos

A lock-off or lock-out condo is something I rate highly when it comes to maximizing rental income.

In a nutshell, it's a condo that's laid out so it can be divided into two individual units. Usually, in a two-bedroom lock-off condo, you can divide it into a suite (a bedroom and bathroom) and a one-bed condo (with a bedroom, bathroom, kitchen and living area). Ideally, both should have a separate entrance.

A lock-off gives you maximum flexibility when it comes to renting. You can rent the condo as a two-bed unit...or rent the suite and one-bed condo separately...or rent one side and keep the other private for your own use.

I've seen folks use this lock-off layout to bump up their occupancy and gross income time and again.

Maximizing Income From Long-Term Rentals

We've seen the world is changing. For a real estate investor, the prospect of generating double-digit yields on long-term rentals is incredibly exciting. It's less work for us than short-term rentals. But you do have to take a different tack than short term. Long-term renters might be locals, expats, or the many remote workers now flooding internationalized places around the world. They typically want the same amenities and vibe as short-term renters but...

Here's how to get the maximum income from a long-term arrangement:

1. Don't over-buy. If an 1,100-square-foot, two-bed, two-bath condo gets the same rent as a 1,400-square-foot, two-bed,

two-bath condo, and your priority is rental returns, stick with the smaller condo. The larger one will cost more to buy initially, more to maintain, and come with higher running costs.

2. Target specific groups of tenants that pay big bucks in the area your home is located in. That might be doctors working at a big hospital close by, overseas students going to an expensive private college, university professors. You may find a big multinational business in your area, for example, looking for good corporate lets.

3. Eradicate anything that is dirty or dangerous that can put prospective tenants off—mold, damp, faulty appliances.

4. Investigate the local market to see if upgrading kitchens or bathrooms will pay off by attracting a higher-end tenant and a higher rental rate.

5. Adding en-suites or extra bedrooms can make the home rent more easily and widen the pool of potential renters.

6. Stay on top of rental rates in your area. Many landlords set an initial rent and then forget to re-price if they have a long-term tenant.

7. Connect with your tenant well in advance of the end of the lease period to see if they plan to stay on. If they don't, start looking for a new tenant immediately.

8. Find out if you are entitled to any tax breaks and utilize them.

9. If you have a bank mortgage or finance loan on the home, see if refinancing will cut overhead costs.

10. Screen tenants properly. Long-term tenants are harder to evict...you should pick those with a good tenancy record.

11. Go for practical finishes that don't need lots of maintenance or frequent replacement. Tile is better than carpet on floors, for example.

12. Inspect the property regularly to make sure it's in good shape. Remember, you usually need to notify the tenant of such inspections: you can't show up unannounced.

13. Keep your tenants happy. If you've got good tenants, they're more likely to stay if you're responsive, promptly deal with repairs, etc.

14. Don't include variables like electricity or water in the rental rate. You'll have to pad the rental rate to cover your potential costs which will make your rate look uncompetitive.

15. Comply with local laws and regulations. Whether it's registering the tenancy, understanding discrimination laws, putting in smoke detectors, or placing the deposit with a government agency, do so.

16. Check to see if your home or area is subject to rent caps or limits on rent increases.

17. Check that local laws don't tie you in. In some countries (such as Costa Rica), you're tied in to a minimum three years on a long-term rental. If you decide to sell after only a year, you're still stuck with the tenant...as is the new owner if you sell. And, if you don't give the appropriate notice three months before the contract expires, it automatically renews...for another three years.

18. If you think an above market rate is achievable, then list at a higher rental rate than you expect to get. Rent is negotiable in most markets, so leave yourself enough wiggle room to give the tenant a discount and not leave yourself short.

The long arm of the law

Before you plump for short-term rental, make sure that you're legally allowed to do that in the area and property that you're buying.

Not everyone is as big a fan of short-term property rentals as investors are.

Some cities with housing crises, particularly in Europe, are banning short-term rentals. Berlin is one of the most high-profile cities to restrict them to just 90 days out of the year if it is a secondary residence. The law doesn't apply to rooms rented in homes while the owners are there. What it does prevent is the renting of entire premises to tourists for more than a short period.

Authorities took the step because of a severe shortage of long-term rentals in the city. It had an immediate effect. Listings on Airbnb for Berlin fell by almost 40% in just one month. Owners had a good incentive to delist their properties: Those found to be in breach of the rules faced fines of up to €100,000. Most sensibly complied.

Other locales are imposing severe restrictions in response to complaints about the impact the business has had on the availability of affordable housing and increased noise and nuisance. In Panama City, Panama, the law states that the minimum rental period is 45 days. In Medellín, Colombia, it's 30 days. These rules are designed to limit short-term rentals and encourage long-term tenants.

Not everywhere has rules like this.

Many growing tourism destinations are welcoming short-term rentals as they help to grow vacationer numbers. Find out before you buy.

You also should consider in-house rules if you're buying in a private community or condo block. The board or association of owners set these rules, and they may limit or restrict vacation rentals. This is more likely to happen in a community or block with mostly owner-occupiers or long-term tenants who don't want the hassle of a revolving door of strangers rolling up. If a majority of owners vote to ban vacation rentals, you're out of luck.

Bear in mind, too, that this is a moveable feast. Authorities act in response to complaints. Just because you can rent by the night all year-round now, does not mean you will always have the right to do so.

Taxes and fees

Rentals are also subject to income tax, lodging tax, and/or corporate tax, paid by the owner to the national or state/provincial government. And different areas of a country might pay different rates.

In some places, renters are on the hook to pay a sales or valued added tax. Sometimes, these tax payments are incorporated in booking sites like Airbnb and sent directly to the government. In other cases, it's up to the owner to build the tax into their nightly rate, calculate and keep track of the tax owed, and submit payment themselves.

There are also rules for financial record-keeping, tax report filing, and the like. Best to let a local accountant or your property management company deal with this paperwork, although you should definitely understand the regulations and what is owed, as it has bearing on your ROI.

Some municipal governments also institute a special tax or fee on vacation rentals. In San Miguel de Allende, Mexico, for example, owners must secure a permit and pay an annual fee of 10,000 pesos, which is about $500.

You will still see folks on various platforms listing their homes in breach of these laws regarding allowed occupancy, permits, and tax collection. But remember...just as these platforms make it easy for potential renters to find you, it also makes it super-easy for officials enforcing these laws to find you, too. They look at your listing and then search the address in government records.

The penalties are usually stiff fines that increase significantly if you're a repeat offender. And, increasingly, officials are cracking down. You could be shut down for a period or subject to back taxes. Don't listen to any real estate agent, developer, accountant, seemingly savvy local, or grizzled expat who tells you it's OK to not pay taxes or not secure the proper permits.

For example, in Costa Rica in 2013 and 2014, in response to pressure from the hotel owner trade association, the government started going after vacation rental owners who had not been collecting the 13% sales tax from renters and sending to the government. This is after years of lax enforcement. Many vacation rental owners were caught quite unawares.

Enjoy Eternal Spring With Travel and Income

For the right person, I think what I am about to tell you is by far my best idea.

At the outset of my real estate investing career, I had a simple idea for how I wanted to live...

I wanted to travel. I wanted good weather all the time, which for me means no need for air con, no need for heating. I like being close to the ocean. I enjoy golf. A vibrant town with good food and reasonable services is a big plus...

And I don't like hassle or excessive travel to and from airports, which in my line of work is a big deal. So I need to be fairly close to an airport.

With these things in mind I went forth...

Today, after years of travel and real estate scouting, I own what I call my "personal bases." Starting out, my plan was:

- Buy properties in beautiful places...

- Earn an income from these properties when I wasn't there...

- Enjoy these properties when it suited me most...

So, here's my big idea...

Using everything you're learning in this book, buy several properties in beautiful locations. Rent those houses out in peak season to cover all your costs, and then spend time in them in the slower season.

I don't quite have the whole thing figured out for myself, but almost...here's how I do it:

Winter: I stay in my condo in Cabo. The crowds of vacationers have thinned somewhat, the weather is ideal for me. Outside of work, I fall into a routine of beach strolls, golf and dining out. I take road trips around the Baja and enjoy the flowering desert.

I bought this two-bed condo in the Copala community of the 5-star Quivira resort in 2015. I did so when the *RETA*-only price was $336,156. In September 2022, I had an agent try persuading me to sell for $600,000. So, it was a good deal.

Spring: Come March usually, I hand the keys to my Copala condo to a property manager. Some years I've rented to a friend of a friend. There's never any shortage of wannabe tenants. My Copala condo could rent from $3,000 to $3,500. I haven't rented this year as I wanted to keep it open for a summer visit and for friends and family. I no longer need a rental/property manager in Cabo as I have a great set of on-the-ground contacts who I can ask to help out. Then it's off to Portugal's Silver Coast...

In October 2020, while on a mammoth scouting trip of Portugal, I bought that two-bed beachfront condo on the Silver Coast that I've mentioned before. I bought it for €300,000.

It's a region of Portugal that I love. The beaches are pristine, there's a treasury of stunning historic towns and fishing villages to explore, I'm spoiled for great seafood... accessible golf...entertainment. And the people here are friendly and easy going.

Not to mention, the value there is very hard to beat...

For my beachfront condo, my total monthly payments (including mortgage, taxes, HOA fees, and golf club dues on two great courses) come in at just under €1,110. That's less that what property tax alone would come in at in California. And I'd argue that the beaches here are nicer. I cover the entire costs just by renting in July and August when I'm not there, plus some random weeks here and there.

While there are a lot of great low-cost resorts on the Silver Coast, Praia D'El Rey, where I own, has an advantage of being close to Lisbon, seeing more weekend and holiday traffic than resorts.

Summer: I like to spend July and August in Ireland. This is my block of time to spend with friends and family, to play golf and recharge with no travel. It's when I try to have a "normal" life. It's important for me personally to stay connected in Ireland...not lose contacts with friends and golf buddies. When (or if) at some point I slow down at work (I hate the word retirement) plugging in here for at least four months of the year will be integral to my plans.

I have a portfolio of rental properties in Ireland. But, I don't stay in any property I own. I rent a vacation home on a golf course that's central to everything for me. I have been shopping for my Ireland summer home on and off for the last couple of years. Nothing I have seen makes sense to buy vs my current rental situation. Come the spring, I will be back shopping in Ireland. Maybe it will be more of a buyer's market there by then. The market has been super hot with chronic scarcity of inventory.

Fall: It's back to Portugal's Silver Coast for a while!

I know of *RETA* members who do something similar, say spend the winter in Cabo and the summer in Canada by the lake...or the winter in Portugal's Algarve and spring traveling... then summer back home...

The truth is, almost anyone can own a profitable home overseas. With the right real estate plays and a lot less money than you might think, you could actually own several...travel among them, rent them for a good income when you're not there, and the day you want to sell, you could lock in a meaty profit.

CHAPTER 9

Use Leverage to Get Really Rich

"Leverage is the reason some people become rich and others do not become rich." — Robert T. Kiyosaki

It's one of the best things about being a real estate investor.

Using financing to buy real estate, you can benefit from a true "money miracle..."

Leverage.

Financing gives you leverage. With leverage, you use borrowed money to buy a property. And with the right deal you can 5X...10X... even 20X your money with this strategy.

Using leverage you can own, control, and profit from a large investment with a relatively small amount of your own money invested.

At the same time using financing, rather than paying 100% in cash, helps you free up capital, allowing you to use your money elsewhere.

Let's say you lock down a $100,000 condo and put in $10,000 of your own money. Then the price of your hypothetical condo rises in value to $200,000. The $100,000 gain you've made equates to a 1,000% return on the $10,000 cash invested.

Or, essentially, you have gotten that condo for free.

I love using leverage. And I get a lot of questions about financing overseas real estate...

Lots of people assume that foreigners cannot get financing abroad and that they must pay cash for a property. This is the case in some places.

In other places, financing opens up all sorts of interesting opportunities.

Financing is what makes the miracle of leverage work, it's the key to maximizing our returns with your real estate investments. It's such an important strategy that I urge you to read this chapter carefully to make sure you understand the concept.

The right deal is key when using leverage. I've looked at lots of deals that have 100% finance at less than 2% and never recommended them to *RETA* because the deals didn't stack up. Don't buy a bad deal just because of cheap and easy credit.

Remember my condo purchase in Vale do Lobo on Portugal's Algarve? My partner and I found a bank fire sale and got 100% financing from the bank. The bankers simply handed us a bag of keys and sat down to their lunch. So we went exploring and found a two-bed condo with an internal elevator for €410,000 in October 2020. The bank gave us 100% financing at a very low rate. I've since seen the same unit type listed for €830,000. And, as I write, this condo is renting for €3,500 a week. (It's peak season. Late in the fall we plan to rent for six months at €2,500 a month before changing back to lucrative short-term summer renting.)

Now that's an amazing deal!

Let's look at another one, an old *RETA* deal from Spain...

North Americans can get mortgages from Spanish banks. Not a possibility in every country on my beat, but in countries where you are able to, it can be the road to those huge profits I'm talking about.

One Sunday afternoon back in 2019, I was reviewing some old recommendations I had made to *RETA* members to see how they were doing.

I came across a listing for an apartment in La Duquesa on Spain's Costa del Sol. A two-bed unit listing for €245,000.

In 2013, *RETA* members could buy here from €95,000.

It was one of the very first Spanish deals I recommended in the wake of the last big global crisis.

Turning €95,000 into €245,000 in six years (from 2013 to 2019) is quite the gain.

But let's assume the buyer bought with an 80% mortgage from a Spanish bank, which was available then—and now—to foreign buyers.

That would have put you into the deal for €19,000 and shows gains of €150,000.

That's nearly eight times your money.

Borrowing in Europe

In July 2009, Sweden's central bank cut its deposit rate to minus 0.25% overnight.

That's right…they started charging to hold funds on deposit.

It was to be a short-lived desperate policy response to the financial crisis. The idea was to encourage banks to lend more. And to create a system-wide disincentive to sit on cash.

The European Central Bank (ECB) soon followed.

For years we have been in an entrenched period of negative rates in Europe. Things look set to change. As I write, rates have just risen again. But that just makes what I am about to say all the more relevant…

Because, at least right now as I write, there has never been a better time to borrow money in Europe. For example, in Portugal,

North Americans can borrow up to 80% loan-to-value on a property at rates of less than 1% in some cases.

The ECB is offering us almost free money…and we can use this to supercharge our returns.

As you've seen, I'm personally using this play in Portugal. As are many *RETA* members.

But Portugal isn't the only place in Europe you can find attractive investment plays in which you can use leverage.

Over the past couple of years, I've sent *RETA* members my scouting reports from Italy and the South of France.

One was in France's largest wine-producing region, the Languedoc. I looked at historic village homes ideal as a base for a few months of the year that could return a 6% gross yield. That's lower than I expect for a *RETA* deal, but it was a way of owning a historic home in France that pays. And, I expect you could see an annualized capital appreciation of 6% over the next 10 years.

That trip also put the city of Montpellier high on my Europe watchlist. It is among the most attractive and exciting cities I have ever visited. It gets 300 days of sunshine a year and offers the strolling visitor a mostly pedestrian old town of winding lanes amid Renaissance-era mansions. You'll find avant-garde architecture too, art galleries, museums, superb nightlife and dining, the city even has its own Arc de Triomphe. Then there's the beach. It takes just 20 minutes or so on public transport to leave the compact city center and have your toes in the sand looking over the Mediterranean.

I've also told *RETA* members that real estate in Italy's major tourist centers is overlooked and how we stand to profit.

Even before COVID, you could find cheap real estate in Italy in places with a surging demand for short-term rentals. The economy was already fragile and there was low confidence and a weak appetite for real estate investing among Italians.

Yet millions of tourists—more than the world has ever seen before—were visiting…and are set to return. And because of the crisis, real estate prices which have been falling for 18 years, are set to fall further. It means we can own in blue-chip tourist destinations like Venice, Florence, and Rome and make a 15% yield or more.

Again, using the miracle of leverage, you can maximize your returns in these plays. It's a strategy that works anywhere you can secure financing.

I've done a deep dive into mortgage financing for foreigners in France, Italy, and Spain. The bottom line is that foreigners can borrow a significant percentage of a property's value at very low rates.

France

The typical French mortgage currently allows a buyer to borrow between 70% to 80% LTV, though some French mortgage brokers have a limit of only 50% for non-European Union buyers. U.K. and other E.U. residents/taxpayers may be able to borrow up to 85%.

Strict Banque de France lending laws state that your total debt (including rents, mortgages, and other regular expenses) cannot exceed more than one-third of your total income. If you are aged over 65, the banks will not include earned income; only passive income or retirement benefits will be considered.

All mortgage interest rates in France are linked to the Euribor (Euro Interbank Offered Rate), which was introduced at the beginning of 1999 along with the European single currency (the euro). French loans can be for between five and 25 years (but, most commonly, 15 or 20 years), depending on your age and the bank you've chosen.

So, for instance, it's possible you can borrow 80% for 15 years fixed at a rate of 1.2%. Or the same amount at a rate of 1.4% for 20 years fixed.

Italy

An Italian mortgage can be granted not just in euro but also in a different currency (such as American dollars or sterling). Current rates vary from as little as 2.05% to 2.35%.

For foreigners, banks usually allow no more than 50% to 60% LTV according to the valuation report drafted by the appointed surveyor. The minimum a bank will lend you is usually €50,000, but some banks have higher minimums. Unlike France, there is no prepayment penalty.

For people over the age of 60, the maximum loan duration is usually reduced to 15 years. If the applicant is older than 60 years, Italian banks usually require the signature of another (younger) applicant that will be jointly liable.

The instalment of the mortgage, added to other potential ongoing financial obligations, should not exceed 35% of customers' net income.

The cost of a mortgage can be quite high, with arrangement fees to pay as well as a government tax of 2% of the amount borrowed, in addition to an extra notary deed fee (usually €2,500 to €3,000).

Watch the Currency Markets for an Even Bigger Boost

Don't forget that financing becomes even more attractive when borrowing in currencies which are expected to fall in value against the dollar, since you'll be paying the loan back with the equivalent of fewer dollars.

Spain

In Spain, foreigners can currently get a mortgage up to 60% or 70% of the value of a property if they are a resident in another country within the Eurozone. As a rule of thumb, you can expect to spend an extra 10% to 14% on the agreed purchase price for taxes and extra expenses—including the full service of a local lawyer.

You need to open an account in a Spanish bank. In order to open your bank account, you will need a NIE "Número de identificación fiscal para extranjeros" or Foreign Resident's Tax Number.

It takes about six weeks to close a loan. There is a "cooling-off" period of 10 days, so this increases the timing for getting a mortgage.

If you buy your property for investment purposes you could have a tax incentive to take a loan, as you have to pay a tax on your "net income," and you are allowed to deduct some charges from your rental income.

Most Spanish lenders require that you have both life insurance and property insurance.

Fixed-rate 20-year mortgages are the most common for foreigners. The standard offering for variable rate mortgages for non-residents is EURIBOR (Euro Interbank Offered Rate) +2%. However, current EURIBOR rates are in "minus" numbers. As of June 2021, the EURIBOR rate is approximately -0.5%.

For foreigners, the fixed rate is between 2.5% to 2.85%.

Loans must be fully repaid before you reach 75 years old, so the duration will depend on your age when you apply for the loan.

100% Mortgages?

You will sometimes come across banks in Spain offering foreigners 100% mortgages. These are usually on foreclosed properties that the bank has on its books. That, to me, is a red flag. Often, the bank inflates the value of the home, so they can offer the 100% mortgage. I recommend you look elsewhere for both the home and your mortgage.

Developer Financing

With many of the special off-market deals I bring to members of *RETA*, members get offered exclusive developer financing. This is especially handy in countries where it is difficult for foreigners to get mortgages, or if they can, the terms are unattractive.

Walk into a bank in Mexico or Costa Rica, for example, and if you are very lucky, they might lend you 60% and charge you 8% or 10% for the privilege. That's after they're done weighing you down with excruciating bureaucratic requirements. Then, and only then, will they decide whether to let you borrow money—they might still refuse.

But, this is where our *RETA* members-only developer finance comes in…

Developer finance is, as the name suggests, where a developer finances a piece of the real estate you buy from him—he's the bank.

It's most commonly offered for pre-construction properties and also in markets where bank finance is extremely difficult to get for foreign buyers and/or prohibitively expensive.

Many of the deals I negotiate exclusively for *RETA* members have developer financing as an option. Often, the financing I negotiate is at interest rates far below what other foreign buyers or even locals will pay on a mortgage with a bank.

Here's how this kind of financing usually works:

Take a pre-construction condo I recommend and that you then lock down. You make a down payment when you sign the contract, usually 20% of the purchase price.

During construction you pay an additional 30% in the form of monthly and balloon payments.

When the condo is finished, you have two options: you can pay the 50% balance in cash, or take up developer finance, which can run for up to 10 years post-delivery of the condo. Interest rates start from 5%…in markets where locals can pay up to 10% on a mortgage from the bank.

When you do this, you can take up the developer finance and rent the condo out to offset costs…while putting your capital to work on another deal. And if the real estate is rising in value at the same time, you've gotten more real estate than you could have done with your own funds at the start of the deal. Again, you get to use someone else's money to finance your gains and to target that capital appreciation.

For instance, *RETA* members could buy homes in Los Cabos, Mexico, at a $152,350 discount. Finance rates on our Copala homes range from 0% to about 8%, depending on the term.

Down south on the Riviera Maya in Akumal, *RETA* members could buy fabulous two-bed, two-bath condos steps from the beach for $174,800, with five years financing available at 6.5%.

In 2020, *RETA* members were able to lock down ocean-view lots in Costa Rica that would retail for $130,000 from just $92,000. (That's a 30% discount on retail.) Upon closing they paid a 20% down pay-ment—$18,400 on a $92,000 lot. After that, payments of $613 per month for a term of 10 years. Then finally, the remaining balance.

I predict the lucky *RETA* members who got in will have the chance to sell their ocean-view lots for a sizeable profit long before 10 years has passed. I reckon gains could be as much as $78,000. (And there is no obligation to build.)

Reducing Risk

Paying 100% cash on a pre-construction deal looks like it saves money on paper, but it's not the best way to reduce risk.

Where possible, I always recommend using financing. This al-lows you to partake in a deal, locking in the potential gains, while minimizing your financial exposure.

It's important to understand that with developer finance, you typically don't own the asset until you have paid off the finance in full. The developer doesn't have to foreclose on you if you stop making your payments, he can simply take the real estate back, and keep the monies you have paid to date. He probably won't even have to go to court to do it, either.

In some countries, such as Brazil, developers must pay back some of the money you have paid on your condo if you stop making finance payments and they take the unit back…but that's not the norm. Make sure you understand the terms of your finance deal wherever you buy and do your due diligence.

Those caveats aside, get this right and it can be one of the most profitable ways in your arsenal to finance a purchase.

Seller Financing

Seller financing is where the seller is willing to finance your purchase. You make an offer. If a seller's home is worth $200,000, you can offer $50,000 now and the balance over 10 years at 5%. Offers like this can work in markets where there aren't many buyers at that moment in time, and the seller just wants out. I've even seen folks make deals where they pay zero interest. To make deals like this you need to fine-tune your negotiating skills.

In this scenario, all, or part, of the purchase price is carried by the owner. Usually, the buyer makes a down payment and then the owner and buyer agree terms on the finance.

They agree an interest rate, the term of the loan, and the monthly payment amounts. In a situation where owners are anxious to sell, that gives you leverage on negotiating good terms.

You'll need an attorney on board to advise you how best to set this up, to make sure it complies with local regulations, and to protect you as a buyer.

The upsides for you as a buyer are shorter close times—no waiting around for bank approvals or detailed credit reports—and the finance can be tailored to suit your situation.

There are some things to consider: You need to make sure the seller has no liens, loans, or mortgages on the real estate. He needs to pay those off. Otherwise, if the seller doesn't stay on top of his loans on the home, you could lose it, even if you're up to date with your finance payments to him. Your local attorney can do this due diligence for you.

Also, think about what happens if the owner sells on the loan to a third party...how will that affect you?

You negotiate the terms one-on-one with the seller. An important consideration here is when you take title. If you take title on signing the deal, you have more protections in the event of a dispute or if you miss payments. (That said, when I'm in the seller's position, I insist that title is only handed over when final payment is made.)

On the right buy and with the right owner, this can give you an edge in some markets on our beat, including Placencia, Belize.

To give you an example, I brought *RETA* members a flash deal in Belize that involved seller financing.

Placencia is a little peninsula with 16 miles of sandy beaches. It's postcard-perfect Caribbean: unspoiled white sands, palm trees swaying in the soft sea breezes, and clear, warm waters.

It's only in recent years that the highway to Placencia from Belize's capital city was paved. That was a huge step forward, making this destination much easier to get to. It's opened access up considerably for tourists, snowbirds, and expats alike.

Yet this is a relatively tiny peninsula, where most of the land is in single family home plots. Demand to own or rent a home there is rising...but there's a lack of inventory. I expect this to drive values and rental rates higher.

The deal I found was a fixer-upper, perfect for someone who doesn't mind rolling their sleeves up and adding value—or a buyer that wants to sit and hold while generating an income stream.

It was a lot with two buildings that were already generating rental income...but could do much better. The list price was $150,000. The lot was in a great central location in Placencia Village, on a quiet street that's a short walk to restaurants, stores, and only a four-minute walk to the beach.

There were two buildings on the lot, laid out as five individual rental units. The buildings were rented to local families, generating in the region of $1,225 a month as they were. That's a gross rental yield of 9.8% on the list price of $150,000. Not bad at all...

But you could target higher yields with an investment of time and money. The property could become a guesthouse or B&B. The existing buildings could be upgraded into units aimed solely at the short-term rentals market.

Alternatively, you could just sit on the property as is. Lots in the center of the village rarely come to market. There are no zoning restrictions on the lot and the central location means it's perfect for rental, long term or short term.

Now for the seller financing. The owner was willing to finance up to $100,000 of the purchase price at a rate of 6% a year. Remember, as it was you could make $1,225 a month renting to locals.

The fact that a seller is offering finance could mean that they are motivated. That might mean wiggle room on the price. For instance, my recommendation on that Placencia flash deal was to offer $130,000 for a quick cash sale.

Leverage Can Make You Rich

However you go about it, leverage is one of the most powerful tools available to a real estate investor. It's an unbelievably good way to profit from your investments.

Of course, you need to use it wisely if you want to use it to make profits. And that means using leverage on the right deals.

Everything else we do at *RETA* to find the best deals is crucial. For example, buying ahead of a Path of Progress that's set to push prices higher...or using our group buying power to negotiate a huge *RETA*-only discount.

Use Your IRA or 401k Funds

You might be surprised to hear this...but contrary to popular belief, you can buy any type of real estate using an IRA or 401K—condos; agricultural land; single family homes; commercial, retail, or office space.

You can do almost everything with the real estate you buy—buy with partners, flip it, rent it out. But some general rules apply: Your retirement fund is meant to benefit you when you retire. So, if you use the funds to buy a vacation home, you'll have to wait until you retire to enjoy your first vacation in it.

But you can buy a retirement home now using your funds and rent it out. Any rental income earned must go back into the retirement fund; however, you can sometimes set yourself up as the property manager and pay yourself a reasonable fee.

You can't purchase real estate that you already own using your funds. And you usually can't purchase from family members or "disqualified persons" (which includes anyone providing services to your fund).

But you can use the funds in your IRA or 401k fund to buy international real estate. You should check with your custodian on the rules and regulations. Some rules apply to every retirement fund, but sometimes custodians apply

---

their own investment restrictions. Even if you have a self-directed IRA or 401K, the custodian may not allow you to buy overseas real estate. You may need to transfer your account to a new custodian or set up a checkbook IRA to do that.

This is another finance strategy to consider, so it's worth checking with your custodian to see what you can do with your funds. (Note, I'm not in the business of IRA or 401K funds—you should talk to your expert advisor before making any changes to your fund set-up.)

CHAPTER 10

The Ultimate Guide to Crisis Investing

"The time to buy is when there's blood in the streets."
— Nathan Rothschild, nobleman and financier

The story goes that Nathan Rothschild was the first man in London to know of Napoleon's defeat at Waterloo.

The communications network of the Rothschild family was critical to their financial success—speedier and more reliable than any other in Europe, including that of the British government.

The Rothschild's traded on information as much as goods and gold.

When Rothschild heard the news of Waterloo in June 1815, he went immediately to the authorities to share it. But they refused to believe him.

Along with the rest of England, they were still reeling from the news two days before of the English defeat at Quatre Bras.

So, not a man to miss an opportunity, Rothschild went to the stock exchange...

There he began selling his console, a form of government bonds. The whisper rippled through... "Rothschild knows. Waterloo is lost." A great sell off began and prices plummeted.

Then Rothschild began to buy...

Rothschild wasn't the first man to make a fortune from a panic or a crisis. Nor the last...

Buying right in a crisis has made vast fortunes throughout history. Think of a crisis as a massive transformation in its own right, a major event that can turn everything upside down...at least for a while.

But you have to play it right and recognize two important things: First, not every crisis is an opportunity. Some are just a mess with no sign of recovery or growth on the horizon. Investing into a crisis without a clear path of recovery in view is pure speculation and let's face it, roulette is an easier way to throw money at chance.

The second thing to recognize is the thing in the crisis that does present enormous opportunity. That is, you need to see the trigger event. The time to buy is not necessarily when there is literally blood on the streets. It might be...or it might be several years into the crisis. Real estate's liquidity or the lack thereof makes playing real estate in a crisis different to other more liquid assets.

Take possibly the best crisis recommendation I ever made close to St. Stephens Green in the Irish capital, Dublin. One with a potential leveraged gain of 1,567% plus a healthy income stream.

Today, the Irish capital is booming. Real estate prices are soaring and supply is scarce and squeezed. The city's docklands have been transformed.

You'll share trendy gastro pubs with youthful tech workers from all around the world. The European headquarters of giants like Google and Facebook are here. The newsstands carry headlines shouting about the country's shortage of housing...rising property prices...

How different to 2009 when the financial crisis flattened Ireland's deeply exposed financial structures. Ireland was in turmoil as banks collapsed in spectacular fashion and the Irish real estate market went "no bid."

The way things played out from there is perhaps the clearest example of what the right kind of crisis can mean for real estate investors like us.

In 2009, I was in Dublin as the biggest corporate losses in Irish history were being reported and I witnessed from the streets of the Irish capital the drama of collapsing banks.

Yet it wasn't until 2011 that I began making my recommendations. It was only then, three years after the crisis had begun, that I recognized the trigger event. This was non-Irish banks exiting the country and offloaded properties in fire-sale auctions. It forced sellers and officials to face reality and kick-started the real estate market.

My predictions at the time were considered by some to be bold, even insane. Time has proven them to have been conservative.

For instance, in February 2012 I recommended to members of *Real Estate Trend Alert* a two-bedroom apartment in Dublin's financial district selling for €135,000 (about $179,000 at the time). I wrote, "Your tenants will be nurses, tech workers (in Google or Facebook), young accountants and lawyers, in their mid to late twenties."

Today, two-bedroom apartments in the same area sell for €450,000 ($449,789). That's a 233.33% gain on capital appreciation alone. With leverage (if you borrowed 80%) that becomes 1,567% (before transactions costs)...and that doesn't even include the €25,000 to €30,000 you would have collected in rents every single year.

In my home city of Cork too, I made recommendations around that time. In 2015, I recommended old, terraced houses in the area at the top of St. Patrick's Hill, which lies just north of Cork city center. At the time I recommended them, a two-bedroom, two-bathroom house on St Patrick's Hill listed for just €60,000. One just listed for €250,000 as I write in August 2022. That's a huge gain in just a few years and all because we found the right neighborhood and the right play.

Why was I bullish? Despite the crisis I saw demand from young professionals was still strong in Dublin. I saw this clearly. I asked the right questions in the right places. Spoke to managers in multinationals and contacts in the new industries. I saw their medium-term hiring plans and understood correctly that Dublin was set to continue its development as an international city. I focused on the right neighborhoods and found the right kind of properties to take full advantage of the bounceback.

In Cork the story was similar. The multinational pharma giants and Apple were expanding, the fundamentals driving demand were still strong. The city center houses I identified as the best opportunities were ideal for the young professionals being attracted to the city. In recent years, Cork has been going through something of a mini-renaissance. An estimated €1 billion is being ploughed into a mix of commercial and residential development in the city's docklands area. And now an ambitious multi-million regeneration project is set to transform the area where we had our opportunity.

Like I've said, the common error to avoid with any crisis is to assume the moment to buy is when the blood is literally in the streets. It might be, but what you're really looking for is some kind of trigger event that signals your buying moment.

In Ireland that trigger event was the 2011 fire-sale auctions. Properties were selling at these auctions in some cases for around 70% less than previous peak prices. From there it became clear where prices were truly at and the market went from nothing happening to bargain-hunters bonanza.

In 2013, the trigger event in Spain was similar to Ireland, fire-sale auctions held by the country's newly created bad bank SAREB. This bank took on a vast and mixed property portfolio and was charged with liquidating it.

Bankers and bureaucrats are not good at selling real estate. It's not their business. And in the case of Spain, there was little incentive to do it well. This created all sorts of outstanding opportunities, albeit difficult to dig out and act on.

Thankfully I had a good layer of contacts on the Costa del Sol, Spain's internationalized southern coast. This is where you'll find Marbella and some of the best golf and beaches in Europe. It's an enormously popular destination. This is where northern Europeans come for vacation and retirement. All the big demographic trends and geopolitics were in their favor. The outlook was stronger than ever.

RETA members who got in on my recommendations from Spain's Costa del Sol have seen a doubling in values from playing that crisis wisely. Banks started selling condos at as much as 80% off right across Spain.

The condos I recommended just outside Puerto Banus for €139,000 would list, as I write in 2022, for €320,000. And, could generate €28,000 a year in short-term rental income. As in Ireland, if you bought with an 80% mortgage you are talking about five times your money.

The global financial crisis has echoed on too…

In August 2020, I was able to recommend bank fire-sale condos in Spain to *RETA* members at 50% off. The backstory was classic financial crisis. A developer got into trouble. The bank bungled its way into the real estate business. They hammered out a big deal with a Scandinavian group to buy every condo, but it fell through…

The bank just wanted out and decided to sell the condos themselves at a fat discount of 27% off. That was a good deal. But it became an amazing deal because the bank's launch was scheduled for March 2020. On March 14 a lockdown was imposed across Spain. Launch postponed.

When the Costa del Sol re-opened, the bank determined to offload everything fast. To do it they knocked another 23% off.

So *RETA* members were able to own these luxury apartments in one of the best locations on the Costa del Sol at 50% off. Our price from just €164,000 ($193,337 at the time).

That was reduced from €325,000.

Penthouses that were €665,000 were ours for just €350,000. But we had to move fast.

It was a killer deal. We were buying for less than the cost of construction. Across the road at the time, smaller apartments were selling for €91,000 more than we were paying. Plus, *RETA* members could take advantage of bank financing in Spain.

The location of these condos is amazing, right opposite one of Europe's most prestigious and luxurious golf resorts, the Finca Cortesin, only a mile from the beach. and less than an hour from the international airport in Malaga. The finishes are immaculate.

Another echo of the financial crisis was my condo purchase in Vale do Lobo, on Portugal's Algarve, which I've told you about. My partner and I found a bank fire sale and got 100% financing from the bank. The bankers simply handed us a bag of keys and sat down to their lunch. So we went exploring and found a two-bed condo with an internal elevator for €410,000 in October 2020. The bank gave us 100% financing at a very low rate. I've since seen the same unit type listed for €830,000. In August, this condo was renting for €3,500 a week. Late in the fall we plan to rent for six months at €2,500 a month before changing back to lucrative short-term summer renting.

Finding out about these crisis deals is not easy. They don't get advertised widely, if at all.

Like Baron Rothschild at the opening of this chapter, it starts with the right information and connections. Which is why I work very hard to nurture my global network of contacts for the benefit of *RETA*.

As you can see, it can be very much worth the effort.

Some Clouds Have No Silver Lining

Like I say, it's important to recognize that not every crisis offers us an opportunity.

Check your newsfeed right now and you'll see a world in turmoil, a crisis in every corner. But you won't find me recommending many crisis deals despite the fact that I love this play.

As an investor I don't want to gamble on a recovery...I want to feel it's a sure thing. And by recovery I mean a post-crisis scenario that will see values soar. It doesn't imply things will be perfect. Just that for a crisis to be an opportunity you have to see a clear end to the crisis and a compelling reason for a bounceback in the future. A clear and easy to understand reason that there will be demand for the real estate we can buy for a song.

Put simply, you want a clear path to profits. In both Spain's Costa del Sol and Ireland's two big cities, there was every sign that demand for the right kind of real estate would continue and grow stronger.

Compare this to crisis-ridden Venezuela, which is stuck in an economic nightmare. I've been keeping a close eye. I haven't moved though. I haven't recommended anything. I won't do so unless or until there's some clear path to profit.

It's a sad state of affairs and I feel for the people. Venezuela should be an economic powerhouse. In 1950, when the rest of the world was struggling to recover from the war, Venezuela was the fourth richest country on earth. It still has the largest oil reserves in the world...vast, rich agricultural plains...stunning beaches and colonial cities…it's just that terrible ideas and corruption have poisoned all that promise.

Yet the country teeters on the edge of economic collapse. The rate of inflation has slowed as I write, though it is still among the highest in the world. Around half the payments for goods in the capital are made in foreign currency.

During the worst of the hyperinflation, my contacts in Venezuela told me restaurant menus came with a separate sheet of prices because those change so often. Things just disappear from the stores…no toilet paper…no milk…then they reappear. You hear of scavenger hunts for daily staples. One contact told me the surreal tale of visiting a supermarket and finding every shelf stocked with ketchup because that's all the store had.

In a strange twist, bullets became so expensive that hardened criminals complained they couldn't afford to fire their guns. The murder rate fell and the kidnap rate plummeted because few people could pay a ransom.

The poverty rate soared to 90%. Millions of Venezuelans left and millions more are trying to follow. It's incredibly sad to see and it's impacting the entire region.

The real estate market is completely dysfunctional. Last I heard, a house in a nice neighborhood can go for $15,000 and a similar property next door might have an asking price of $500,000. It entirely depends on the personal situation of the seller and how desperate they are for cash. Some folks will sit it out in the hopes of better days…others want out right now and will take what they can get.

So, in Venezuela we have a deep, intractable crisis. And we can find real estate going for a song. Yet no one can accurately predict when/if reform and stability will come to Venezuela. Things could get much worse before they get better. Right now, there is no clear path to profits…no compelling sign of a bounceback.

In this case, bounceback means when will vacationers feel safe to return in big numbers, or foreign oil companies come back and need housing for their foreign workers and executives.

In the meantime, all we can do is prepare for when/if the sign of bounceback comes. Keep watching. One place I have my eye on is Isla Margarita, an island off the coast of Venezuela in the Caribbean Sea. It has 198 miles of coastline and around 80 beaches. It was once a destination for the jet set. Tourism took off in the 1970s when the town of Porlamar became a duty-free port.

Throughout the 1980s and 1990s it was a popular spot. Direct flights from Europe, the U.S., and Canada made for an international mix of vacationers. They came for classic fun in the sun on a Caribbean island.

It still has the pristine beaches that once drew thousands of tourists. And they aren't making any more Caribbean islands. When things stabilize, tourists will flock back. I'm not talking about the return of a Venezuelan golden era—just a sense of security. Venezuelans will flock back too. There are millions overseas and a lot of Venezuelan capital has also been moved to safety, some of it will be going home once the bounceback comes.

I'm interested in beachfront land on Isla Margarita, little hotels and condo buildings, or hotels that can be converted to condos. We could buy using all the tricks and strategies we learned in previous crises like Ireland and Spain.

But we need to see the bounceback...the road to recovery... before committing any money.

In every crisis we need a picture in mind about how the market is likely to recover—and how the property we buy is likely to perform in that market.

The Crises of Christmas Past

You don't always need a crisis to benefit from crisis-level pricing. Sometimes the reputation of a crisis is enough to depress prices long after a crisis abates.

It's a form of perception hacking. All we need to do is see things for how they truly are and filter out the noise.

That's what's happened in Medellín, Colombia. Medellín existed in the shadow of its violent past for a long time meaning that prices were way below what they should have been. Most people looked at Medellín as a place for drug cartels and violence.

But in 2011, I was hearing things from my contacts. So, I visited and found a city set to boom. I could clearly see the big unstoppable trends at work. Money had been spent on infrastructure, security was good, and the climate was perfect year-round. The expat scene was small but growing. International companies were setting up, executives were coming, digital nomads, too…

I spent time looking at real estate in the city and soon focused on the high-end neighborhood of El Poblado. I recommended condos there going for $800 per square meter. Since then, values have doubled. And rents have grown strongly, too.

Exchange rate movements may have eaten in to some gains but while the exchange rate bounces around, folks can keep making income. Airbnb monthly and three-monthly rentals to the flood of digital nomads are particularly strong say my contacts on the ground.

From there, the opportunity to buy low ahead of the transformation spread to neighboring Laureles. There I recommended big homes for around $150,000 that today are worth $350,000 to $400,000.

Today, Medellín's reputation has changed. Foreigners, once a rare sight, are now commonplace. And real estate prices rose to reflect the value of the city today—a cosmopolitan and sophisticated international place. By getting in after the true crisis, ahead of the crowd, *RETA* members were set up for a big win. It was the perfect buying moment.

By the way, one of the expats who discovered Medellín and now lives there is our *RETA* Concierge, Nancy Kiernan. From Massachusetts originally, Nancy and her team help *RETA* members get the best out of our group. You can arrange a chat with Nancy or another of the *RETA* concierge team at: *https://realestatetrendalert.com/concierge/* or by scanning the QR code:

Turn on camera app   Frame the QR   Click the pop-up

Special Situations: A Crisis Around Every Corner?

It's not just countries or the global economy that can tumble into crisis. In every market, no matter how buoyant, you can often find special situation deals—the chance to buy below market value.

The best of these special situation deals can be easy to find as long as you have the right contacts and a good understanding of the local market. This is at the core of why I've spent nearly two decades carefully cultivating relationships with a multitude of insiders in markets all over the world.

Special situation deals are usually "blink and you miss 'em" deals when a seller wants out fast and is willing to sell under market value to do so.

Sometimes the opportunity comes out of the blue or on the back of a scouting trip I've taken. Like when I traveled to Costa Rica's lake district, Arenal, a few years back.

The deal there was that you could own a five-bedroom, three-bathroom guesthouse just a few minutes' walk or bike ride from the town of Nuevo Arenal. The house was in need of serious refurbishment. It needed someone who had the time and will to take on a project. For the right investor, it was a great buy. There was a shortage of rooms to rent short term in downtown Nuevo Arenal, and this guesthouse could make you up to $50 a night from each of those five rooms. At full occupancy for just a third of the year, that's a gross yield of $30,000.

The guesthouse initially listed for $200,000. But the seller had dropped the price to $145,000. He was experiencing some personal issues that motivated him to sell. I recommended offering $100,000 for it and—if accepted—spending $30,000 to $50,000 on refurbishment.

This was a complete one-off—the type of opportunity you only hear about from being dialed in to a real estate market and having the contacts who can tip you off about these kinds of deals.

Another example was a luxurious ocean-view villa in Nicaragua…

In May 2020, I got a tip off from my contact in San Juan del Sur, the most popular beach-town in the country about this bargain. I immediately sent details to *RETA* members.

From an original price of $789,000, this six-bed, three-story home overlooking the Pacific in San Juan del Sur, Nicaragua, was down to $250,000.

I reckoned an offer of $220,000 could get you the property. I didn't even count the cost of the land it was built on.

Within days the villa was reserved. I think the final price was indeed $220,000.

It was a familiar story. The owner had passed away and his family back in the States simply weren't interested in owning a luxury villa in Nicaragua. They wanted a quick sale.

Whenever I get word of deals like this, I send a flash announcement to *Real Estate Trend Alert*. It's a good reason to tune into your email!

The Flip Side of Crisis: How to Protect Yourself

We both know it makes sense to diversify your portfolio. That way, if you take a hit on one, life goes on.

I've diversified through real estate with exposure to different markets across the world. If something happens to the euro and Portugal, I still have income coming in dollars and a condo in Cabo...and so on. If British vacationers can't rent my Silver Coast condo because COVID stops them flying, the Portuguese and Spanish can still drive.

One of the biggest advantages to investing overseas is that if things were ever to go belly up in the U.S., having some of your money outside the U.S. could be the only thing to save your hide. You're not leaving your entire nest egg at the mercy of one market. As I've told you, in 2008 and 2009, as real estate and stock market values imploded back home, we were hitting home runs in north east Brazil. The market there was on a tear.

If your portfolio is entirely reliant on one single currency's staying strong, you could be in for a shock if things take a turn for the worst. If you have an entirely dollar-denominated, stock-heavy retirement portfolio, you're exposing yourself to two big risks: Inflation and currency devaluation. Both of these can erode your buying power and force you to dip into your savings sooner and more often than you'd planned. By investing in real estate markets that don't use the dollar, you minimize your risk and have greater potential to maximize your returns.

CHAPTER 11

The Most Important Rule
of Real Estate Investing

"Diligence is the mother of good luck". – Benjamin Franklin

"I wired the money for the house I was buying to my attorney. Now he has a new car and is on vacation in the Caribbean. He's not answering his phone or email. He has all my money and I don't have the house."

None of us want to be the guy who sent that email to one of my team a few years back.

That's why this chapter is about the most important thing you can do to ensure you're set up for a slam-dunk venture.

It's the number one rule for successful real estate investing. And it's just three words: do your homework.

Doing your homework (also known as doing your due diligence) means thoroughly investigating an opportunity before you make a decision to buy. With a clear process for doing due diligence you'll save time and energy.

This is especially important when you're buying in an unfamiliar market. I wager you and I are savvy enough to know we'll find a few scoundrels in every corner of the world. I bet you know a few in your home town. The thing is, on our home turf most of us can spot a deal that's too good to be true. We have years of experience, we know people. We know how it all works.

After decades deep-diving into real estate markets across the globe, I know how "it" works pretty much everywhere. I have built a team around me to help untangle and assess potential real estate opportunities. And I can tell you a few of the toe-curling stories of fraud and deception I've heard on my travels. Much more common though are not criminal scams, but tales of title issues, problems with water, utilities, and infrastructure…a result of not doing enough or any due diligence.

So, I've prepared a checklist. Your basic blueprint for due diligence. You can apply this list to any real estate purchase and you'll be doing smart things to safeguard your money.

Before I give you this checklist though, let me explain that I'm a big picture guy. I start with the big picture long before getting into the nitty gritty. I want to be sure that unstoppable trends are at play and that a massive transformation is truly underway. Getting in ahead of these is step one, that's before I bring in my team and the lawyers to pour over any paper details.

Most of the top-level due diligence I do these days is on the developers and the people behind potential opportunities. I often don't meet them face-to-face until I've spent dozens of hours forming a view of them.

That said, the following checklist forms sound principles to use whenever you buy—principles that have helped me to make strong investments, and that have prevented me from investing in questionable or downright dodgy deals. It's also something used successfully by many members of my *Real Estate Trend Alert*. Among us I know we have applied this to hundreds of overseas property purchases. If you're serious about investing in real estate, this checklist is your most valuable tool.

Your Due Diligence Checklist

1. Avoid the "Margarita Effect"
2. Hire a local attorney
3. Buy title insurance
4. Check the sale contract
5. Check the title deed
6. Check permits and approvals
7. Check access
8. Check infrastructure essentials
9. Check the developer's background
10. Check the master plan
11. Check the CCRs and HOAs
12. Investigate tax issues and wills
13. Use approved escrow services

These 13 steps are the building blocks of buying well overseas. Let 's go through them one at a time.

Step #1: Avoid the "Margarita Effect" When Buying Overseas

There's a strange phenomenon I've seen time and time again. Sensible, cautious people take a vacation somewhere exotic. When they're taking an evening stroll on the beach, they see a "For Sale" sign. Suddenly all their common sense goes out the window. There and then, they decide they must have the little house by the beach. This phenomenon happens to otherwise careful people. They don't speak the language. They can't read or understand their contract. And yet they commit to buying a new house in a country they don't know all that well, without ever consulting a lawyer or doing the necessary checks.

Maybe it's the effect of too much sun—or a margarita too many.

Whatever it is, it often leads to buyer's remorse. And it's not something you should let happen to you. Your approach to buying in any country should be the same no matter where it is: measured and rigorous, with all your homework done.

The rules for purchasing may be different, and the way the sale is conducted differs from country to country but the basic principles are universal. Do your homework and keep your head.

At home, you wouldn't trust some guy you met in a bar who tells you his friend has a great deal on some land. It's been in the family for generations, he tells you. The only problem, he says over a cold beer, is that it doesn't have permitting yet so that you can build. But that will be no problem, he promises. It's a quick and easy process. He knows someone who can move the process along…for a fee, of course.

Except after you meet this guy's friend and hand over the cash, you hit problems. Maybe someone else claims the land you've just paid for. Or the permitting process is restrictive, slow, or a complete no-go for new builds.

Reading this, you might wonder who would buy property from a stranger they met in a bar? And without checking title or permitting? The answer: more people than you would think.

You wouldn't spend hundreds of thousands of dollars to buy a place back home without digging deeper into the deal, so why would you act any differently when you're buying overseas.

Follow the same tried and true steps you would at home.

Step #2: Hire a Good, Local, In-Country Attorney

Using an attorney to vet your deal is good. In fact, it's essential. But it's not a good idea to use your attorney back home when buying overseas.

Sure, you've got a comfort level with the attorney you've used for years. They know you. Know your personal situation. Right down to the name of your partner, your kids, and your dog. And your attorney might know a lot about real estate in your part of the world.

What they don't know is the legal system or the buying process in other countries. Without country-specific legal knowledge and experience, an attorney can walk you into trouble. Some legal terms used overseas sound very similar to ones you use back home—but don't mean the same thing.

Additionally, the type of legal system overseas is likely different from the one you're used to. In most of the U.S. and Canada, common law is used. In the world of real estate, common law is very forgiving if you make a mistake or something goes wrong. You argue your case, plead for forgiveness, and reach a compromise with the seller.

Overseas, most countries use civil law. Civil law is much less forgiving. It's black and white. There's no grey area. You are either right or wrong.

Your home attorney just won't cut it. A different system of law; different clauses and terms; and a different buying process. To make sure you're getting the best legal advice overseas, you need to find a competent in-country attorney.

The way you find an in-country attorney is the same way you find one back home. Look for word-of-mouth recommendations. If you have friends, family, or colleagues who have bought in a certain country, ask them which attorney they used and whether it was a good experience.

Don't just take any recommendation, though. Do not—I repeat—do not use the attorney the broker or a developer recommends. And you should make sure, when you find your attorney, that he or she works only for you. To most of us, that may sound like a given. But it's not a given overseas. In many countries, an attorney can legally represent both sides in a transaction. In their country, it may not be seen as a conflict of interest. So, feasibly, the attorney could be representing you as the buyer, and also the seller, without telling you. Ask your attorney specifically if they have any connection with, or represent, the seller.

If you're having trouble finding an attorney and you're a member of my *Real Estate Trend Alert* service, then remember you have access to my rolodex of contacts from around the world. Inside you'll find the names and contact details of attorneys that I and other *RETA* members have used in different countries. Go to *Realestatetrendalert. com/rolodex*.

Tips on Getting the Right Attorney

Look for an attorney who is bilingual. You should be able to understand exactly what your attorney is telling you and make sure that he's carrying out your instructions to the letter.

Find an attorney with an interest in real estate or one who regularly handles real estate transactions. He or she is going to be more familiar with local laws, good (and bad) developers, neighborhoods with issues, etc.

Ask your attorney to make sure that every promise the seller has made to you about the property is covered in the contract. Don't just take a seller's word for it.

Ask your attorney to explain any clauses in the contract that you don't understand. Your attorney may not think to explain a clause that is normal procedure in his country—but it may be very different to how you'd do things back home.

That works in the other direction, too. Sometimes you will see a term that looks like one you're familiar with back home. But never assume it means exactly the same thing. Commonly used legal terms can have different meanings from country to country.

Step #3: Buy Title Insurance

In some locations overseas, getting title insurance can be a good idea. That's why I've added it to this checklist. Your attorney can advise you best in this regard.

What is it? Title insurance is designed to protect a buyer from title claims, liens, and other unforeseen issues that may exist pre-purchase but only become apparent post-purchase. It covers defects in title, property taxes, boundary disputes, hidden defects (fraud, forgery, and unknown heirs)—up to the point when you buy the property.

Title insurance does not cover events (including political risk) that arise after you purchase. You are protected up until the point you buy the property. A big caveat here: Anything that you are aware of at the time of purchase is not covered.

Title insurance is available in many countries overseas. You pay a one-off payment upfront and that lasts as long as you (or your heirs) own the property. In the case of a claim, your insurer will cover the defense costs and/or actual loss. If someone challenges your title, based on a past event—forgery of documents, fraud, someone selling a property who was not entitled to do so—then the insurer has a duty to defend that title.

As with any kind of insurance product, not all title insurance policies are equal. Do your research to find the best kind for you. Be aware that specific situations may be excluded from your insurance policy. And they may be the very things that are most likely to go wrong. Check exclusions in your title insurance cover carefully, and be aware they vary from country to country.

Title insurance isn't just for constructed properties. It works slightly differently in the case of pre-construction property. You can get a commitment to title insurance on pre-construction property. That commitment has to be renewed every six months.

Don't rely on the fact that a developer has a master title insurance policy in place. It is a great sign if a developer has one, but it does not cover you; it only covers property he owns. Once the developer has sold you a property—whether that is a lot, a condo, or a home—his insurance cover on that piece of property ends. You need to get individual title insurance when you're ready to buy.

By the way, it's not necessarily a red flag if a developer doesn't have a master title insurance policy, but you should always ask why. Sometimes the answer is simple: He may be dealing with local buyers, who don't ask for title insurance. Or the developer may never have even heard of title insurance—not unusual in some countries.

Today, some of the better-known title insurance companies are no longer offering cover in Latin America, Mexico, or the Caribbean. Others are only offering limited cover or raising their minimum charge per policy. This is not because they see these as high-risk locations; they're simply not profitable enough for these companies (most locals don't buy title insurance). If you have any questions about title insurance, contact Tuey Murdock. *Email: tueymurdock@gmail.com.* Tuey, an attorney who worked with First American Title Insurance for a couple of decades, now runs her own company to help buyers find the best title insurance policy on the market.

Step #4: Check the Sale Contract

The sale contract spells out your agreement with the seller. It covers who pays what, how much, and when. It details what you get—the kitchen cabinetry, the air conditioners, perhaps the light fixtures. And it lays out what happens if either you or the seller fail to comply with any of the contract clauses.

Ensuring that you understand your contract is essential. If you don't understand what you're buying, or you're not happy with any part of it, don't sign the sale contract. Trying to renegotiate after you have signed that contract is pointless. Once you've signed, you're legally committed to what's in the document.

Make sure that the contract you're reading is the legally binding version. Sometimes a developer or seller will give you a sale contract or purchase agreement in English. That's a nice courtesy but it may not be the binding contract. Only a contract that is in the official language of the country that you are buying in is legally binding, whether that is Spanish or Portuguese or French. If you have a dispute with the seller, if you need to go to court, then the contract in the language of the country will be the one that you use.

Have your attorney translate the sale contract for you. Ask your attorney to explain any clauses or terms that you are not sure of.

Here are some major ones to look out for:

- Check that the property details, description, and price are correct.

- Check that the seller's name matches the name on the current title deed.

- Ask your attorney to check that your sale contract/purchase agreement gives you title, free and clear, on closing. That may seem obvious but sometimes contracts don't give you title on closing. I've seen a few that give you possession of a condo, and the keys, but not the actual registered title. Instead, the developer simply stated that he would register it at some point (with an undefined time period). Have a specific timeframe in the contract for you to get your title deed—and hold money back until that happens.

I've also seen a few contracts that gave title but did not include a mechanism for the seller paying off his mortgage related to the property. The mortgage stays with the property in most countries overseas. For that reason, if a seller has a mortgage, have him pay if off in full before the property title transfers to you. Also make sure that there are no outstanding taxes, fines, HOA fees, water rates or liens on the property.

- Check for any unfair penalty clauses in your contract. Sellers like to incorporate penalty clauses into your contract. It's normal overseas that once you sign the contract, if you default for any reason you will lose the property and whatever monies you have paid to date. I have seen contracts where they not only keep the property and the money, but make you pay the full purchase price—and sometimes add a fine on top.

Penalty clauses should work the other way, too. Ask what happens if the seller defaults (say, by not transferring title to the property to you within the agreed timeframe). You should ask for all penalties to be reciprocal.

- Check any price adjustments. These apply to pre-construction property. In some countries, such as Brazil, Costa Rica, Panama, and Mexico, for example, some developers include a clause stating that if construction costs rise during the build period, they can charge an additional fee, based on a percentage of the property's purchase price. That percentage can be as high as 10%. So, in that case, if you agreed a purchase price of $100,000 for your condo, you could end up paying $110,000.

The additional fee is payable on closing in many countries. Developers are supposed to prove that construction costs have actually risen, using government figures and statistics. In Brazil, the adjustment is monthly, if you are making monthly payments to the developer during the construction period.

Step #5: Check the Title Deed

A retiree showed one of my team photos of a house in Costa Rica he planned to buy. It looked luxurious. He loved its ocean views, its wide balconies, and its fancy finishes. But there was one big glitch...

It wasn't titled. And it was in a zone where foreigners are not allowed to own property.

Another expat approached one of my team to ask about a project in Panama. Again, it wasn't titled. It was in a concession zone where you're not supposed to build residential homes. Unfortunately, we were too late in this case. The guy had already paid $500,000 for a condo. Ouch…

Freehold titled ownership is just one type of ownership, the one you're likely most familiar with back home. But you'll see other ways of owning property overseas.

One is rights of possession property, known as *derecho posesorio* or ROP. The name says it all. With ROP, you get the right to live on the property, use it and enjoy it, until someone with a better claim shows up. In some cases, that doesn't take long. One buyer contacted us about a ROP property they purchased and enjoyed—for all of a week, before someone showed up and laid claim to it. They lost the property and the money they had paid for it.

ROP land is sometimes common or shared land, given by the government to locals to farm.

Other times it's land acquired through squatter's rights, where folks move onto a property and stay there unchallenged for long enough to acquire rights, called adverse possession.

Occasionally it's land that a family has lived on and used for generations and simply never got round to titling.

If you're considering a ROP property and the seller says that he can get a freehold title for it, great. But get him to do that as a condition of purchase. No title, no closing. Don't try getting it titled yourself. It's often complicated, costly, and time-consuming.

The other type of property you'll come across is concession property. In many countries overseas, beaches are public. They're inside a maritime zone. Governments often grant concessions, a type of lease, in this zone.

But beware the word "lease". This is not the same as buying leasehold property back home where you get the benefit of laws and regulations governing how much you pay per year, automatic renewal of the lease and the cost of renewal.

That's not the case with leases in concession zones. New governments sometimes decide they don't like the decisions of previous officials—and may revoke the leases, change the terms or hike the cost. There are some other restrictions with concession zone property. Foreign ownership of concession land is often restricted. And normally only tourist-type development is allowed—resorts and hotels, perhaps a dive shop or beach bar. But developers sometimes ignore this basic requirement.

So, before you get into the nitty-gritty of your sale contract, take a few minutes to ask your attorney the basic question: Is this fee simple/titled property? It can save an awful lot of headaches and hassle later on.

Then, when it comes to checking the title chain to make sure it's good...In some countries the registry is online. Buy in Panama or Costa Rica, and your attorney can check the title chain for a property anywhere in the country from the comfort of their office. In other countries, the attorney (or a notary or trusted contact) will have to search through physical documents to check the title.

From that title check, your attorney should be able to tell you the current registered owner and value, the boundaries, previous sales and transfers, whether there are any liens or mortgages or taxes outstanding on the property, and if there are any annotations such as rights of way, etc.

Some things that you should have your attorney check when investigating title:

- Make sure that your seller is the property owner. This is an obvious one, but important. Make sure the person you're buying from has the right to sell the property.

- Check if your title is registered or possessory. In some countries as I say, they can seem similar. You can live in a Rights of Possession property, record your claim to it, and you can sell it. There is a difference, however. Registered title means you own the land. Possession means you have the right to occupy the property, until someone with a better claim to it turns up. When they do, you may lose the property and the money that you paid for it. I recommend that you only purchase freehold, titled, fee simple property.

- Check the title chain. Be careful if there's a record of *co-operativa* (shared ownership) or confiscation. Similarly, in Mexico, if land was formerly *ejido* (indigenous-owned) land, tread carefully. Both issues can be a potential landmine, as they could indicate that someone may lay claim to your property in the future. In these instances, your attorney will have to do extra checks to make sure that the title is clear, and all transfers were done correctly.

- Make sure you can own that piece of beachfront. The right piece of beachfront land may sound like a great buy. But be careful that you can actually own it. Most countries overseas have a section of the beach related to the high-water mark where you cannot legally own a property.

That caution doesn't just apply to owning beachfront land. I've come across cases of people buying beachfront condos, just meters from the water. The only problem was that it was illegal to build or own residential property there.

- Check if you can legally own as a foreigner. Occasionally you, as a foreign buyer, will be barred from purchasing what a local can buy. Foreign buyers are usually not allowed to own property close to a country's international borders. The distances for these zones are not standardized, but vary from country to country, so be sure to double-check what that distance is if you are planning on buying near the border.

Foreigners may face restrictions, too, on Caribbean islands for example. They may not be able to buy investment property (where they rent the property out rather than keeping it for personal use), or they have to purchase a property in certain areas or of a certain value.

In some countries, too, particularly in Asia, foreigners cannot legally own property outright. There are sometimes ways around this, but ask your attorney to investigate thoroughly.

Step #6: Check the Permits and Approvals

Never take a seller's or developer's word that all the necessary permits are in place. I don't care if they seem to be the most trustworthy individual. It doesn't matter if they're a respected businessman, someone with political connections, or a billionaire.

A verbal contract about permitting isn't worth anything. Get your attorney to check that all the promised permits are in place.

If a developer is open with you that they are waiting on a permit or two, that is not necessarily a black mark against him/her. In many countries, patience is a must-have when it comes to permits. Especially in the aftermath of the global pandemic, there were tremendous bureaucratic backlogs in many corners of the world. Add to this that in some countries, there are far more bureaucratic hurdles to get through before a permit will be granted.

There are a number of necessary permits to get in any development. The standard ones are environmental, water, construction, and municipal permits.

(By the way, if you're buying land with a view to developing it, you need to be even more familiar with the country's permitting requirements and processes. You need to know how long the process takes, how much it costs, and what you will need to do to comply with regulations.)

Have your in-country attorney check to make sure that your seller/developer has all the permits and approvals he needs to comply with current regulations.

Many countries require projects to have developmental and environmental pre-approval before they can be legally marketed or sold. That process can take up to two years, and until pre-approval is granted, the developer cannot start selling—or construction.

If you're in a country that bans marketing and selling before that pre-approval is granted, and a developer is selling without it, take that as a red flag. If a developer hasn't done things correctly at that early stage, it could be a sign that there will be problems further down the track.

But the lack of a particular permit doesn't always mean a developer is crooked. As I said, permitting processes can be slow in a lot of countries. If you're buying abroad, you need to be aware of that. If you're offered the chance to buy in a development that has all but one final permit granted, you may decide it's worth the investment and go ahead, anyway.

That's fine. In most cases, that permit is likely to come through. But never take it as a given. And make sure you protect yourself in that situation. If you find yourself in a situation where you want to buy but the developer is waiting for one last permit, tell him that you're putting your money (whether it's a deposit or the full purchase price) in escrow until the permit is granted. That way, you're protected if he doesn't get the permit—and you won't have to fight to get your money back.

Permitting issues don't just apply to pre-construction properties. Just because something is move-in ready doesn't mean it has all the necessary permits.

In some countries, you can see houses for sale that have either never applied for planning approval, or had initial approval but subsequently added an extra unapproved bedroom or garage. This is particularly true in rural areas. It can lead to problems if the authorities fine you or order the home to be demolished. Have your attorney check for you, and ideally get the seller to legalize the property before you buy it.

Step # 7: Check Access

Never assume that you have automatic access to the property that you are buying. The broker/seller might have taken you on a certain road to view a property. But that doesn't mean he has permission to. If access to the property is via a right-of-way through someone else's property, that needs to be stated in the deed.

And don't assume only you have the right of way through your property. Have your attorney check this for you, and ask neighbors and locals if anyone has been using your property as a right of way for any time period.

Step #8: Check Infrastructure Essentials

No matter what you're planning to do after you buy a property overseas, you need to make sure you're comfortable with the infrastructure in place. That applies whether you plan to live in it yourself, rent it out, or develop a piece of land.

Infrastructure may be way down your list when you're thinking of buying property. But in the long run, the infrastructure—or lack thereof—can have a big effect on how comfortable or hassle-free your purchase is, and how valuable the property is.

You may be willing to buy initially without some of the essential infrastructure in place for the sake of a good deal. The lack of infrastructure might not be a deal breaker in that scenario. But you should always ask the questions below before you buy.

Water:

- Is there a source of potable water on the property?

- What's the water pressure?

- What's the purity?

- If there isn't a mains supply, who will drill a well? If it is you, can you get a permit to do that, and if so, how deep will you have to drill—and how much will that cost?

- How is waste treatment being handled? And does it comply with local regulations?

- Will there be a municipal system, a system put in place by the developer, or will you need to put in a septic tank?

- If a septic tank needs to be installed, check local regulations to see how much you will have to spend. (Some environmentally sensitive areas require a very high-tech, and very expensive, tank.)

Electricity:

- Is it in place, and if not, what timeframe (and cost) are you looking at? In rural Latin America, it can take a long time to get hooked up even if you are relatively close to the nearest supply and happy to pay the fee.

- Is it reliable, or will you need a back-up generator?

Roads:

- Are roads and pavements already in place?

- If not, when will they be, and what standard will they be?

Remember, developers often leave roads until last, as road surfaces can be damaged by heavy construction equipment.

Internet:

Ask what the speed is in MB (megabytes) and how much it will cost. Ask locals about its reliability. "High speed" internet in some countries I have visited is at a snail's speed compared to parts of North America and Europe. In some destinations, internet services can cut out for large portions of the day.

Ensuring that you get what you were promised goes back to your sale contract. You can try to cover yourself by ensuring that your contract has firm timelines, standards, and commitments for the essentials.

And when you're buying pre-construction, never pay in full for the property. Hold money back until you get what you were promised in the contract. You can add a clause to the contract that states specifically that you are holding back, say, 15% of the purchase price until you get whatever you are being promised (roads, electricity, water, the fancy gourmet kitchen, the clubhouse and swimming pool).

Step #9: Check the Developer's Background

You wouldn't send money every month to a guy off the street just because he said he was a banker. You'd never start a business with some woman you'd never met before because she sent you a flyer that said you'd get rich. You wouldn't buy a flashy sports car without taking it for a test drive.

So why would you hand over hundreds of thousands of dollars to someone you don't know? When you put it like that, it sounds obvious. But people do. They see a nice brochure or get the grand tour from a charming sales guy. And they put their trust in someone they know nothing about. Sounds crazy, right? It is. And it's not something you're going to let happen to you.

Making an investment in real estate is a business transaction—whether you're buying the property for personal use or to make a profit.

Before you even think of handing money over to a developer, make sure you know as much information as you can about that developer and their track record.

As I've said, most of the top-level due diligence I do these days is on the developers and the people behind possible opportunities. I often don't meet them face-to-face until I've spent dozens of hours forming a view of them.

These days I have a lot of contacts around the world, people involved in real estate and business I can quiz long before my team and I get into paper trail details. But even if you're starting from scratch, here's some of the basic information you should find out:

What is the developer's track record?

Knowing a developer's track record can give you some idea of the probability of success of his development. Find out whether your developer has finished a project before. A developer with no proven track record to his name isn't necessarily a bad thing. Still, you're taking a greater risk with an unproven entity. Ask yourself if that risk is worth it.

If the developer has completed a project, ask where it is and when it was constructed. If you have the time and the funds, visiting one of the developer's finished projects could give you an indication of the quality of his past work. That's not a guarantee that the current development will be of the same quality, but it can give you an insight into what his standards are.

How happy are past and current customers? Ask the developer upfront if he can provide you with written testimonials from previous buyers. If he has dozens of testimonials from happy buyers, that's encouraging. And get some email addresses from buyers you can contact to verify that they are indeed happy with their purchase.

In addition to requesting testimonials and emails from the developer, do your own digging. If you have an opportunity to talk to previous buyers (whether at any previous project or the developer's latest one), take it. Ask them for their honest opinion about their experience.

How is the developer financed?

Knowing your developer's solvency is a must. You never want to put yourself into a situation where a developer starts a project you've bought in and then runs out of money before completing it.

To be clear, buying pre-construction is always a risk. There's no way to protect yourself 100% against that risk. By buying pre-construction, you're taking a risk that a project will be completed as promised. But pricing for pre-construction property is generally lower than buying a finished property. The trade-off for that lower pricing is accepting the risk.

That said, there are ways you can ensure your chosen developer is as robust as possible. To do that, you have to dig deeper into the developer's finances.

First, you need to find out how the developer is financed. (You do that by asking the developer and checking the title deed of the land for the project, which your attorney can do.) Does he have loans or mortgages on this development or any other? If so, how is he proposing to pay them off?

If he is committed to repaying those before he starts construction, that is not ideal: You'll likely wait a long time before your home is built. If he needs money from sales to finance the project, how likely is he to achieve the sales level he needs in the current market? Bank financing often kicks in when a developer has a certain amount of inventory sold. That percentage could be anywhere from 20% to 80% of the project being sold. A bank will give a developer financing based on a number of factors, including the developer's track record and the market he is operating in. Why is this important to know? Because if you're one of the first buyers, it's preferable for you if the developer starts construction when he is 20% sold rather than 80%.

Who's building the project?

Some developers have their own team for construction. The majority, though, do not. Usually a developer will hire a construction company to build his project. If that's the case, you should find out about the construction company. What is their background and track record? Can you see some of their finished projects to confirm whether you are happy with the quality of their work?

And you need to find out if the developer has insurance that covers him in the event that his constructor goes bankrupt or can't complete the work or fails to complete it satisfactorily.

Insurance means a delay while the developer waits for the funds to restart construction, but it's better than the alternative of a half-finished project.

Step #10: Check the Master Plan

If you are promised something by anyone—whether that is a real estate agent, broker, seller, or developer—get it in writing. When it comes to pre-construction, you should take that advice and apply it to what's promised in the master plan.

A master plan is the plan a developer puts together for a whole project. It will show amenities like swimming pools, clubhouses, barbecue areas, tennis courts, and landscaping. When it's on the plan, it's only a promise. And promises can easily be broken. A contract is much harder to break.

If you can, get the developer to put in writing in your contract, details of the promised amenities. That should include, where possible, standards, sizes, and timelines for completion. Otherwise, don't be surprised when that massive pool with a giant water slide that you were promised ends up being a kiddies' paddling pool.

Amenities are usually the last items installed in developments, and the first that suffer if a developer is running short of cash. You should also ask questions about any reserve areas or green spaces on the masterplan. Just because it's a green area now doesn't mean the developer hasn't earmarked it for something else at a later date. Ask whether the green spaces or reserve areas will be preserved or used for future development. Similarly, if there's empty land next to the property, find out what plans are in place for it. You don't want to wake up one day to discover a new factory is being built beside your new condo.

Check the local municipal developmental and zoning plan, if there is one, to see if roads or factories are planned nearby. Similarly, check out the local area to see if there's anything that might disturb your enjoyment of your new property. Is there a municipal dump close by, for example, or a truck park, close to your new home?

Step #11: Check the HOA

Homeowners Associations (HOAs) apply when you purchase a condo or a home in a gated community. They enforce the rules and regulations of the community.

HOAs typically outline their rules in the Covenants, Conditions, and Restrictions (CCRs for short). The breadth and depth of CCRs differs from one HOA to another. Make sure there is nothing in the

CCRs that you can't live with. Some are relatively easygoing; others are mapped out with military precision and enforcement.

CCRs can cover what kind of pets, if any, you can keep. Some have restrictions on working from home; if you intend to work from home, find out what those restrictions are.

Some set out standards for maintenance—including how often you have to carry out work and how it should be completed. CCRs can dictate down to the smallest detail how you should maintain your home—right down to the color you can paint your house or what you can plant in your garden. (I've heard of one recently that even dictated what direction a car could be parked in. Front bumper to curb was fine, apparently. Trunk side to curb would get you a stern warning from the HOA.) Of course, those restrictions can work in your favor, too. If you're not happy that your neighbor has painted his house purple or that he bought a rooster for his yard that wakes you up at 4 a.m. every day, the CCRs could be your best friend. The rules of a CCR should be loose enough that you can enjoy your home, but tight enough that your neighbor can't decide to start an all-night club next door.

If you're thinking of subleasing your property for vacation rentals, find out if you're allowed to do so before you buy. There's no point investing in a property to earn rental income only to find that short-term rentals are strictly prohibited.

What do your HOA fees pay for?

I like to golf. I golf whenever I can. That's why it makes sense for someone like me to buy a home that sits right next to a golf course. Non-golfers sometimes choose to buy in a golf community. They do it for a variety of reasons. Some appreciate the quiet, manicured green space on their doorstep. Others might want to rent their home out, and a golf course is an added attraction for many renters. If the golf course is a completely separate business they're not paying for, they get all the upside of golf course proximity with none of the expense of a golf club membership.

But if you're a non-golfer, you might want to think carefully about buying in a golf community, even if you're told at the beginning that you don't have to pay. I know of one court case highlighting why caution is advisable.

In a California community, the community's homeowners association (HOA) was left footing the shortfall after the community's golf course got into trouble. Last I heard, some of the homeowners affected were suing the HOA.

The community's HOA asked owners how they felt about supporting the struggling golf course in their community. A narrow majority (63% of the 94% of owners who voted) agreed to support the golf course. So, the HOA tacked on $250 a month to the $1,050-a-month dues each owner already paid, just to support the golf club.

That wasn't so bad for the golfers who owned a home in the community. Golf club members got a $250 monthly credit on their membership that offset the additional charge. Owners who were not golfers felt they were carrying the burden. A group of those non-golfing owners launched a lawsuit against the HOA.

You could argue that keeping the golf course in good shape is in everyone's interest. A badly maintained, un-watered course, or one that's closed, can negatively impact property values. But the question remains, who should pay if the golf course can't fund itself? Or what happens if it goes bankrupt?

This is something you need to consider when you're buying in a community with an amenity such as a golf course or equestrian center or wellness center. Even if you're not using the amenities right now, and it's a free bonus that bumps up the value of your home, how would you feel if you were asked to pay toward it in the future?

If it's a dealbreaker, you might want to consider buying a home in a community with few or no shared amenities—or ensure you have enough disposable income to foot increased HOA dues at some point down the line.

How the HOA is run and managed

Besides CCRs, there are some other things you should know about the HOA. First up is how it is managed and financed. Know exactly who will manage the HOA (Homeowners Association) initially. If it is the developer, find out when the handover to owners happens.

Then you need to find out what the projected monthly dues are. Are they likely to change? And can the HOA legally enforce collection?

If not, those lovely shared amenities could deteriorate very quickly. If other owners are refusing to pay—and the HOA can't force them to—who's going to pay to keep the road surfaces in good condition or the elevator in working order?

But there's another question to ask: Who is or will be managing the HOA finances—and are there checks and balances in place to ensure that funds are managed correctly?

Find out if there is a reserve fund set up. Ideally, you should make at least two extra monthly payments a year that should go into a reserve fund, just in case any serious, costly maintenance issues come up. Many owners ditch the reserve fund to cut their monthly bill. Then when a big-ticket expense crops up, there's no money to fund it, and many owners will refuse to pay, even if it's an essential, like urgent repairs to the roof of a condo building.

Last thing to consider: Are the CCRs and HOAs tied into the property deed? Are they enforceable against future owners if the current owner sells? Don't assume that because CCRs are in your deed that they are enforceable. They must also be set up under a proper statutory regime that varies country by country. Your attorney can check this for you.

A Cautionary HOA Tale

If you're buying somewhere that has a Homeowners Association (HOA), you need to be sure you know exactly what your obligations are.

HOAs are typically found in private or gated communities. They're the bodies that enforce the rules and regulations of the condos or houses in those communities. They also set the monthly fees every owner must pay to cover the cost of maintenance and repair of shared amenities like roads, elevators, and swimming pools.

The monthly fees are a bone of contention for many owners. More so when you're buying pre-construction. It's often hard to get a handle on how much you'll pay per month. Plus, while the community is under construction, the developer normally runs the HOA until most of the homes are sold, when control passes to the owners. Owners don't always agree with the developer's decisions and price-setting. But there's no guarantee that things will go any better once the owners take charge.

Some owners think the easiest solution when they're at odds with the HOA or they're cash-strapped is to simply stop paying their monthly fees.

But, as one owner in Texas discovered, that can lead to all kinds of problems—such as losing your home. The homeowner was busy setting up a new business. Her HOA fees slipped through the cracks. She racked up $1,800 in unpaid HOA fees. The HOA ultimately sold her home at auction to recover the fees. The owner hadn't missed any mortgage payments, by the way. The foreclosure and sale by auction related only to the $1,800 of unpaid HOA fees. The owner didn't understand the consequences of not paying the fees. She certainly had no idea it could lead to her losing her home.

> My advice when you're buying in a condo block or gated community is to do your research.
>
> Ask lots of questions about who will run the HOA, how board members are elected, and how decisions are made and implemented. Find out how much you'll pay per month in HOA fees and how that money is spent. Investigate what happens if you're late paying or can't pay the fees. And make sure there's a reserve fund. Extra cash from HOA fees should go to the reserve fund, to pay for big-ticket expenses like replacing an elevator.
>
> If you're buying pre-construction and the HOA rules have not been set up, ask the developer (in writing) what rules he plans to implement, how the HOA will be run, and an approximate level for monthly fees.

Step #12: Investigate Tax Issues and Wills

As Benjamin Franklin once wrote, there is nothing certain in life but death and taxes. It's not pleasant, but you have to consider both when you're buying property overseas.

To start with the arguably less unpleasant of the two (though opinions on that one vary), you should get an idea of your tax obligations before you buy property overseas.

Your attorney or a good CPA/financial adviser with foreign real estate experience can discuss with you the best way to hold your property overseas. This is a very personal matter that depends on why you're buying the property, what you plan to use it for, and your current tax circumstances.

The other thing you need to consider is what happens to you in case of your death. You may need to have two wills, one in the country you are buying in, and one back home. If you are a couple, how would the death of one partner affect the property ownership? Make sure to get good advice from both your in-country attorney and your tax advisor back home.

Step #13: Use Approved Escrow Services

Before you start making payments to the seller, you should consider escrow services. Escrow is the best way to protect your money when you're buying overseas.

You should never pay the seller directly. Nor should you send the money to your real estate agent or attorney in-country. They may not have a separate client account—and there are likely no protections or insurances if they decide to take your money and run.

You should use an approved escrow service. That way, your money is protected and only released to the seller when certain conditions are met—getting the final permit, finishing construction, title transferring to your name, etc.

A Word on Emotion...

Emotion. Remove it from the equation. Have your process and be rigorous and true to it.

In the world of real estate, a healthy dose of skepticism is a good thing. All that glitters is definitely not gold. It doesn't matter how good a deal a property appears to be. You need to make sure that the deal stacks up. And you can do it systematically.

Don't let fear of missing out affect you. FOMO is your enemy. Don't let greed get to you. Don't let any of your emotions get in the way or drive your decision-making.

Earlier in this book, I spoke about profiling or interviewing yourself. Doing so means you can develop your personal investment criteria. As a reminder:

- What are your reasons for making the investment…

- Your tolerance for risk, and how much you have to invest

- How you intend to finance the property

- The needs of your existing portfolio

- Your level of experience in the market

- The level of involvement you want to have managing the property

Now you also have my 13-step due diligence checklist, which means you are streets ahead of 99% of people when it comes to having an awesome process for buying real estate anywhere.

How My Team and I Vet a *RETA* Deal

I've told you I'm a big picture guy. That doesn't mean the details outlined in my checklist aren't crucial. But it only makes sense to bother with the details *after* the big picture stuff stacks up.

What do I mean by big picture?

Drilling down to find out all about the major transformation underway…we want a big Path of Progress event. We seek incredible demand driven by unstoppable trends.

Then, who are the players in the real estate industry? What about their track records. Can we do business with them, should we? I've told you: Most of the top-level due diligence I do these days is on the developers and the people behind possible opportunities. I often don't meet them face-to-face until I've spent dozens of hours forming a view of them.

Months, even years, of research can go into producing this big picture. Lots of boots on the ground visits. Lots of conversations and observations. Research. Research. Research. We want to be in at the ground-floor of upswings and growth that will continue for a long time. We only want to deal with developers we can trust to deliver.

When I started out on my journey as a real estate investor I didn't have a big rolodex of contacts all over the world. I've spent decades making the right connections and building fruitful relationships.

Doing so has led me to incredible opportunities to buy, sell, rent and spend time in stunning real estate in beautiful places. Plus, I now have a network I can tap into to be "on the inside" in all sorts of destinations.

As my *Real Estate Trend Alert* group has grown, word has got out among developers. When I started out years ago, I was doing most of the door-knocking to get deals for *RETA*. These days developers come to me. And my team has grown too, our reach has never been wider. I can put people on the ground in places like Turkey to scope out the effect of inflation on real estate there...in the mountains of Ecuador to look for bolt-hole escapes...on the beaches of Portugal and Spain... the villages of southern France...the hill-towns of Italy...in Belize, Thailand...wherever there's a sniff of opportunity, my team and I go.

My team and I vet hundreds of potential deals a year. Yet *RETA* members will only ever hear about a fraction of these.

Because—after doing our homework—we reject most of them. The truth is the bar is very high, and only a few developers tick all the boxes. It says a lot about our group, too, that many developers, once they've done business with

RETA, seek to do it again and again. They recognize a good relationship when they see it...

But here's the nub of it when it comes to vetting a *RETA* deal: The deal is the very last piece I put in place. I long ago decided that conversations with developers should be at the end of my process. First, I find the right transformation, the right location...remember my five R's? I look for these...

- **Right Transformation.** As a risk averse and conservative investor, I purposely seek out opportunities in the world's most desirable and internationalized places. That's because these are destinations where people come from around the world in good times and bad. Millions of people driving demand. And tied to a major transformation making it easier for those people to get there. A virtuous circle. A crisis like COVID or the global financial meltdown of 2008/09 are just temporary blips on the growth trajectory of these internationalized places. They bounce back stronger. All the fundamentals that make these places attractive are even more attractive after a crisis.

- **Right Location.** Then you drill down, where exactly makes the most sense. It might be several or even a dozen different spots. Close to the beach, or golf...airport...in a certain micro-climate or sought-after neighborhood.

- **Right Developer.** I'm only interested in doing deals with people with a long track record of delivering. The more storms they have weathered the better. A developer who's been delivering for 30 years has seen a thing or two. I like developer's who are creative, yet conservative. They don't take chances but they do like to innovate. Passion for creating beautiful communities is a must.

- **Right Real Estate.** The longer you are a *Real Estate Trend Alert* and the more familiar you get with our international beat, the more you'll realize how much real estate I don't recommend or talk about. I'm only ever interested in the best in class, that means we retain a competitive edge. So, I seek out the best amenities, the best-designed condos...nothing cookie cutter or pedestrian. By owning the best real estate, your real estate stands the best chance of always being in high demand.

- **Right Price.** All of the above is pointless if you aren't buying at the right price. And that is a lower price than anyone else. The lower your price, the bigger your potential gain and the higher your potential yield. Buying at the right low, low price is the entire point of *Real Estate Trend Alert*. We buy in exclusive off-market deals and use our group buying power to get lower prices than anyone else will pay, and before anyone else has a chance, too.

Why do developers give us first dibs at lower prices than anyone else? Why do they often offer *RETA* members exclusive financing? What's in it for them? What's the catch?

You might be surprised! It's all quite scientific. There is a financial equation underpinning the perfect *RETA* deal. And in the next chapter I'll go into details on that equation. But basically, it's a simple win-win for each side. The developer gets quick and discreet sales from our group allowing him to go to the local market with sales under his belt and the confidence to charge higher retail prices (i.e. the price everyone else pays)...and we get a deal at a price no one else can even dream of.

Like I say, more on this in the next and final chapter...

Not Every *RETA* Deal Is A Winner

The vast majority of exclusive deals I bring to *RETA* members work out amazingly, often better than I predicted. I'm conservative.

By that I'm talking about six-figure uplifts in value in a matter of a few years. Red-hot rental income once delivered and established. Throughout this book you've heard about some of those deals. *RETA* members have shared their thoughts with you too.

I've been bringing exclusive deals to our *Real Estate Trend Alert* group since 2008. I stand on our track record, just as I expect developers we deal with to be able to stand on theirs.

Try as we might though, not every deal is a winner. Least you think I lie by omission, let me tell you about two that fell through and how that worked out for *RETA* members.

In January 2021, I brought *RETA* members an exciting deal in Playa del Carmen. The community was called Sunrise in the stunning master-planned community of Corasol. *RETA* members could buy luxury two-bed condos from $192,800. I predicted that these condos would be worth $300,000 three years after delivery. I reckoned members could gross annual rental yields of $24,000 after the community was established.

The developer had a stellar track record of delivering. They are a family-run group who have been developing for close to 30 years. You need to be seriously good to do business with Walmart. And their group have been doing business with the giant U.S. retailer for three decades.

Everything looked good. But shortly after I launched the deal to *RETA* members, advanced engineering works discovered a large underground cave on the site. This had significant implications for the planned project and associated costs. It meant the project was cancelled.

Rare events like this are the reason my team and I negotiate protections on behalf of *RETA* members. In the case of this Sunrise deal, *RETA* members had reserved using an escrow service as insisted upon by my team and I. As per that escrow agreement, money was returned. I also worked hard on finding other deals for disappointed members and getting them priority access.

And I managed to bring members another deal in Corasol in a community called The Village. Members could own in this luxurious, amenities-rich community, including a well-regarded 18-hole Nick Price golf course and access to a secluded secret beach, from $258,600. I expect these condos to be worth $400,000 just three years after delivery—a $141,400 boost. Even at that I'm being conservative (it is very much a $500,000-level community and then some).

In Panama we had a different disappointment. *RETA* members had been able to buy in a beachfront community called Playa Caracol in exclusive off-market deals taking advantage of a major tax incentive I called "the bailout."

This was a tax break given to developers to encourage tourism. It meant the developer behind Playa Caracol could offer incredibly low pricing on fully furnished condos close to the beach. A condition was that the condos had to be in a five-year rental program. I viewed this as a huge benefit, as did many *RETA* members. I bought alongside *RETA* members and was looking forward to spending time in my new condo then handing the keys to the rental people to do their thing and send me income.

Cue craven government back-tracking on the scheme, which essentially cancelled the bailout deal. Again, *RETA* members were fully refunded and my team and I doubled down on finding deals in Panama to make it right.

The above deals are exceptions to the *RETA* rule. And despite the dreadful disappointment, in both cases as you see, being a member of *RETA* ultimately offered a protection.

With all investment comes some risk. I firmly believe that with *RETA* our risk is mitigated considerably. This is because, firstly, my team and I are out there figuring stuff out, getting ahead of the big transformations and filling in the big picture. This exhaustive and relentless process is no easy task to take on alone. It's a big benefit of *RETA* to have the right destinations homed in on for you.

From there my team and I are vetting developers and deals in such a way that the vast majority turn out extremely well. We only ever want to do business with developers that are honorable and have a reputation to protect.

And lastly, as the above examples show, my team and I negotiate protections on behalf of *RETA* members that are hard or impossible to find when you go it alone.

CHAPTER 12

A Special Kind of Club: How to Use Your *RETA* Membership

"The first man gets the oyster, the second man gets the shell." — Andrew Carnegie

"Alone we can do so little; together we can do so much." — Helen Keller

Warning: If you're not a member of *Real Estate Trend Alert*, this chapter is going to make you want to be! I'm going to tell you how this *RETA* malarkey works. How do we get the best real estate deals? As a member, how do you get your piece of those deals? And, what comes after you buy?

First...

Whatever your business or profession, I expect you know what a huge advantage it is to be first. First with an idea. First to develop a product. First to market it.

The same goes for making truly staggering profits in real estate.

To be a *Real Estate Trend Alert* member is to be first on the very best real estate deals in the world. First to get wind of a big transformation, a big trend or major Path of Progress event, first to get in on the ground floor of that transformation...first to get in on a best-in-class real estate at off-market prices.

That's why I have a team of researchers and analysts. It's why we spend a small fortune on travel and research. It's why I have two chartered accountants to run the rule on things. To be *first*.

But to be first is not enough of an advantage…

We must be first *together*.

And the core strength of our *RETA* club is our group buying power. It's by acting in unison with like-minded investors that we get the incredible deals that we do.

Alone, I can't bring much to the table when I negotiate with developers besides my charm. I might as well be some guy with a clown tie and an empty briefcase bluffing about what's inside. I might not even get into their office. With you at my back though, I can bow developers to our will, craft insanely good terms and prices, and leave everyone a winner. And after 14 years in existence, our *RETA* group now has a heavy-hitting reputation in the right circles.

Our group buying power is highly respected and sought after. It's how we get deals no one else gets, deals that even the most informed local real estate insiders can't believe.

Here's a story for you…

Back in 2017, when *RETA* members locked down condos in Siempre Playa in the heart of Playa del Carmen's Zona Dorada, the calls starting coming from local brokers.

These guys had heard wild rumors of condos in Siempre Playa being sold off-market to our *RETA* group for just $193,800. Bear in mind, within a few months the developer was having his "friends and family" launch at prices from $250,000 or so.

They were not happy. This is normal. We have haters. Lots of folks don't like what we at *RETA* do. It undermines what they do which is charge big fees for adding less value.

It plays out like that with many of our *RETA* deals. We're the real insiders. After the shock and disbelief comes the question: "Who are these *RETA* people and how did they pull this off?"

Let me tell you.

In *RETA* we have doctors, lawyers, dentists, business owners... busy professionals. We have software engineers, chemists, real estate agents, financiers...we have retired army and navy officers, actors...

We have some celebrity members but it would be indiscreet for me to name names. We have incredibly wealthy retirees, and folks on a modest budget looking for a dream home somewhere sunny...

Our club is international. We have Australian and English members. Folks in Singapore and Dubai.

Among us we have differing investment goals and budgets. Some want real estate to live in, others seek rental income. You might want to sell for a fat profit, or you might be content to have blue-chip real estate to leave to the kids...our portfolios are different.

But we all have one thing in common: We're comfortable looking for opportunities out in the big wide world.

RETA members don't want to mess around trying to find an edge in our local real estate markets. An edge that tips a deal from marginal to economic, or even reasonably good.

That's the shell as billionaire Andrew Carnegie put it. *RETA* members want the oyster.

We want to buy at the point where, thanks to a major transformation, a raging torrent carries us along and drives our income into the double-digits, and capital appreciation into the six-figures.

Ours is not a new idea.

In fact, it's one of the oldest ideas there is. Ever since the first men, people have sought opportunity beyond their small corners of the world. They have strode, rode, and sailed toward the horizon in search of a better deal. It's just got so much easier in our globalized world. The internet, smartphones, and air travel make it straightforward.

Of course, someone still needs to get their boots on the ground. That's where I come in, along with the team I've put together.

It's been tremendously exciting to be a part of a growing and vibrant group of like-minded real estate lovers for so many years. It's given my travel a noble purpose.

I founded *Real Estate Trend Alert* in 2008 amid some irritation and bewilderment. I couldn't understand how a club like ours didn't already exist. I badly wanted to join such a club. Here I was, an ordinary small-scale investor who loved real estate. I looked everywhere. Where was my tribe and how could I take my place among them to prosper and thrive?

I had my "aha!" moment in the depths of the financial crisis on the beaches of north-east Brazil. As I've mentioned earlier in this book, while the world seemed in financial meltdown in the U.S. and Europe, there was a boom going on in northeast Brazil. No crisis there. Instead, a major transformation was underway creating huge opportunities for investors.

I knew there had to be many others like me who, given these kinds of opportunities, would recognize a great deal wherever it was in the world and act decisively.

What I did not know, was just how *RETA* would evolve. Today our *RETA* club is bigger than I ever imagined it would be, and it's become a unique deal machine. As I've told you, I get in on the ground floor. I get my boots on the ground.

What do you get when you're in the *RETA* club?

I'll email you frequently with news of deals, reports from the road, analysis of markets, that sort of thing. We also have a dedicated *RETA* app you can have on your phone or tablet. This is particularly useful for keeping up to date on current deals. *RETA* members have a website, videos, reports...a vast library of resources.

A few years back, I hired a special concierge for *RETA* members. She's available to help you with anything. And there's a buyer's liaison too, to help you out after you've bought in any *RETA* deal.

I like things simple and smooth. And that's what I want *RETA* to be for members.

The real juice of *RETA* membership though...the biggest benefit of them all...

That has to be the off-market *RETA*-only deal.

An off-market *RETA* deal is one I negotiate exclusively on behalf of *RETA* members on real estate I expect will rise in value. I use our awesome buying power as a group when negotiating.

For a deal to cut my muster, I have to see clear potential for us to double our money invested in five years. I particularly love deals that offer us rapid appreciation and enormous income potential should we chose to rent upon delivery.

All Sorts of Deals

Besides the off-market deal, we have other sorts of deals. Flash deals for instance are one off and urgent. Remember for instance the luxury ocean-view villa in Nicaragua I mentioned earlier in this book that went for less than the cost of construction? Or just before this book went to press, I was able to tell *RETA* members about a townhouse selling at a big discount in Spain. You get the point.

> Also, from time to time I might bring you some vicarious dream real estate my team have found, something that's good value but not a red-hot *RETA* deal—think a castle in Italy or a cottage in Ireland. Something special with a lifestyle twist that often stacks up as a respectable investment, just not the stellar yields and gains we focus on for *RETA*. An example, in 2016, I scouted historic village homes in the south of France that were ideal for renting out in the summer and spending time in yourself the rest of the year. You could figure on a 6% gross yield doing that. Not bad for your own slice of history in a fairy tale French village.

It all starts with my team and I identifying up-and-coming markets and major transformations with potential. For months or even years before I send you details of a members-only deal launch, I've been researching...putting boots on the ground...and meeting high-level contacts in the destinations where I feel there could be a hot opportunity.

I go places. For instance, as I write, I'm packing a bag for a scouting trip to Croatia and Montenegro. Why? Because I hear things. I first visited Croatia in 2005 just before real estate prices took off. Now there are murmurs about Montenegro which shares the same stunning Adriatic coast. Around the Bay of Kotor I hear there's a drive on to attract wealthy yacht-owners. Montenegro is said to be the next country to join the EU.

What does this mean? It means I ought to go spend some time in Montenegro.

I do these sorts of trips all the time. It's how I identify the places where we can buy low in a market that's set to take off, undergoing some kind of massive transformation.

It's also how I build up the *RETA* rolodex. It's taken me decades and millions of air-miles to create my global insider network. This is another core benefit of *RETA*.

My contacts from around the world are constantly feeding me potential opportunities by email, WhatsApp, in phone conversations, Skype, Zoom, you name it...

My team and I dig deeper on this intelligence, then hit up other contacts in the area for a second, third, and even fourth opinion on the opportunity.

Years of boots on the ground, scouting, have primed me to filter through to the most exciting opportunities pretty fast. If something stacks up, then I or one of my most senior colleagues visits the opportunity in-person.

If it sounds promising, I want to see the opportunity with my own eyes, kick rocks on the site of projects...speak directly with the key people involved. I want to walk the streets of the town, explore the wider region, and spend time in the markets, the hotels, resorts, on the beaches, in the mountains...I want the entire context of the potential opportunity. I talk with local business owners, homeowners, expats...everyone from taxi drivers to government ministers.

From there, I look for the best-in-class developer. This is a key step. I'm looking for someone with an impeccable track record. I like developers who have been around a while, for example, if they survived the 2008/09 crisis and came out stronger and smarter. Here's a taste of the things I look for in a developer:

- An instinct to be extra conservative...

- But creative and dynamic at the same time. They will be innovators, but only through a succession of small incremental changes.

- They need to put their customer first.

- They must show that they know how to make money…if not, the first puff of crisis will blow them over…

- They need to be able to see the bigger picture. Be comfortable with selling at a huge discount to *RETA* members in pursuit of a bigger agenda. Greedy developers won't work.

- They must take a long-term perspective…picture how they would feel living in the community they are building themselves 10 years out…

- And they must have a strong track record of delivering on their promises.

Then I uncover the best project they have in the works. Next, I have my lawyer check the paperwork and permits, etc.

If things still look good, it's time to talk numbers. Because of the combined group-buying power of all *Real Estate Trend Alert* members, I'm able to negotiate some serious discounts on retail pricing.

An off-market *RETA*-only deal must see us paying much less than anyone else, which means we're locking in significant gains from the get-go.

It's usually pre-release, off-market, meaning that we're buying way in advance of the developer's official wide-scale retail launch.

Why do these developers agree to offer us the unbeatable pricing they do?

It's a simple win-win for each side. The developer gets quick and discreet sales from our group…allowing him to go to the local market with sales under his belt and the confidence to charge higher retail prices (i.e. the price everyone else pays)…and we get a deal at a price no one else can even dream of. More on this in a moment…

When the deal is finally ready I launch it to *RETA* members.

Over the course of about a week, I share everything about the new opportunity with *RETA* members in the form of reports, photos, sometimes renders, maps, podcasts, and videos…everything you need to assess my analysis and the deal.

I'll tell you what makes this deal so good, why it makes sense as an investment, and why I expect it will be profitable. I tell you to be ready on a certain day and certain time—when the deal will be open.

Normally, I will send several emails over the course of a launch because one email is easily glanced over or missed.

After reading my research, it's up to you whether to act on the deal or not. Since most deals have limited inventory, you need to act quickly when the deal goes live, so you should carefully read all of my alerts beforehand.

If the deal is for you, you inquire, and the developer's team walk you through picking the best available home or lot, figuring out the payment plan and financing, and any other questions that you might have.

Every deal won't suit your personal investment needs. That's OK. *RETA* is designed to bring you a range of deals so that you can choose the ones that suit your needs best. But all of them come with big profit potential.

The good news is, most deals can be reserved for a small, fully refundable deposit. So, you can lock down a unit without fully committing to anything.

Though I and my team have vetted the deal, it's ultimately your responsibility to decide if it is right for you—or not. Remember, the number 1 rule of real estate investing: Do Your Homework. This goes for any deal—including a *RETA* deal.

Normally when you reserve, you have a couple of weeks to do your own due diligence before making any commitments. I always recommend that you speak to a lawyer. (I share the contact details of the attorney I use in the area the deal's located in, to make it easier for you.)

To the best of my knowledge, there is nothing like *RETA* anywhere and never has been. As I say, that's the precise reason I founded it.

My team and I vet many hundreds of real estate deals every year and most don't cut muster for *RETA*. The tiny number that do have passed months (and sometimes even years) of vetting. They are the cream of the crop.

Of course, you might feel *RETA* is not for you. The truth is that going it alone is not easy. You can, of course. And I have met savvy real estate adventurers on my travels who do go it alone.

The single best piece of advice I—or anyone else—can give you if you go solo is to find a local partner you can trust. And make sure you have the time and resources you need to do your scouting, your homework, and follow through.

Why Do Developers Give Us These Deals?

Why do developers agree to offer us the unbeatable pricing they do?

The short answer is because of our *RETA* group buying power. By that I mean our capacity as a group to buy out communities in the space of a weekend or even less time. That's why.

Our deals need to be a win for everybody. A win-win-win. The developer gets fast sales, *RETA* members get incredible pricing, first dibs and often exclusive financing, and my company receive a fee, which helps keep the lights on and the deals flowing.

By all buying together at the same time, our group can change the developer's business.

When developers decide to proceed with a project there are typically two numbers they target.

One is the profitability, the other is Internal Rate of Return (IRR). Without getting too technical, IRR is the annualized rate of return on their cash invested.

Developers look for the lowest-risk route to hit their targets.

By doing a deal with us at *RETA*, it means the developer gets a quick chunk of sales under his belt. That's because we bring our phenomenal group buying power to bear. And that cuts the project lifespan significantly.

In other words, the developer can get the project done much quicker, which has a huge impact on the IRR number. It boosts it (conversely, stretching out a project reduces the IRR proportionally).

Cutting the timeframe of the project also reduces costs because sales and admin offices are staffed and open for a much shorter period of time.

Meantime, because the developer has less inventory to sell to the local market, they can charge a higher price.

This all adds up to a very simple equation for a developer: They can offer really big discounts to us and still hit their numbers, while reducing their risk (and, by extension, our risk).

That's the win for the developer and it's the win for *RETA* members. By way of full disclosure, the third "win" in our win-win-win is that my company get a fee for playing our part. Much of which gets ploughed back into travel and research and is the reason I've been able to grow *Real Estate Trend Alert*.

And as you can see, the stronger our group, the more amazing deals I can negotiate for us.

This is the big strength of *RETA*—our capacity to change the game for a developer. In lots of cases, in the space of hours, a developer who's cut us the right kind of deal has sold more condos in an afternoon than he and his team had expected to sell in a year.

Now you can see why, as word got out about *RETA*, developers started to come looking for us.

It's worth talking about land here...

In many cases the most outstanding *RETA* deals are those we get because, back in the mists of time, a developer did a great land deal.

It's a question of margins. A developer who is late to the party buys land in say, downtown Playa del Carmen and starts building. He will have paid for the land many times what the smart developer next door paid a decade ago.

I actively look out for developers who get ahead of major transformations in their own right, buying land ahead of a Path of Progress, buying low, and waiting.

Those guys can afford to cut us big discounts. But if a developer's margins are extremely tight, it's impossible for them to do the kind of deal we demand.

EPILOGUE

Time to Exit

"The entrance strategy is actually more important than the exit strategy." — Eddie Lampert, billionaire

"Exits are great but it's better to do it as a choice, not a consequence of bad moda operandi."
— Richie Norton, entrepreneur

No one's born an investor. Not even Warren Buffett. The events of our life and the circumstances of our place and time put us on our path.

I entered into the world in a town with no road in or out, where winters are 50 F below freezing. Maybe that's why I hate the cold so much and make sure I'm usually in the perfect 67 to 77 F range with low humidity and soothing sea breezes.

Gillam is in Manitoba, Canada, on the banks of the Nelson River. It's a snow-bound hardy place. I don't remember much. Like many Irish people, my parents—both teachers—had escaped a grim economic outlook in Ireland for opportunity overseas. After nine years teaching in Canada they moved home, taking me—then three years old.

So, I grew up in Cork, in the south of Ireland, where among my earliest memories are those of my parents investing their hard-saved money from Canada in real estate. My parents continued to invest in real estate as I grew up. I remember my father explaining how he'd got financing for a house. I thought it was wonderful! How neat and tidy it was…you borrow from the bank. You buy a property. And your tenants pay your mortgage. Free house!

School bored me but I did love geography and economics. I was fascinated by far-off places and big ideas. And golf…my young life was defined by golf.

We had a golf course close by the house. Dad played. The neighbors played. I caddied. At the age of 13 my nickname around the club was "the Prospect." I lived for golf until my mid-teens when I stalled out and didn't make the jump to the next level.

In retrospect, this became a valuable life lesson. As a young golfer I had wanted to do it all fast and find shortcuts. I had no interest in working out the faults in my swing, which is the only way to go forwards.

I've since learned how richly rewarding it is to embrace the long grind. Have a process, hone it, and be true to it. Day in, day out. Having a process enables me to filter deals rapidly. And this is only possible if you love what you do

Admittedly, I didn't arrive at my process overnight. It took time and experiences.

My first ever real estate launch was in the midst of Ireland's big Celtic Tiger boom. I entered a fine office in a Georgian mansion near Dublin's Merrion Square. Agents in expensive suits were busy on the phone. Reservations were being taken amid a frenzy.

I was just a guy in off the street looking for a deal.

It was the wrong place and the wrong time. The agents were dismissive. The market was going crazy. Who was this kid trying to find an edge? And what kind of edge could I truly have found…

The frenzied market of Celtic Tiger Ireland taught me a few things, among the most valuable was that it paid to be an insider.

Brand-new apartment buildings were being launched in Dublin amid fanfare yet the choice units were already sold before they ever hit the market. Those on the inside had already snagged the best deals…people with the right contacts.

It was an eye-opener. I thought about how to get inside…to get first choice and the best property. I vowed one day that would be me.

And I knew I'd be smart to broaden my horizons. My brushes with the American Dream had convinced me as a youngster that perseverance and patience paid. My first encounters with the American Dream were on the golf course caddying for Americans. I was always excited by the sense they gave me that with hard work anyone could achieve anything.

In the late nineties I traveled to the U.S. and got a job caddying in the Westchester Country Club, in Nantucket. The clubhouse— which I was never let inside—was full of wealthy folk. Membership fees were in the region of $250,000. There were $10-million homes dotted around the course. Some of the people I met weren't happy. They obsessed about money, moaned and complained. That taught me that money can own you in all the wrong ways if you let it. But the U.S. felt like a land of opportunity at the time. Like a place you could make it at whatever you wanted to do.

This early sense of possibility was important to my future.

My friends were all leaving Ireland to funnel into the corporate rat race in London. I wanted a different path. I set up and successfully ran emerging tech businesses in Ireland, fascinated with the internet and its possibilities. But I found consultancy frustrating. Not being able to follow through and realize a vision.

Then I got a call. It was a head-hunter: "I want you to meet some people from a company called *International Living* about a job."

OK. Turned out *International Living* wanted a real estate scout. None of it made much sense but it was interesting. Exciting.

I knew one way or another I was destined to travel and seek out opportunities where they were strongest and purest, so why not try it with these *IL* guys?

A couple of days later I was on a plane to Nicaragua and my life as a roaming real estate investor had begun in earnest.

Getting my boots on the ground around the world was the best thing that ever happened to me.

Everything I saw confirmed what I'd long thought, that when you're comfortable investing wherever the best opportunities are to be found, then you can find them all the time in all sorts of stunning destinations.

Over the years I have come to value simplicity and clear thinking in all aspects of life, especially in investing.

When I listen now to Jack Nicklaus talk about moving a golf ball around Augusta I recognize how phenomenally complex it is in a way my teenage self couldn't. Yet, he describes how to play that course in unbelievably simple steps.

I approach investing in the same way. Keep it simple and focus on the truly critical things. Only a few things really matter to make for a brilliant deal. In this book I've tried to share them with you.

If those things are in place then it's my belief it's very hard to go wrong. If they aren't, it's very hard to do really well. This has been my experience in close to 20 years of real estate investing.

When I look at some of the most successful investors that I know I see this reflected. While good at many things, they always seem to have one key ingredient that makes the difference. One accomplished guy for example, is really good at land deals. He gets the land deal right, which means everything else works out. Permitting may run longer on him for instance, but it doesn't really matter. He got in at the right price.

The real estate equivalent to value investing is "the no brainer deal." A deal where you're getting such a good price that even if things don't work out exactly as predicted you'll still make out OK.

With *Real Estate Trend Alert*, I've found a way for a group of fellow real estate investors and I to band together to do high-margin, high-impact investing with low risk.

I don't ever want to be playing a game where I'm selling to a bigger fool. I was in an investment club in the dotcom era and I realized all that was truly being traded was hype. It was highly speculative. I got lucky but that was all it was, luck. And it's much harder to recognize mistakes you've made in deals where you made money.

Emotions such as greed and fear are neither good nor bad. They simply are what they are. The very successful investor will make a significant move at the right time. They will ignore fear and greed. Fear makes you sell at the wrong time, greed can stop you selling at the right time.

As legendary value investor Benjamin Graham said: "Investing isn't about beating others at their game. It's about controlling yourself at your own game."

A young guy starting out on his real estate investing journey recently asked me about my exit strategy.

I thought about it for a while.

And here's the answer I gave him: If you get your entry strategy right it means you have the option of changing your mind on how you exit. Buy right and you can do pretty much anything that suits you with your real estate.

To steal another line from Ben Graham: "The value of any investment is, and always must be, a function of the price you pay for it."

At the outset of this book I told you my process is deceptively simple. And as you can see, my life's journey has informed it.

I follow big unstoppable trends. Then I position myself ahead of these big unstoppable trends. I find the right location…the right real estate…at the right price. And I make a point of doing business with the right people.

I get in on the ground floor. I get my boots on the ground. And I have made a lot of money doing it.

And you can too.